Louis Malle: Interviews

Conversations with Filmmakers Series
Gerald Peary, General Editor

LOUIS
MALLE

I N T E R V I E W S

Edited by Christopher Beach

University Press of Mississippi / Jackson

The University Press of Mississippi is the scholarly publishing agency of
the Mississippi Institutions of Higher Learning: Alcorn State University,
Delta State University, Jackson State University, Mississippi State University,
Mississippi University for Women, Mississippi Valley State University,
University of Mississippi, and University of Southern Mississippi.

www.upress.state.ms.us

The University Press of Mississippi is a member
of the Association of University Presses.

First printing 2022
∞

Library of Congress Cataloging-in-Publication Data

Names: Beach, Christopher, 1959– editor.
Title: Louis Malle : interviews / Christopher Beach.
Other titles: Conversations with filmmakers series.
Description: Jackson : University Press of Mississippi, 2022. | Series: Conversations
    with filmmakers series | Includes index.
Identifiers: LCCN 2022003389 (print) | LCCN 2022003390 (ebook) |
    ISBN 9781496839602 (hardback) | ISBN 9781496839619 (trade paperback) |
    ISBN 9781496839657 (epub) | ISBN 9781496839626 (epub) | ISBN 9781496839633 (pdf) |
    ISBN 9781496839640 (pdf)
Subjects: LCSH: Malle, Louis, 1932–1995—Interviews. | Motion picture producers and
    directors—20th century—Interviews. | Motion picture producers and directors—
    France—Interviews.
Classification: LCC PN1998.3.M34 A5 2022 (print) | LCC PN1998.3.M34 (ebook) |
    DDC 791.4302/33092—dc23/eng/20220211
LC record available at https://lccn.loc.gov/2022003389
LC ebook record available at https://lccn.loc.gov/2022003390

British Library Cataloging-in-Publication Data available

Contents

Introduction

Louis Malle's place within the history of French filmmaking, and more generally within the history of world cinema, is difficult to summarize. A French director who spent some of the most productive years of his career making films in the United States, Malle was never strongly associated with any group or movement. Although he is sometimes included in discussions of the French New Wave, Malle was not a member of the group of filmmakers that includes François Truffaut, Jean-Luc Godard, Claude Chabrol, and Eric Rohmer, nor was he part of their *Cahiers du cinéma* circle. Unlike many of his French contemporaries, Malle did not work as a film critic.

Malle twice left France to break free of what he felt was a constraining social and cultural environment in his native country. In 1968, he traveled to India, taking a hiatus from his rising career as a fiction filmmaker to make a series of documentaries. Less than a decade later, after having established himself as one of the most respected directors in France, he moved to New York City. He directed five narrative films and two documentaries in the United States before returning to France for the final years of his career. During his American period, Malle became what he described as a "voluntary exile" from his native France, developing productive working relationships with writers, actors, and crew members in the US and displaying an unusual talent for observing diverse aspects of American life with the sharp eyes of a European outsider.

Malle's career took a number of fascinating twists and turns, but it is helpful to think of it as divided into four major phases, each of which is covered by interviews in this volume. In the first phase (1957–67) Malle established himself as one of the brilliant young French directors of the era. The second phase (1968–74), which includes the documentaries in India and the French fiction films of the early 1970s—*Murmur of the Heart, Lacombe, Lucien,* and *Black Moon*—cemented his reputation both in France and abroad. In his third, American phase (1978–86), Malle directed five narrative features, including the controversial *Pretty Baby,* the more commercially successful *Atlantic City,* and the art-house hit *My Dinner with Andre,* as well as the feature-length documentaries *God's Country* and *And the Pursuit of Happiness.* Malle's fourth and final phase (1987–94) saw the director at an artistic peak with the much-celebrated *Au revoir les enfants* and the acclaimed filmed stage production *Vanya on 42nd Street*.

Au revoir les enfants, which is set in a Catholic boarding school during World War II, and *Murmur of the Heart*, about a boy with a heart condition, both have recognizable autobiographical elements. Many of Malle's other films were based more loosely on aspects of his life and social milieu. Born into a wealthy family in 1932, Malle had a social and educational background that differed in significant ways from those of French contemporaries like Rohmer, Truffaut, and Chabrol. His mother, Françoise Malle (née Béghin), was an heiress of the Béghin sugar dynasty, and his father was one of the directors of the Béghin-Say sugar refinery. Malle grew up amidst the upper bourgeoisie, enjoying a privileged upbringing as heir to one of the wealthiest industrial families in the north of France. His early education included attending two Catholic boarding schools, but a heart murmur caused him to be taught privately at home. Afterward, Malle studied history at the Sciences Po in Paris before enrolling at the prestigious national film school, IDHEC (Institut des Hautes Etudes Cinématographiques). His elite education ended when Malle volunteered to work as a cameraman for the underwater explorer and filmmaker Jacques-Yves Cousteau. Several months on board Cousteau's ship, the *Calypso*, led to the documentary *The Silent World*, which won the Palme d'Or in Cannes in 1956 with Malle credited as co-director.

After working briefly as an assistant to Robert Bresson, who was shooting *Un condamné a mort s'est échappé*, Malle felt ready to take on the task of directing his own film. At the age of twenty-five, he had acquired an excellent training in cinematic technique through his work with Cousteau, but he had very little experience working with actors or with a large film crew. His first film as a solo director was the crime thriller *Elevator to the Gallows*, starring two of the rising stars of the period: Jeanne Moreau and Maurice Ronet. The film was released in January 1958, shortly before the first features by Chabrol and Truffaut. With strong performances, stylish black-and-white cinematography by Henri Decae, and an atmospheric jazz score by Miles Davis, the film was a distinctive debut, and it earned Malle the Louis Delluc Prize for the best French film of the year. In rapid succession, Malle went on to direct a series of narrative films: *The Lovers* (1958), *Zazie dans le métro* (1960), *Vie privée* (1962), *The Fire Within* (1963), *Viva Maria* (1965), *Le Voleur* (1966), and *William Wilson* (a segment in the three-part 1967 omnibus film *Spirits of the Dead*).

As a rising filmmaker in the late 1950s and early 1960s, Malle showed little interest in becoming part of a group such as the *nouvelle vague*, and even less interest in engaging in what were then extremely fashionable debates about film theory. At a 1959 roundtable on the future of French cinema, Malle expressed skepticism about the existence of a revolution in French filmmaking: "A new school is characterized by the overturning of aesthetic rules. And up to now *Hiroshima mon amour* is the only film in which the material of cinema has been transformed."[1] He went on to assert that there was no unified generation of French directors, but instead a group of young filmmakers "who come from all over and are going in different directions."

The source of Malle's reluctance to be associated with the *nouvelle vague* is somewhat unclear. Hugo Frey speculates that Malle's artistic ambition militated against any desire to be lumped in with potential rivals, which might detract from his status as an independent filmmaker (Frey, 8). As his interviews suggest, Malle continued to feel a distance between his own career and those of his New Wave contemporaries. His references to other French directors of his generation remain relatively rare, and while there is an inevitable overlap between his interests and those of directors like Truffaut, Godard, and Rohmer, their career paths were very different. Malle's decision to travel to India and shoot the documentary footage that would later be edited into a stand-alone film, *Calcutta* (1969), as well as a televised series, *Phantom India* (1969), distanced him further from the New Wave. But there were dividends for Malle. Later, he would argue that the experience of making these documentaries led to a decisive change in his approach to filmmaking, and that he could not have directed his fiction films of the early 1970s—*Murmur of the Heart* and *Lacombe, Lucien*—in the way he did without having made his documentary portraits of contemporary India. Today, *Murmur of the Heart* and *Lacombe, Lucien* remain among his most enduring achievements: both Wes Anderson and Noah Baumbach claim *Murmur of the Heart* as an influence, while *Lacombe, Lucien* is regarded as one of the most chilling depictions of collaboration in Vichy France.

Nonetheless, Malle's renown as a filmmaker has no doubt suffered from his refusal to be part of the *nouvelle vague*. Though Malle directed nearly thirty films—some of which can be counted among the most important of the second half of the twentieth century—his work has received far less critical and scholarly attention than that of contemporaries such as Truffaut, Godard, and Rohmer. Malle's critical reputation has been hurt as well by his reluctance to define himself as an "auteur"—at least if auteurism dictates that a filmmaker stay within a relatively narrow and consistent thematic and stylistic register. Malle has been dismissed for his extreme eclecticism and for a wide-ranging artistic palette that has at times been regarded as a form of dilettantism. But it might instead be read as a strength that he displays a far greater range—in terms of both subject matter and cinematic form—than most of his peers.

Despite the wide variety of the films and the absence of a single identifiable style, one can identify certain consistent tendencies. Malle's films are generally set within definite historical, cultural, or social contexts, and they often deal with intense psychological, erotic, or interpersonal situations. A number of the films involve characters who are either children or adolescents, and several of them treat themes of maturation and the loss of innocence. On a stylistic level, we can see Malle's use of music as a unifying element. Both jazz and classical music play an important, even central role in Malle's films, starting with his groundbreaking use of an improvised jazz score by Miles Davis in *Elevator to the Gallows*. He made effective use of pieces by Johannes Brahms (*Les Amants*), Erik Satie (*Le Feu follet* and *My Dinner with Andre*), and Franz Schubert (*Au revoir les enfants*), and he included various jazz musicians in the soundtracks of *Murmur of the Heart*, *Lacombe, Lucien*, *Pretty Baby*, *May Fools*, and *Vanya on 42nd Street*.

Additionally, Malle's films often explore controversial social issues and difficult moral boundaries, including suicide in *Le Feu follet*, mother-son incest in *Murmur of the Heart*, collaboration with the Nazis in *Lacombe, Lucien*, child prostitution in *Pretty Baby*, and the tensions surrounding Vietnamese immigrants on the Texas coast in *Alamo Bay*. Malle was not afraid of offending his public or of courting controversy. His second film, *The Lovers*, threatened the standards of censorship boards in both France and the United States. The French culture minister, André Malraux, attempted to impose restrictions on the film, and it was ultimately forbidden to viewers under the age of sixteen. In the United States, the film's overtly sexual content led to a landmark Supreme Court case regarding the definition of obscenity. The case is perhaps most famous for the declaration of Justice Potter Stewart: "I do not know how to define pornography, but when I see it will recognize it, and the film in question is not pornography."

With *Murmur of the Heart*, Malle took on the even more controversial subject of incest. When the film came out in 1971, the French Censorship Board objected both to its brief scene of intimate relations between and mother and son and to its "accumulation of erotic and perverse scenes." The film was ultimately allowed to be shown in theaters but was restricted to viewers eighteen and over. Finally, *Pretty Baby* pushed the censorship boundaries of several countries: though the film was released with an R rating in the United States, it received an X rating in Great Britain and was entirely banned in other parts of the world. While several prominent critics defended the film, others accused Malle of engaging in child pornography because of the overtly sexual content and nude scenes involving the twelve-year-old Brooke Shields.

Seeing Malle's filmmaking in terms of controversy can make one forget his passionate commitment—greater than that of any other narrative French director of his generation except Agnès Varda—to an ongoing project of documentary filmmaking. While his documentaries vary widely in both setting and focus, they generally adhere to the style of *cinéma direct*, a term Malle preferred to the more familiar *cinéma verité*. As Malle makes clear in several of the interviews in this book, his work as a documentary filmmaker not only provided a respite from fiction filmmaking at several junctures in his career but also informed his conception of narrative films, which over time displayed a greater realism in their approach to character, setting, and performance. Breaking down the barrier between documentary and fiction, he often used small, flexible crews and handheld synchronous-sound cameras for his narrative films, and he liked to cast non-professional actors alongside professionals.

The interviews in this volume, a number of which have been translated into English for the first time, cover the entirety of Malle's career. The chronological progression of the interviews—from a 1960 interview in the now defunct cinema journal *Cinéma* to an interview conducted in 1994, the year before Malle's death, by the prestigious film journal *Positif*—provides an excellent window into the different stages of Malle's career. In some cases, the interviews focus on a single film; in others, there is an attempt to put the entirety of his career in perspective. As the interviews collected here demonstrate, Malle was an extremely intelligent and articulate filmmaker, one who thought deeply about his own choices as a director, about the ideological implications of those choices, and about the often-controversial themes treated in his films. Among the many topics addressed are Malle's approach to casting and working with actors; his attitude toward censorship and controversial subject matter; his understanding of the relationship between documentary and fiction film; and the differences between French and American film industries.

In addition to the interviews conducted by various film journals, Malle participated in two seminars at the American Film Institute in Los Angeles. The first of these, from 1975, has never appeared in print, and the second, from 1988, appeared only in a very condensed version. The AFI graciously provided me with access to the original recordings of these sessions and granted permission for their use in this volume. In both cases, the full transcripts of the recorded seminars have been edited for the sake of both brevity and clarity. All the other interviews in this volume have been included in their entirety and have not been substantially edited for republication. Explanatory footnotes have been added in cases where cultural references may not be familiar to non-French readers.

CB

Note

1. Louis Malle, "L'Avenir du cinéma francais: une table ronde imaginaire entre producteurs et réalizateurs," *Le Monde*, November 8, 1959, section 1, page 9.

Chronology

Louis Malle is born on October 30 in Thumeries, a small town in northern France, to Françoise and Pierre Malle. His father is the director of a highly profitable, family-owned sugar refinery. Louis, one of seven children, is educated by a private tutor in the family's mansion.

1940   The family moves to Paris, where Louis attends a Jesuit school.

1943   Transfers to a Jesuit boarding school outside the city.

1945   After contracting scarlet fever, Louis is diagnosed with a heart murmur, and his parents withdraw him from school. For the next two years, he is taught privately at home and develops a passionate interest in literature.

1947   Inspired by films like Jean Renoir's *La Règle du jeu*, begins making short films with a camera given to him by his father.

1951   Passes the entrance exam for IDHEC, the prestigious national film academy.

1953   Accepts a position as an intern working for the underwater explorer and filmmaker Jacques-Yves Cousteau.

1955   Serves as underwater cinematographer and co-director of *Le Monde du silence* (*The Silent World*).

1956   *Le Monde du silence* wins the Palme D'Or at the Cannes Film Festival and Best Documentary at the Academy Awards. Malle serves briefly as an assistant to Robert Bresson on *Un condamné à mort s'est échappé* (*A Man Escaped*), but resigns before the end of shooting.

1957   Shoots *Ascenseur pour l'échafaud* (*Elevator to the Gallows*). Wins Prix Louis-Delluc.

1958   *Les Amants* (*The Lovers*). Wins Special Jury Prize at the Venice Film Festival.

1960   *Zazie dans le métro* (*Zazie*).

1961   *Vie privée* (*A Very Private Affair*).

1962   Travels to Algeria to make a film about the end of the Algerian War, but is not satisfied with the footage and decides not to complete the film. Makes a documentary short about the Tour de France bicycle race (*Vive le Tour*).

1963   *Le Feu follet* (*The Fire Within*) released. Wins Special Jury Prize at the Venice Film Festival and the Italian Film Critics Award.

1964   Travels to Thailand, where he shoots footage for the documentary short *Bons baisers de Bangkok*.

1965   Marries Anne-Marie Deschodt; they will divorce in 1967. Shoots *Viva Maria* on location in Mexico. Jeanne Moreau wins Best Foreign Actress at the British Academy Awards (BAFTA).

1967   *Le Voleur* (*The Thief of Paris*).

1968   *William Wilson* released as part of the anthology *Spirits of the Dead*. Malle travels to India, where he shoots the footage for both *Calcutta* and *L'Inde fantome* (*Phantom India*).

1969   *Calcutta* is released in cinemas; the seven segments of *Phantom India* are broadcast on French television.

1971   *Le Souffle au coeur* (*Murmur of the Heart*) released; Malle's screenplay is nominated for an Academy Award. Travels to Mexico to explore a project dealing with young men enlisted by the police to infiltrate student demonstrations, but abandons the project when it becomes clear he will not be allowed to shoot the film in Mexico.

1972   Shoots documentaries in the Citroën automobile factory (*Humain, trop humain*) and the streets of Paris (*Place de la République*). Travels to Brazil to research a planned documentary about the Amazon region, but abandons the project.

1973   *Lacombe, Lucien* released. Wins Best Film at BAFTA. Receives Golden Globe and Academy Award nominations for Best Foreign Language Film.

1974   *Humain, trop humain* and *Place de la République* released in French cinemas.

1975   *Black Moon* released. Wins César Award for Best Cinematography and Best Sound.

1976   Moves to Los Angeles and signs a two-picture deal with Paramount.

1977   Shoots *Pretty Baby* on location in New Orleans.

1978   *Pretty Baby* released.

1979   Shoots footage for a documentary in the town of Glencoe, Minnesota (*God's Country*); the film will not be completed for another six years. Begins work on *Atlantic City*.

1980   Marries actress Candice Bergen.

1981   *Atlantic City* released. Wins Golden Lion at Venice Film Festival. Academy Award nominations for Best Picture, Best Actor (Burt

Lancaster), Best Actress (Susan Sarandon), Best Director, and Best Original Screenplay (John Guare). *My Dinner with Andre* released.

1982 Begins work on a political comedy to be entitled *Moon Over Miami*, with both John Belushi and Dan Ackroyd to star in the film. When Belushi dies of a drug overdose in March 1982, the project is cancelled.

1983 Shoots *Crackers* on location in San Francisco and on Universal Studio sets.

1984 *Crackers* released. Despite the largest budget of any of Malle's films, it is the greatest critical failure of his career. Shoots *Alamo Bay* on location on the Texas Gulf Coast.

1985 *Alamo Bay* released. Travels to Sicily to begin work on a political thriller with a screenplay by John Guare; the film is never made.

1986 *God's Country* completed. Travels around the United States to shoot footage for the documentary *And the Pursuit of Happiness*. Returns to France to begin work on *Au revoir les enfants*.

1987 Shoots *Au revoir les enfants* in January and February; the film is released in the fall. The film wins a number of awards, including the César from the French Academy for Best Cinematography, Best Director, Best Editing, Best Original Screenplay, Best Production Design, and Best Sound; the Prix Louis-Delluc; the Venice Golden Lion; and the BAFTA for Best Director. The film is nominated for Best Foreign Language Film and Best Original Screenplay at the Academy Awards.

1988 Begins work on *Milou en mai* (*May Fools*).

1989 Shoots *Milou en mai* in the south of France.

1990 *Milou en mai* released. Wins César Award for Best Supporting Actress (Dominique Blanc), with nominations for Best Actor (Michel Piccoli), Best Actress (Miou-Miou), and Best Supporting Actor (Michel Duchaussoy).

1991 Undergoes open heart surgery.

1992 *Damage* released. Miranda Richardson wins BAFTA for Best Supporting Actress, and is nominated for Golden Globe and Academy Awards in the same category.

1994 *Vanya on 42nd Street* released.

1995 Begins work on *Dietrich and Marlene*, to star Uma Thurman. Before the film can be made, Malle dies of lymphoma on November 23.

Filmography

This filmography lists all the films directed by Louis Malle, including short films, documentaries, and films made for television. The information provided here is not meant to be exhaustive: those interested in more complete information about the films can consult the website imdb.com.

CRAZEOLOGY (1953)
Production: Institut des Hautes Etudes Cinématographiques (IDHEC)
Director: **Louis Malle**
Cast: Nicolas Bataille, Pierre Frag, Bernard Malle
Length: 5 minutes

SECTION 407 (1954)
Production: Jacques-Yves Cousteau
Director: **Louis Malle**
Length: 18 minutes

LE MONDE DU SILENCE / THE SILENT WORLD (1956)
Production: Société Filmad, Requins Associés, Titanus (Rome), FSJYC Productions (Denmark)
Co-directors: Jacques-Yves Cousteau and **Louis Malle**
Screenplay: Jacques-Yves Cousteau
Cinematography: Edmond Séchan, Philippe Agostini, and **Louis Malle**
Editing: Georges Alépée
Sound: Yves Baudrier
Length: 86 minutes

ASCENSEUR POUR L'ECHAFAUD / ELEVATOR TO THE GALLOWS (US) / LIFT TO THE SCAFFOLD (UK) (1958)
Production: Nouvelles Editions de Films
Director: **Louis Malle**
Screenplay: **Louis Malle** and Roger Nimier, based on the novel by Noël Calef

Assistant Director: Alain Cavalier
Cinematography: Henri Decaë
Production Design: Jean Mandaroux and Rino Mondellini
Editing: Léonide Azar
Sound: Raymond Gaugnier
Music: Miles Davis
Cast: Jeanne Moreau (Florence Carala), Maurice Ronet (Julien Tavernier), Georges Poujouly (Louis), Yori Bertin (Véronique), Jean Wall (Simon Carala), Lino Ventura (Chief of Police Cherrier), Ivan Petrovich (Horst Bencker), Elga Anderson (Mrs. Bencker), Charles Denner (Deputy Chief of Police)
Length: 90 minutes

LES AMANTS / THE LOVERS (1958)
Production: Nouvelles Editions de Films
Director: **Louis Malle**
Screenplay: **Louis Malle** and Louise de Vilmorin, based on the novel *Point de lendemain* by Dominique Vivant
Assistant Director: Alain Cavalier
Cinematography: Henri Decaë
Production Design: Bernard Evein
Editing: Léonide Azar
Sound: Pierre Bertrand
Music: Johannes Brahms, *String Quartet No. 1 in B Flat Major*
Cast: Jeanne Moreau (Jeanne Tournier), Jean-Marc Bory (Bernard Dubois-Lambert), Alain Cuny (Henri Tournier), José Luis de Villalonga (Raoul Flores), Judith Magre (Maggy Thiebaut-Leroy), Gaston Modot (Coudray)
Length: 88 minutes

ZAZIE DANS LE METRO / ZAZIE (1960)
Production: Nouvelles Editions de Films
Screenplay: **Louis Malle** and Jean-Paul Rappeneau, based on the novel by Raymond Queneau
Assistant Director: Philippe Collin
Cinematography: Henri Raichi
Production Design: Bernard Evein
Editing: Kenout Peltier
Sound: André Hervé
Music: Fiorenzo Carpi
Cast: Catherine Demongeot (Zazie), Philippe Noiret (Uncle Gabriel), Carla Marlier (Aunt Albertine), Jacques Dufilho (Gridoux), Vittorio Caprioli (Pedro

Trouscaillon), Hubert Deschamps (Turandot), Annie Fratellini (Mado), Yvonne Clech (the widow Mouaque)
Length: 92 minutes

VIE PRIVEE / A VERY PRIVATE AFFAIR (1961)
Production: Progefi, Cipra, CCM (Rome)
Director: **Louis Malle**
Screenplay: **Louis Malle**, Jean Ferry, and Jean-Paul Rappeneau
Assistant Director: Philippe Collin
Cinematography: Henri Decaë
Production Design: Bernard Evein
Editing: Kenout Peltier
Sound: William Robert Sivel
Music: Fiorenzo Carpi
Cast: Brigitte Bardot (Jill), Marcello Mastroianni (Fabio Rinaldi), Eleonore Hirt (Cécile), Nicolas Bataille (Edmond), Jacqueline Doyen (Juliette), Ursula Kubler (Carla), Dirk Sanders (Dick), Gregor von Rezzori (Gricha), Antoine Roblot (Alain), Paul Sorèze (Maxime), Gloria France (Anna)
Length: 103 minutes

VIVE LE TOUR (1962)
Production: Nouvelles Editions de Films
Director: **Louis Malle**
Cinematography: Ghislain Cloquet, Jacques Ertaud, and **Louis Malle**
Editing: Kenout Peltier and Suzanne Baron
Music: Georges Delerue
Length: 18 minutes

LE FEU FOLLET / THE FIRE WITHIN (US) / A TIME TO LIVE AND A TIME TO DIE (UK) (1963)
Production: Nouvelles Editions de Films
Director: **Louis Malle**
Screenplay: **Louis Malle**, based on the novel by Pierre Drieu La Rochelle
Assistant Director: Volker Schlondorff
Cinematography: Ghislain Cloquet
Production Design: Bernard Evein
Editing: Suzanne Baron
Music: Erik Satie
Cast: Maurice Ronet (Alain Leroy), Jeanne Moreau (Jeanne), Bernard Noel (Dubourg), Léna Skerla (Lydia), Hubert Deschamps (D'Averseau), Jean-Paul

Moulinot (Dr. La Bardinais), Yvonne Clech (Miss Farnoux), Mona Dol (Madame La Bardinais), Pierre Moncorbier (Moraine), René Dupuy (Charlie), Ursula Kubler (Fanny), Alain Mottet (Urcel)
Length: 110 minutes

BONS BAISERS DE BANGKOK (1964)
Production: ORTF (French television)
Director: **Louis Malle**
Cinematography: Yves Bonsergent
Editing: Nicole Lévy
Length: 15 minutes

VIVA MARIA (1965)
Production: Nouvelles Editions de Films, United Artists (France), Vides Cinematografica (Rome)
Director: **Louis Malle**
Screenplay: **Louis Malle** and Jean-Claude Carriere
Cinematography: Henri Decaë
Production Design: Bernard Evein
Editing: Kenout Peltier and Suzanne Baron
Sound: José B. Carles
Music: Georges Delerue
Cast: Jeanne Moreau (Maria I), Brigitte Bardot (Maria II), George Hamilton (Flores), Gregor von Rezzori (Diogène), Paulette Dubost (Madame Diogène), Claudio Brook (Rodolfo), Carlos Lopez Moctezuma (Rodriguez), Poldo Bendandi (Werther), Francisco Reiguera (Father Superior)
Length: 115 minutes

LE VOLEUR / THE THIEF OF PARIS (1967)
Production: Nouvelles Editions de Films, United Artists (France), Compania Cinematografica Montoro (Italy)
Director: **Louis Malle**
Screenplay: **Louis Malle** and Jean-Claude Carrière, with dialogue by Daniel Boulanger, based on the novel by Georges Darien
Cinematography: Henri Decaë
Production Design: Jacques Saulnier
Editing: Henri Lanoë
Sound: André Hervée
Cast: Jean-Paul Belmondo (Georges Randal), Geneviève Bujold (Charlotte), Marie Dubois (Geneviève Delpiels), Françoise Fabian (Ida), Julien Guiomar

(Abbott La Margelle), Christian Lude (Urbain Randal), Marlène Jobert (Broussaille), Paul Le Person (Roger Voisin, aka Roger-la-Honte), Bernadette Lafont (Marguerite)

WILLIAM WILSON (in the anthology film *Histoires extraordinaires*/*Spirits of the Dead* (US) / *Tales of Terror* (UK) (1968)
Production: Les Films Marceau, Cocinor, Produzioni Europee Associati (Rome)
Director: **Louis Malle**
Screenplay: **Louis Malle** and Clément Biddle Wood, with dialogue by Daniel Boulanger, based on the short story by Edgar Allan Poe
Cinematography: Tonino Delli Colli
Production Design: Ghislain Uhry
Editing: Suzanne Baron and Franco Arcalli
Music: Diego Masson
Cast: Alain Delon (William Wilson), Brigitte Bardot (Giuseppina), Daniele Vargas (the Professor), Renzo Palmer (the Priest), Marco Stefanelli (William Wilson as a child)
Length: 40 minutes

CALCUTTA (1969)
Production: Nouvelles Editions de Films
Director: **Louis Malle**
Cinematography: Etienne Becker and **Louis Malle**
Editing: Suzanne Baron
Sound: Jean-Claude Laureux
Narrator: **Louis Malle**
Length: 105 minutes

L'INDE FANTOME / PHANTOM INDIA (1969, television series; 1975, cinematic release)
The series was broadcast in seven episodes of 50 minutes each. The credits are the same as for *Calcutta*.

LE SOUFFLE AU COEUR / MURMUR OF THE HEART (US) / DEAREST LOVE (UK) (1971)
Production: Nouvelles Editions de Films, Marianne Films, Vides Cinematografica (Rome), Franz Seitz Filmproduktion (Munich)
Director: **Louis Malle**
Screenplay: **Louis Malle**
Cinematography: Ricardo Aronovich

Production Design: Jean-Jacques Caziot and Philippe Turlure
Editing: Suzanne Baron
Sound: Jean-Claude Laureux and Michel Vionnet
Music: Charlie Parker and Sidney Bechet
Cast: Lea Massari (Clara Chevalier), Benoît Ferreux (Laurent Chevalier), Daniel Gélin (Charles Chevalier), Michael Lonsdale (Father Henri), Fabien Ferreux (Thomas Chevalier), Marc Winocourt (Marc Chevalier), Ave Ninchi (Augusta), Corinne Kersten (Daphné), Jacqueline Chauvaud (Hélène), Liliane Sorval (Fernande)
Length: 110 minutes

LACOMBE LUCIEN / LACOMBE, LUCIEN (1974)
Production: Nouvelles Editions de Films, Universal Pictures France, Vides Cinematografica (Rome), Hallelujah Films (Munich)
Director: **Louis Malle**
Screenplay: **Louis Malle** and Patrick Modiano
Cinematography: Tonino Delli Colli
Production Design: Ghislain Uhry
Editing: Suzanne Baron
Sound: Jean-Claude Laureux
Music: Django Reinhardt
Cast: Pierre Blaise (Lucien), Aurore Clément (France Horn), Holger Lowenadler (Albert Horn), Therese Giehse (the Grandmother), Stéphane Bouy (Jean Bernard), Loumi Jacobesco (Betty Beaulieu), René Bouloc (Faure), Pierre Decase (Aubert), Gilberte Rivet (Julien's mother)
Length: 137 minutes

HUMAIN, TROP HUMAIN (1974)
Production: Nouvelles Editions de Films
Director: **Louis Malle**
Cinematography: Etienne Becker
Editing: Suzanne Baron
Sound: Jean-Claude Laureux
Length: 75 minutes

PLACE DE LA REPUBLIQUE (1974)
Production: Nouvelles Editions de Films
Director: **Louis Malle**
Cinematography: Etienne Becker

Editing: Suzanne Baron
Sound: Jean-Claude Laureux
Narrator: **Louis Malle**
Length: 94 minutes

BLACK MOON (1975)
Production: Nouvelles Editions de Films, Bioskop Film
Director: **Louis Malle**
Screenplay: **Louis Malle**, with dialogue by Joyce Bunuel
Assistant Director: Fernand Moszkowicz
Cinematography: Sven Nykvist
Production Design: Ghislain Uhry
Editing: Suzanne Baron
Sound: Nara Kollery
Music: Richard Wagner
Cast: Cathryn Harrison (Lily), Therese Giehse (the Old Woman), Joe Dallesandro (the Brother), Alexandra Stewart (the Sister)
Length: 100 minutes

CLOSE UP (1976)
A documentary portrait of the model and actress Dominique Sanda.
Production: Sigma—Antenne 2
Director: **Louis Malle**
Cinematography: Michel Parbot
Editing: Suzanne Baron
Music: Erik Satie
Length: 26 minutes

PRETTY BABY (1978)
Production: Paramount
Director: **Louis Malle**
Screenplay: Polly Platt and **Louis Malle**, based on the book *Storyville, New Orleans* by Al Rose
Assistant Director: Donald Heitzer
Cinematography: Sven Nykvist
Production Design: Trevor Williams
Editing: Suzanne Baron and Suzanne Fenn
Sound: Don Johnson
Music: Jelly Roll Morton, Scott Joplin, and other jazz composers

Cast: Keith Carradine (Bellocq), Susan Sarandon (Hattie), Brooke Shields (Violet), Frances Faye (Nell), Antonio Fargas (Claude, the pianist), Gerrit Graham (Highpockets), Diana Scarwid (Frieda)
Length: 110 minutes

ATLANTIC CITY (1980)
Production: Denis Héroux and Gabriel Boustani (Selta Films), Cine-Neighbor (Canada), Canadian Film Development Corporation, International Cinema Corporation, Famous Players Limited
Director: **Louis Malle**
Screenplay: John Guare
Assistant Director: John Board
Cinematography: Richard Ciupka
Production Design: Anne Pritchard
Editing: Suzanne Baron
Sound: Jean-Claude Laureux
Music: Michel Legrand
Cast: Burt Lancaster (Lou Pascal), Susan Sarandon (Sally Matthews), Kate Reid (Grace Pinza), Michel Piccoli (Joseph), Hollis McLaren (Chrissie), Robert Joy (Dave), Al Waxman (Alfie)
Length: 105 minutes

MY DINNER WITH ANDRE (1981)
Production: The Andre Company, Saga Productions
Director: **Louis Malle**
Screenplay: Wallace Shawn and Andre Gregory
Assistant Director: Norman Berns
Cinematography: Jeri Sopanen
Production Design: Stephen McCabe
Editing: Suzanne Baron
Sound: Jean-Claude Laureux
Music: Erik Satie
Cast: Wallace Shawn (Wally), Andre Gregory (Andre), Jean Lenauer (the Waiter), Roy Butler (the Bartender)
Length: 111 minutes

CRACKERS (1984)
Production: Universal Pictures
Director: **Louis Malle**
Screenplay: Jeffrey Fiskin, based on the Italian film *Big Deal on Madonna Street*

Assistant Director: James Quinn
Cinematography: Laszlo Kovacs
Production Design: John L. Lloyd
Editing: Suzanne Baron
Sound: Richard Dior and Robert Hoyt
Music: Paul Chihara
Cast: Donald Sutherland (Weslake), Jack Warden (Garvey), Sean Penn (Dillard), Wallace Shawn (Turtle), Larry Riley (Boardwalk), Trinidad Silva (Ramon), Christine Baranski (Maxine), Charlaine Woodward (Jasmine), Tasia Valenza (Maria), Irwin Corey (Lazzarelli), Edouard De Soto (Don Fernando), Ann Maria Horsford (Slam Dunk)
Length: 92 minutes

ALAMO BAY (1985)
Production: Tri-Star, Delphi III Productions
Director: **Louis Malle**
Screenplay: Alice Arlen, based on a series of articles by Ross E. Milloy
Assistant Director: Fred Berner
Cinematography: Curtis Clark
Production Design: Trevor Williams
Editing: James Bruce
Sound: Danny Michael
Music: Ry Cooder
Cast: Amy Madigan (Glory Sheer), Ed Harris (Shang Pierce), Ho Nguyen (Dinh), Donald Moffat (Wally Scheer), Truyen V. Tran (Ben), Rudy Young (Skinner), Cynthia Carle (Honey Pierce), Martin Lasalle (Luis), William Frankfather (Mac), Gary Basaraba (Leon), Bill Thurman (Sheriff Buzz Welty), Michael Ballard (Wendell Gunderson), Buddy Killen (Reverend Disney), Lucky Mosley (Crankshaw), Harvey Lewis (Tex)
Length: 99 minutes

GOD'S COUNTRY (1986)
Production: PBS/National Endowment for the Arts
Director: **Louis Malle**
Screenplay: **Louis Malle**
Cinematography: **Louis Malle**
Editing: James Bruce
Sound: Jean-Claude Laureux and Keith Rouse
Narrator: **Louis Malle**
Length: 95 minutes

AND THE PURSUIT OF HAPPINESS (1987)
Production: Pretty Mouse Films
Director: **Louis Malle**
Screenplay: **Louis Malle**
Cinematography: **Louis Malle**
Editing: Nancy Baker
Sound: Danny Michael
Length: 80 minutes

AU REVOIR LES ENFANTS (1987)
Production: Nouvelles Editions de Films, Marin Karmitz (MK2 Productions), Stella Film (Germany), NEF (Germany)
Director: **Louis Malle**
Screenplay: **Louis Malle**
Assistant Director: Yann Gilbert
Cinematography: Renato Berta
Production Design: Willy Holt
Editing: Emmanuelle Castro
Sound: Jean-Claude Laureux
Music: Franz Schubert, Camille Saint-Saens
Cast: Gaspard Manesse (Julien Quentin), Raphaël Fejtö (Jean Bonnet), Francine Racette (Madame Quentin), Stanislas Carré de Malberg (François Quentin), Philippe Morier-Genoud (Father Jean), François Berléand (Father Michel), François Négret (Joseph), Peter Fitz (Muller), Pascal Rivet (Boulanger), Benoit Henriet (Ciron), Richard Leboeuf (Sagard), Xavier Legrand (Babinot), Arnaud Henriet (Negus), Jean-Sébastien Chauvin (Laviron), Luc Etienne (Moreau), Irène Jacob (Mademoiselle Davenne, the piano teacher), Jacqueline Paris (Madame Perrin), Jacqueline Staup (Nurse)
Length: 103 minutes

MILOU EN MAI / MAY FOOLS (1989)
Production: Nouvelles Editions de Films, TF1 Films, Ellepi Film (Rome)
Director: **Louis Malle**
Screenplay: **Louis Malle** and Jean-Claude Carrière
Assistant Director: Michel Ferry
Cinematography: Renato Berta
Production Design: Willy Holt
Editing: Emmanuelle Castro
Sound: Jean-Claude Laureux
Music: Stéphane Grappelli

Cast: Michel Piccoli (Emile Vieuzac, known as Milou), Miou-Miou (Camille), Michel Duchaussoy (Georges), Dominique Blanc (Claire), Harriet Walker (Lily), Bruno Carette (Grimaldi), François Berléand (Daniel), Martine Gautier (Adele), Paulette Dubost (Madame Vieuzac, Milou's mother), Rozenn Le Tallec (Marie-Laure), Renaud Danner (Pierre-Alain), Jeanne Herry-Leclerc (Françoise)
Length: 108 minutes

DAMAGE (1992)
Production: Nouvelles Editions de Films, Skreba Films, StudioCanal, Channel Four Films, Canal +
Director: **Louis Malle**
Screenplay: David Hare, based on the novel by Josephine Hart
Assistant Director: Michel Ferry
Cinematography: Peter Biziou
Production Design: Brian Morris
Editing: John Bloom
Sound: Jean-Claude Laureux
Music: Zbigniew Preisner
Cast: Jeremy Irons (Stephen Fleming), Juliette Binoche (Anna Barton), Miranda Richardson (Ingrid Fleming), Rupert Graves (Martyn Fleming), Leslie Caron (Elisabeth Prideux), Ian Bannen (Edward Lloyd), Peter Stormare (Peter Wetzlar), Julian Fellowes (Donald Lindsay)
Length: 110 minutes

VANYA ON 42ND STREET (1994)
Production: Channel Four Films, Mayfair Entertainment, The Vanya Company
Director: **Louis Malle**
Screenplay: Andre Gregory, based on David Mamet's adaptation of Anton Chekhov's play *Uncle Vanya*
Assistant Director: Gary Marcus
Cinematography: Declan Quinn
Production Design: Eugene Lee
Editing: Nancy Baker
Sound: Tod A. Maitland
Music: Joshua Redman Quartet
Cast: Wallace Shawn (Vanya), Julianne Moore (Yelena), Brooke Smith (Sonya), Phoebe Brand (Nanny), George Gaynes (Serybryakov), Larry Pine (Dr. Astrov), Jerry Mayer (Waffles), Lynn Cohen (Maman), Andre Gregory (himself), Madhur Jaffrey (Mrs. Chao)
Length: 119 minutes

Louis Malle: Interviews

Do You Know Zazie?
An Interview with Louis Malle

René Gilson / 1960

From *Cinéma*, no. 51 (December 1960): 5–11. Translated from the French by CB.

Louis Malle is leaving the studio where they recorded the music for *Zazie*, and I just had the surprise of hearing the passage from Brahms that has been very familiar to you ever since *Les Amants*. No, Louis Malle hasn't gotten the film wrong: we hear these few measures of Brahms again in *Zazie*. Seriously? But this film is so "unreasonable," as we will hear Louis Malle himself say in a little while!

René Gilson: What explains your long silence since *Les Amants*?

Louis Malle: It was a question of bad luck, that's all. I worked for a long time on two projects that were never completed. The second one, in particular, caused me a good deal of regret: it was an adaptation of a novel by Conrad, *A Victory*, and it was also a remake, since an American film of it had already been made. I had transposed the action of the film to Greece. I went there to work on location and, in the end, for reasons having to do with the rights, the film could not be made. I was so fond of it that I tried to transpose its themes into an original screenplay. But there is a mystery in Conrad, and I failed. It was really naive and pretentious on my part to imagine that one could remake Conrad. In any case, it wasn't wasted time: Alexandre Astruc was correct in saying that, in filmmakers' filmographies, you should also include the films that were not made. Conrad is one of the novelists who is the subtlest in his novelistic technique, and I consider that the work I did in adapting his piece of writing was enriching for me.

RG: You take a book by Raymond Queneau, the comedy of which depends essentially on language and even spelling, you turn your back on all of those people—nine out of ten—who call you a daredevil, and you listen to Alain Resnais, who tells you, "The only problem with *Zazie* is a problem of distribution." You,

Louis Malle, were one of the first people to read the novel *Zazie dans le métro*. Roger Nimier had handed you the manuscript. . . .

LM: I took it with me to Greece, after having told my producer Napoléon Murat: "You should buy the rights." But by the time I came back, the book was famous, and the overbidding for it had begun. Raoul Lévy had bought the rights, and René Clément was going to make the films. Then, Lévy let it go and gave the rights to Murat. Things had come full circle, and I put myself to work on it with Jean-Pierre Rappeneau. I like Rappeneau: I liked his screenplay for the second Arsène Lupin film which Yves Robert directed, and the one for *The Three Musketeers*, which Becker directed. He's a gagman: he has a real sense of comedy. We had decided to make a small, inexpensive film in black-and-white, but it wasn't long before we ran into problems with the work on the film, which turned out to be a long process [since August 15, 1959, Malle has devoted his entire life to *Zazie*], and which ended up being a color film that cost 200 million francs. We were ready for a winter shoot, but we preferred to wait until spring: you don't shoot comic films in the winter, right? Also, we had to rework the script: I made a number of cuts, and I shot kilometers worth of takes with the actors. . . . The shoot ended up taking four months.

What fascinated me in *Zazie*, which isn't the best book by Queneau, was this internal criticism of literature and language. I tried in my way to base my film on another form of autocriticism, that of cinematic language, of *découpage*, combined with the idea of telling a false narrative, a narrative that isn't one. You can easily imagine the little resumé of the film's subject that would appear in *La Semaine de Paris*. . . . An outspoken little girl comes to Paris for forty-eight hours and makes trouble everywhere she goes. *Zazie*, whether it is the book or the film, is obviously something very different from that!

To replace the comedy that was on the level of literary language, I tried to substitute a form of comedy based on cinematic language. I tried, for example, to play with one comic mode: the contraction of time and space, which is a kind of research that is going on now in the cinema. The result was not comic, but it gave the film a curious rhythm, which I was happy to have discovered. I learned more from making *Zazie* than from any of my other films. It's fascinating to make a comic film, and it's also exhausting: it drains you, because you have to be five times as inventive. I understand why Tati only makes a film every five years! It also requires an amount of work on my part—and that of the entire crew—that is much greater than what other films require. And now I'm afraid that all this research, the subtleties I wanted to have in the film, go by too quickly, and that the film is a bit byzantine. A friend of mine said to me, in effect: "If people laugh at anything, they'll miss half the film!" But that doesn't matter: the plot is so linear and the film is so unreasonable. The important thing is that people laugh, because with a comic film that is an absolute criterion. At least children will laugh: I have seen it happen, and *Zazie* will surely be a film that children will like!

We definitely made the main character younger by four years. I wanted to avoid the "Lolita" side of things. Our *Zazie* is therefore a little girl of ten, who will say anything, without equivocation, and who is absolutely outside of the world of adults and is never wrong with respect to it. That world seems to her to be strictly absurd, made up of people who don't know anything about themselves and who live in chaos. Her entrance into the film comes with the music of a Western in the background, and there is a side of her which is like the sheriff of a Western. She arrives in the town and starts to become less in solidarity with its inhabitants. The more she provokes them, makes fun of them, and insults them, the more the chaos is increased. She judges them severely; she will never play their game. But by the end of the film, it was time for her to go: she had begun to let herself be influenced by them. She says, "I got older."

People should be reassured: the little girl who played Zazie was not perverted by her role or by her foray into the cinema. She never identified with the character. She really "interpreted" her role with a perfect sense of distance from it, with an idea about her relationship to the character that was strictly Brechtian. She even talked about her in the third person, saying, "Zazie did such and such. . . ." For her, Zazie was strange, rather spoiled, and unnecessarily aggressive, even though she was right about things.

The other actors came from everywhere. They came from both the theater and the cabaret, and some were amateurs. All of them acted in very different ways, often parodically. Annie Fratellini did a parody of Giulietta Masina, and we also notice that at a secondary level it is a parody of Chaplin. Philippe Noiret plays Uncle Gabriel, a very broad character. He doesn't play him as the crusty old dog—he is a *young* uncle—but with a solemn side that is more in the mode of the Comédie Francaise. The taxi driver is one of my friends, who in real life goes around doing a natural parody of the Actors Studio, but he didn't completely find that naturalness in front of the camera.

In order to accentuate the divide that exists between Zazie and the adult universe, I tried to use the sets to create a world that is a bit fluid, changing its appearance; but these changes still have a realist justification. So the bistro is a dirty, dark, old bistro at the beginning of the film so that it can become, over time, through a process of modernization that is completely in line with what is happening today, a shiny snack bar. So there is always a transformation taking place in the décor of the bistro. It's the same thing for Gabriel's nightclub. In the fight at the end, they break through the walls of the set and we discover the original bistro, as if the modern transformation had just happened within the interior of the old one, just twenty centimeters from its former space. It was Bernard Evein who came up with the design for the sets.

Gabriel's apartment is a glass conservatory where all the neon signs of the city are reflected: it is green, then violet. It's horrible. I wanted to play on the horrible aspect of the city, its impossible side, its absurd inconveniences.

I used the new Eastman film stock, which allowed me to shoot in color with the same freedom as in black-and-white. The arrival of this film stock is as important as that of the Tri X stock was five or six years ago. Using it, my cameraman used four times less light than Clouzot's, and we were able to shoot a night scene in Pigalle without artificial light. Until now, in color films—other than documentaries—we have been condemned by cinematographers to a kind of academicism. Now, we can dare to do the same things in color as we do in black-and-white. And we still never dare to go far enough. We can stop treating color in such a realistic way.

I shot some scenes at eight frames per second: this inexhaustible virtue and this eternal comic vice of speeding up the action is extremely curious. Perhaps the essence of the comic resides in it: we always make reference to the real, but at the same time to its deformation. But it was also a way of using three times less light, and, by allowing the actor to play in slow motion, you can in fact get the same movement as you would at twenty-four frames a second. I'm sure that you don't notice that certain shots were done at eight frames per second. But it gave me the possibility of creating an unexpected kind of burlesque: the movement of the actor playing in slow motion remains the same, but the box of matches that he drops . . . or the car moving on screen!

You see, you can constantly make new discoveries in filmic language, and you take more and more satisfaction from moving away from the faithful reproduction of reality. For the filmmaker, an apple can't simply be an apple, just as the burghers painted by Franz Hals could not simply be the people whose portraits he painted. And, with a comic film, one can do anything. At the beginning of the shoot, my script girl was being driven crazy; by the end, she was the one who was encouraging me to make continuity errors!

Breathless, Pickpocket, and *Hiroshima mon amour* certainly represent the modern cinema movement. We are searching for a new representation of time and space. (I am less in agreement with the kind of research that is done in *L'Avventura,* despite the admirable talent of Antonioni.) But it is not so much the problems of construction that interest me; it is on the inside of the cinematic material itself, on the inside of a shot, that I like to discover something new. Personally, this kind of work has brought a real enrichment on the level of both *mise en scene* and cinematography. When I think that I learned cinema with this obsession with the rational representation of reality! And the freedoms that filmmakers are not using are accepted very naturally by the public. It's the technicians who are often more difficult to convince.

Interviewer's note: Traditionally, these kinds of interviews end with compliments and wishes for future success. At the moment, I am thinking about what we exchanged concerning American burlesque, W. C. Fields, and also this curious hiatus between Louis Malle's first two films and his third film. *Elevator to the Gallows* and *Les Amants* are now listed in one of my film categories, and by no means the least precious one: the category of films that I was not enthusiastic about when I saw them for the first time but that, on a second viewing—especially when it came after a long pause—acquired a maturation and an expansion of their qualities, making me want to see them again, whereas certain other films are quickly forgotten fireworks. Today, Louis Malle is enthusiastic and happy about this strange film he has just completed, while at the same time experiencing that disquieting feeling which especially affects the director of a comic film during the period between the end of his work on the film and the film's first contact with the public.

Interview with Louis Malle

André-Georges Brunelin / 1962

From *Cinéma*, no. 63 (February 1962): 9–27. Translated from the French by CB.

Louis Malle: What I call the "Bardot myth," and which is certainly a very important phenomenon in modern mythology, is something that can be explained, even though I'm not completely persuaded by it. But, in any case, that is a matter for sociologists, not for storytellers. I am willing to believe that there is a lot to say about the studies of sexual myths that have intervened in the career of Brigitte Bardot, but I don't believe that it's a phenomenon that is easy to explain in cinema without the risk of falling either into an intellectual analysis—which ends up being a *film à thèse*, and which I am personally against, since the cinema is really not designed for that kind of analytical demonstration—or into the genre of explanation, which brings up the mindset of a certain kind of journalism, like that of *France-Dimanche*.

What interests me in this film, *Vie privée*, is that I believe—I'm even sure—that Brigitte Bardot is a character. I don't have an answer for all the questions that this character raises. I do, however, have some of them. And I think that you don't fascinate millions of people around the world, as is true in her case, without that fascination corresponding to something real about her. As a consequence, if you make a film with her, it's interesting to make her play a character who allows her to be the closest to herself, to what she is in reality. In that way, there is the least amount that has to be "composed," to be "shifted." In the end, the film could be explained by the fact that for one and three-quarter hours we are showing Brigitte as she really is. There can be as much invention as you want, and as much "creativity" as you can imagine, but you still see a character evolve who is, I believe, in quite a real sense, what Brigitte is in life.

André-Georges Brunelin: Basically, it was not the life of Bardot that interested you and that you wanted to show so much as the character she is playing.

LM: In fact, yes. . . . There is a very "documentary" aspect to the film: it is a documentary about Brigitte Bardot. We never leave her side. The camera stays relentlessly fixed on her. And we can already draw a conclusion from that: that this character has to be extremely solid, contrary to what many people say, because I think that the character "holds up" admirably well. There is a television show called "Reading for Everyone" which has already impressed me in this sense. The hosts, Pierre Dumayet and Pierre Desgraupes, put writers who come to talk about themselves and their books on the spot. The camera scrutinizes their faces and their hands in close-up. What is striking is that some of them come in with a studied look or a certain attitude, and then, as the minutes pass, and as they are put on display by the camera, which "searches" them, we discover, little by little, certain tics, or a trembling of their hands, as the questions Dumayet and Desgraupes ask them take away their masks. And often, when what the person came in with was fabricated or superficial, he can't hold up under the analysis. He falls apart, and we become aware that the guy who had come in encased in a shell that he thought was solid, with an attitude that he had composed for the circumstance, leaves the stage almost naked, remaining just a poor specimen, with no scope, no real depth. The experience of that show taught us something, because at the beginning of the shoot we were asking ourselves, deep down, "Who is this girl?" On the walls of our office, we were writing a kind of statement about her each day, as we studied her case. In fact, it came to pass that we were quite violently against this story. We would say, for example, "This isn't possible . . . we can't make a film about this girl. . . . She won't hold up. . . . She must be faking it." On the contrary, on other days, we found her to be great: she fascinated us. It was funny. Basically, she represented a big question mark . . . and the film, more than any other, rested completely on her shoulders. And the film proves, conclusively, that Brigitte is an uncommon heroine of the cinema. If it hadn't been for that, you understand, we would have fallen into a caricature in the style of *France-Dimanche*. We definitely felt the danger of that in the screenplay.

AGB: Can we talk about the screenplay? Wasn't it more or less a theme where Brigitte was the object being studied and you were leaning over her, using the methods of an entomologist?

LM: We tried to play that game, and it was Brigitte, in part, who was leading it. I improvised a lot. It's the film that I have the improvised the most on, and I really don't like doing that. It's too tiring for my nerves. It's the difference between trapeze artists who do their act over a net and those who do it without a net: our net was the script, the screenplay.

AGB: The theme of the film, and the idea of the film itself, lent themselves to that method.

LM: I wanted, at the beginning of the film, to show this character in the context of her childhood. She is a young girl from a good family, who lives in a charming old house next to Lake Geneva. She has a mother, an old servant, a bicycle, a goat, dancing, games, swimming, friends: it's the whole "before the original sin" side of things. And I wanted to show her as it was written in the screenplay, in the time of her memory, with stops, jumps ahead, and a slight fogginess in the cinematography, like old photos that have become yellowed with time, and music that is happy and a bit jaunty.

AGB: And that's what you did.

LM: Yes, that's what I did. I like that whole beginning of the film. But afterwards, I wanted to jump over the rest of the story, and show the young woman going to Paris, with a card saying, "Three Years Later." She has become an idol, a kind of monster of popular culture, whose every act and gesture unleash people's passions. I took out the middle part of the story, you see. I wanted to postulate that this young woman whom we had seen living a happy life in Geneva abruptly becomes a kind of golden calf. I was playing on the fact that the whole world knew the basic outline of her rise to fame. That was a theoretical impression we had, but we couldn't trust in it completely. So we chose a middle ground. Since we had to tell what had happened, we were led to divulge a few keys to the situation, without explaining the actual reasons. We did it in a rapid way.

AGB: It's true that in this part of the film—which is, I grant you, quite brief—we find certain situations that she really experienced, and we can even find sketches of characters who are caricatures of famous people whose lives crossed hers. So I will ask you a question that everyone will be asking themselves: "Why isn't Roger Vadim in it?"

LM: Vadim isn't there, in any part of the film, because we didn't want to make a movie that was a *film à clé*. We knew from the start that everyone would be looking for him, which was another reason not to put him in. In addition, as I've told you, that part of the story didn't interest me. It was a bit of a mission statement for me. Including Vadim would have made me lengthen the film. Also, I don't share the generally accepted opinion that someone "made" Brigitte. Vadim helped her, that is clear. Without him, she wouldn't have had the will and the courage to persevere.

AGB: Is it fair to say that the biographical aspect of your film ends at the point of her return to Geneva, after the major breakdown which follows the riot?

LM: Yes, there was definitely a portion of interpretation and an invention of details. Basically, I think the film is divided into three time periods: the beginning, in Geneva, which is set "before the original sin," is the past time frame. There is a bit of a prolongation of this time period, which is the part shown in flashback, where I use a voiceover commentary as well as magazine clippings that show her rise. Then there is Paris, her success, the disorder and chaos that her life starts to be: that is the present time. The whole second half of the film, which is, I believe, the most important part, is a projection into the future. The essential theme of the film is: let us imagine that Brigitte Bardot, after a serious and violent breakdown—that's really what we wanted to show with the scene of the breakdown that comes right after the scene in the elevator with the insults from the cleaning woman—falls in love, and is loved by someone who doesn't have anything to do with her, who would have come out of another walk of life, another universe, as in the case of Odette and Swann in Proust. He doesn't have the same preoccupations as she does, or the same life. We therefore chose a character—the character of Fabio, played by Marcello Mastroianni—and we made him closer to us, because it's better to talk about things you know about. He is an intellectual who lives in the world of spectacle, the theater world. He is passionate about his work, and as with all people who are passionate about their work, the problem of his love life is a real problem to the extent that he cannot abandon everything, sacrifice everything to the woman he loves. We went on from there. The door was wide open, because it was no longer a question of autobiography. And also, from the moment when Brigitte's nerves are "broken" or "shattered," the moment when she finds Fabio again, we started to have a very different tone.

AGB: In the part in Geneva, the first of the two parts that take place in Geneva. . . .

LM: That was the part that made the most work for me. First of all, it was at the beginning of the shoot. And then there was the fact that, for a fairly long period of time, Brigitte and I didn't like each other. In other words, I believe that she was bored with shooting films. She had gotten to a point where she had really had enough, not just of cinema, but of everything that surrounds it. She had had enough of being stalked. She wanted to stop making films, with the thought— wrong in my opinion—that she would stop being a person who was constantly in the spotlight, and that then she could lead a normal life, be a normal girl.

In the first part of the film, for example, I had to fight with her a bit to get her not to wear makeup. She did manage, little by little, to gain a certain consciousness about her character. You know, they say that it always took four hours for Marilyn Monroe to "make herself into" Marilyn Monroe, there was an enormous job of doing the makeup and the hair. Brigitte is a much simpler kind of person, much less sophisticated, but she has still become, over time, a certain type of character, one from whom she can't separate herself without an effort. I really wanted to have a "fresh" Brigitte, a very "young girl" version of her (which I did by glossing over the part of the story that fell between her departure from Geneva and her success—the auditorium scene, for example).

That theme interested me a lot! It was the side of Brigitte as the anti-Hollywood star. That's a very particular and interesting aspect of the Bardot myth. She's not the girl whose childhood was unhappy, who was dying of hunger, and who took control of her life out of revenge. The classic type of that character is

Marilyn, isn't it? Brigitte is the opposite. She is a girl who came from the bourgeoisie. All of that gives her a certain assurance. We know that she didn't care that much, deep down, about her career. Above all, she loved to dance, and she loved music. That attitude gave her a great ability to stay relaxed. In the film, we showed one scene where she is doing a screen test. She doesn't care whether she gets the part or not. That gives her an impertinence that corresponds with how she really was.

AGB: You said before that there was a change in tone in the film from the moment when, after the nervous breakdown, which led to the verge of insanity, she runs into Fabio again in Geneva. You imagine her future, and the tone becomes more tragic.

LM: The story that we imagined couldn't end well, I mean, not in a "happy ending," and that can be felt from the beginning of the film on. I'm not against the principle of the happy ending, but in this case, it would have been absolutely against the grain. This film, this long downward slide into infinity, may not really signify her death. It is a lyrical conclusion, an ending for a mythological heroine. You know, I love endings that are left open-ended. I couldn't have shot a scene where we really see her fall and crash to the ground. To tell the truth, I'm not sure that she dies in the literal sense of the word. It may be just a part of her that goes away, that detaches itself and falls away. It's a bit like in a dream. I believe that we made it very clear, in the part of the film that takes place in Spoleto, that there was no future for their love, in the way the noose is tightening around them and in the way they are putting themselves into it. Because it would be superficial to believe that all of that is coming from other people: from the crowd, from journalists. It comes just as much from the two of them, from the difficulty they have in loving each other, in living. It comes from him, for example: from his egotism as a creative person and as a man who is obsessed by his work, and from his whole character, which is very Italian, very authoritarian; and it comes, just as much, from this taste for—and in Brigitte, the real Brigitte, it is even stronger—this need to be with other people, to not move away from them. In Brigitte, there is a certain fear of solitude.

AGB: So you have the feeling, as far as the second half of the film is concerned, that, at least in spirit if not in the facts, the character of Jill intimately "matches" that of Brigitte?

LM: The Brigitte who returns to Geneva, from the moment when she starts to love Fabio, and above all during the part in Spoleto, is, if you will, a Brigitte out of a tragedy by Corneille. You recall the line of La Bruyère: "Racine depicts heroes as they are; Corneille shows them as they should be." I think that the character we told the story about is a bit ahead of where Brigitte really is, and of what she is feeling right now. It's that projection into the future that I was talking about earlier. We have shown a kind of ideal Brigitte, as she should be, and also as she thinks she already is. I am not interested in mediocre characters. I intensified the character of Jill because I prefer heroes. Jill is the heroine of a novel, a true one, like in Stendhal. Too bad if Brigitte isn't exactly like that.

AGB: How did she react when she had to play scenes which presented situations that were like the ones she had really lived through?

LM: One example is the scene where she tries to commit suicide. I had a terrible time getting her to do it. She didn't want to. You understand, she was always colliding with this character who was upsetting her, who was stalking her. I had to empty the set. She had an extraordinary modesty in her. And perhaps she was also afraid.

AGB: It seems like it is a given that *Vie privée* is not "the life of Bardot"; however, could you have made the film with an actress other than Brigitte?

LM: No, I don't think so. The film as it stands benefits too much from the presence of Brigitte, from this dreamlike emotion, from this confrontation, if I dare to put it in this way, between her and her. In order to play certain scenes, she put herself into a state of rebellion, and sometimes certain words came out of her with such a violence! At other moments, she was withheld, with the feeling of being on edge. It was really astonishing.

AGB: For this film, you adopted a pointillist and fragmented style, which is quite surprising.

LM: First of all, there is the idea that we were telling a story which, starting at the beginning, went on over a number of years. I was therefore led to tighten things, to choose only the moments that seemed essential to the understanding of the character and her story. Nowadays, I look more and more for ways to break through a certain dramatic convention of the cinema, which owes a lot to the theater, and which I personally believe we need to move beyond. A lot of films become terribly dated, because they are filled with constant references to a classic form of dramaturgy. On the contrary: if you are telling a story that is based on current material, you can very easily take just parts of it. You can certainly take entire blocks of the story; but if I go further, if I take just brief instants in the story, then I am breaking the basic principle of traditional cinema, which is the "scene," in which, as in the theater, there is the entrance of characters who take us little by little toward a crisis, and to the point of either force or rupture, before they exit. Between the moment when the characters enter and the moment when they exit, something happens, which forms a kind of whole. It is obviously a convention that you bring them to this place so that they can say what they have to say. I'm exaggerating a bit. I try to turn my back on all that. I believe that the cinema corresponds better to the Stendhalian definition of the novel. It is a mirror that moves along a road. *Vie privée* is something like that. All through this story, all through this character of Jill, we are walking along, walking next to her. It is a long tracking shot, and, from time to time, we press the button on the camera. We only film her from time to time.

AGB: How did you proceed in your work on the set, in terms of *mise en scene*?

LM: It would be very dangerous to make actors feel that only *parts* of the scenes they are playing will be used in the film. They shouldn't be aware of it. If the actors played the game of "pointillist" style, it would have disastrous consequences, because they would not be able to put themselves in the right situations. Actors are like a motor: you have to throw them into gear. I was able to discover a shooting technique, through making both *Zazie* and *Vie privée*, that I could almost patent! It consists of doing fairly long shots, like sequence shots—in other words, a shot that lasts a minute or two minutes, and which follows all the action from several camera positions, and with different positions of the actors. I know, while shooting it, which parts of this shot will be used in the final edit. It's not just a question of the editing, but a calculation about the *mise en scene*. I need to have this just about in place at the time of shooting. I take into consideration the "shortcuts" I have foreseen. Let's imagine two characters going from a bed to a table; I am intentionally simplifying. I film all the action, and I indicate to the actors how I want them to play the whole scene, even though I know that I will be cutting out the part, for example, where they are moving across the room. I pay just as much attention to them moving, even though I know I won't be using it, because it can create the exact tone that I'm looking for at the moment when they get to the table. Thus, I get a rhythm of normal acting which follows a classical dramatic progression, but this rhythm, in my mind, has already been broken or accentuated. I am faced with a living material, out of which I can carve an edit that follows my idea of the scene; and the *mise en scene* will not have disturbed the performance of my actors at all.

AGB: In this way, I think that *Vie privée* comes close, in dramatic tone, to the style of *Zazie dans le métro*.

LM: There is a connection between *Zazie* and *Vie privée*. That might surprise people, but for me it is both obvious and intentional. As in *Zazie*, there are major ruptures in rhythm: brief moments, dead times, and then long sequences that develop in a more classic way.

As my cinematic style has evolved, it has changed. I couldn't make *Les Amants* today, and I had warned my producers that *Vie privée* would be more like *Zazie*. I think they took it as a joke, but it's true. *Zazie* made me discover many things on the level of technique. That's our material as filmmakers, just like the painter has his paints and his colors. Moving forward, one discovers infinite possibilities of expression, and *Vie privée* certainly benefits a great deal from my experience of making *Zazie*, even if it's just in the way time is treated. It is fairly linear, but it is captured as if in sudden bursts, with a kind of violence, an aggressive aspect. Since nearly all the films we make involve dealing with our own time, what is most striking in our time is its violence and its disorder, which are represented in the compositions of modern painters. I don't see why, in order to please the public, we have to make films that have perfect synchronization of movement—where everything runs smoothly, well oiled. It would be as if painters were still painting in chiaroscuro. I'm very sensitive to the absurd side of contemporary life, to the disorder and violence that characterize it, and I think that shouldn't be lost in the story, in the subject of a film, and especially in the writing itself, in the style, particularly when it is a question, as in *Vie privée*, of a theme of love rendered impossible by a number of circumstances which come from the life we live, and from the terrible influence of the mass media of the press. I'm not saying that *Vie privée* is a pamphlet, or a social satire, but even so. . . .

AGB: Do you think you still described a social phenomenon?

LM: Yes, I think so. That wasn't exactly my intention, but I think it will affect people because it is there, as a kind of watermark. And what interests me is that it is expressed not only in the basic story, but also in the technique itself. Some novelists write revolutionary books with very daring ideas, but their technique has remained the same as that of Balzac. I know that I am working in a more "disintegrated" cinematic style, and I will not go backwards. I hope that the public will follow me. But they have bad habits. We have made it too easy for them. There is nothing astonishing about the fact that the public was surprised, even shocked, by the aggressive aspect of *Zazie*. Note that *Zazie* was a very concerted effort to shock: there were a lot of provocations in it. *Vie privée* is very different. I would like to say that the aggressive aspect still exists, and it might even irritate some people, but it is no longer a trick: the form corresponds more closely with the subject matter. There are still sequences that are slow, soft, set in the present, and classically edited.

AGB: Is there only one rear projection shot in *Vie privée*?

LM: Alas, yes! There is one, in one car scene, because it was easier. But I don't like rear projection. I think it is ugly and always looks fake. And putting real people on the street brings out what I was talking about just now: in the street, you have the feeling of this absurd life, of people running, and bumping into each other, without seeming to know where they're going.

AGB: You made Fabio an intellectual who was enamored of the theater. The play that he puts on at the Spoleto Festival has an important role in the film. Why did you choose Kleist's *Katie of Heilbronn*?

LM: Well! Because we needed a play which would allow us to have that kind of spectacle—that would enhance the scenic representation of Spoleto—and also because I love Kleist's plays, and I feel very close to this theater.

AGB: You seem—not only in your films but also in your theories—to be the least intellectual of the young directors of recent years, in the literary sense of the word. What do you think?

LM: Yes, perhaps. I had a different education: in other words, I really learned my craft as a technician, especially with Cousteau. I worked on all the techniques of cinema. As for making comparisons, I would prefer a comparison with painting rather than with literature. There is—in painting as in cinema—the same combat with our material. I feel closer to being a painter than a novelist.

AGB: We feel that in *Zazie* as well as in *Vie privée*.

LM: I think it's a mistake to put yourself in the position of being an intellectual who expresses himself through the cinema, and who could just as easily say what he has to say in a novel. There are a lot of guys from my generation—some of whom have an enormous amount of talent—who have taken that route. Twenty or thirty years ago, they would have written novels, and now they make films. The cinema is a bit abstract as a vehicle. I myself have preoccupations that are more visual, more pictorial. What interests me is not so much telling a story, but the way of telling it. What fascinates me in cinema is seeing how this filmic material is both beautiful and resistant. There are infinite possibilities in our work, and we are only gradually grasping both the difficulties and the solutions.

AGB: What differences do you see between you and the filmmakers of the older generation?

LM: None. Except that you don't make the same films at twenty-five as you make at fifty. The new French cinema strongly resembles the cinema that the older generation made when they were young. Godard makes references to the René Clair who made *Quatorze Juillet* [*Bastille Day*, 1933], Truffaut makes references to the films of Jean Vigo, and *Last Year in Marienbad* could have been a film by Germaine Dulac.

AGB: What cultural traditions do you feel part of?

LM: Alas, how do you escape from the tyrannical tradition that, since childhood, has taken us into its mold—this western tradition of Christian humanism, which is rational and powerfully determined by Descartes? How do you escape from it other than through a very lively curiosity about other forms of thought, especially those of Africa? But our intelligence and our sensibilities are too structured by the disciplines of the Sorbonne for us to be anything more than admiring travelers through other forms of culture.

I have the feeling of being part of a major transition—that which marks the end of the domination by the West—and I am appalled by the self-righteousness and the deafness of many European and American intellectuals, who, at the dawning of the atomic age, still persist in having systems of moral and psychological values that have absolutely expired (and I don't make an exception for the

Marxists of our countries). But what can be done about it? There is an irreversible historical process, which makes us look a lot like the Sages of Byzantium. In any case, our incoherence is itself a testimony, whether it is voluntary or not.

AGB: What are your fundamental principles?

LM: My only rule up to now has been my curiosity, which spreads out a bit in all directions. For a filmmaker, as for a painter, all subjects are good ones, even to the extent that the subject doesn't matter. There is that eternal and ridiculous question about the content and the form, which, unfortunately, the spectators and critics of film have not entirely resolved. It is appalling to think that we usually classify filmmakers based not on their style (even though it's true that few possess one), but on the abstract content of their work.

AGB: Do you think you capture our times through your films?

LM: I think it would be difficult not to express the disorder, the violence, and the absurdity of our lives, even if you wished not to express them, and even when we are analyzing traditional emotions.

AGB: What are the main obstacles that you encounter?

LM: The only true obstacles are the ones we find inside us. The cinema is such a vast art—so mysterious, so difficult to master—that disappointment builds up. My films, once they are finished, are never more than the caricature of what I had dreamed of making a few months earlier. Reality is so difficult to grasp, to transpose, to dominate: it is an inert and resistant material, which tramples my imagination. That's why, with each new film, I have to recharge my batteries. I try to make each one a different adventure from the one before, through the subject matter, the shooting conditions, et cetera. In the background, there are the same uncertainties, the same curiosity, and the same disappointments.

If I continue to make films, it's because, going through this maze of incoherence, I have the feeling of a progression. Each time, the split between the dream and the realization of the dream gets smaller. The material resists a bit less. Each film brings me its share of simple truths, and of things that suddenly become obvious. In ten or twenty years, perhaps I will be a good director.

Malle from India

Guy Braucourt / 1969

From *Cinéma*, no. 135 (April 1969): 27–31. Translated from the French by CB.

Calcutta is a document of an hour and thirty-five minutes which Louis Malle has brought back to us from a four-month journey to India (from January to April 1968). It is the first part of a mass of forty hours of 16mm footage out of which Malle hopes to get a five-to-six-hour film devoted to the rest of India, and that he will release either in segments on television, or (if possible) as a unit in theaters. The least that can be said of this film is that it is uncomfortable: it is the kind of film that breaks through the screen to come and hit you as you sit on your couch, and which forces you to plunge into all the misery of the world.

Guy Braucourt: In leaving aside fiction-based cinema to go and capture the reality of India, have you in fact gone back to the source, since you came to the cinema through documentary?

Louis Malle: Well, I have always been divided between these two temptations: let us call them, in order to repeat the divide that has always existed within French cinema, the Lumière tendency and the Méliès tendency. At the beginning of my career, when I started, it was the Lumière aspect of cinema that interested me. And then I wanted to be an auteur of films: I wanted to tell stories, to research different areas of life. . . . But I always kept a nostalgia for the extraordinary freedom that direct cinema can give. What is exhilarating in this kind of cinema is that the image usually comes before the idea. And I have already felt the temptation to do this several times: in 1962 in Algeria (which didn't work out), in 1964 in Bangkok (for the television series *Cinq colonnes à la une*), and I also made a short documentary of the Tour de France.

GB: One has the impression, seeing *Calcutta*, that it will be very difficult for you to make cinema as you did before.

LM: Yes, I think so too! But perhaps I am wrong. Also, there is one thing that has really struck me in Rivette's last film, *L'Amour fou*, and which is also very striking in the films of Godard, but with a different approach. That is, that you could apply this same mentality, this same conception of the cinema—it actually doesn't have that much to do with the technique of shooting—to fictional subjects. In Rivette's film, which is in certain respects highly crafted, he has managed at certain moments to give the impression of a freedom that I have rarely felt in cinema. I believe that this is the case because he knew how to place conditions on a fiction film which are very close to the ones we had when we filmed in Calcutta.

GB: And why did you privilege Calcutta over the rest of India?

LM: I didn't originally have the intention of making a separate film, but when I got home, watching everything we had filmed, I realized that the process hadn't been the same for Calcutta as for the rest of the country. Whereas I had gone there to make something very subjective—because I presumptuously thought I could explain India to viewers—and whereas the rest of the footage was a kind of very personal take on "Indianness," the reality of Calcutta imposed itself as something stronger, something more shocking, which absolutely doesn't make you want to try to express the state of its soul, but makes you be content to record it as objectively as possible, even if at some moments there is of necessity a choice that has to be made. I had even thought, initially, that I would not put the commentaries in it at all, as is the case in the first few minutes of the film. But I believe, after all, that it is indispensable to give information to the viewer at certain moments: things like statistics, general facts about the country, et cetera.

GB: In several sequences, most notably the one involving the cremation, with the husband who performs all the acts of the ritual without apparent emotion, there is the feeling that these people are detached from their material circumstances, that they are ready to accept anything: their poverty, their hunger, and even their death. And it is frightening because they say that no political solution is possible, not even a revolutionary one—at least in the near future.

LM: Yes, that's exactly right! And it is a very difficult thing to understand, for a Western mind. I don't like to use the word "fatalism," which has taken on a somewhat peculiar meaning, but let's say that it has to do with a certain notion of duty, with the idea that man lives in a fixed world, that he is in passage through the world—this passage being in a secondary and illusory state—in order to accomplish a mission, that he has been assigned to be part of a caste, and thus that he has to live within the rules and limits of that caste. It may be a case of religion as opium of the masses, but we have to believe that this system brings people something that satisfies them in a certain way, because it has resisted everything for centuries and centuries, including colonization and industrial civilization. If not, there would have been a revolution a long time ago! And now, you really have to be an optimist to envision any kind of political solution for the problems of India. But to come back to the sequence of the cremation: I think you have to take your attention to one element that at the same time de-dramatizes the serious, theatrical, definitive event which death is for us Westerners, and also makes us understand the particular climate in which it takes place. That element is the synchronous sound, which allows us to hear the sounds of the street and the conversations between people, and that gives this death the familiar, everyday, and "normal" character it has for Indians. It's in that way that direct cinema is really fascinating: you don't have to say things, and explain them, since everything is implicit in the image and the sound. And this kind of cinema matches so well with reality that in the end we want to project the images as they are, and to let the spectator deal with them! What interests me personally in this kind of cinema is that at the very least we move past this notion that is sacrosanct in France of the *cinéma d'auteur,* in the sense that it's not really the vision that a creator or an "artist" imposes on you, but a lived experience that frees you. It demands of viewers a participation that is more complete than in a normal film, and it gives them the task of defining themselves in relation to the reality shown in the film. In some ways, it can be the point of departure for a personal reflection.

GB: You know, you are completely in line with the ideas that Rossellini declared ten years ago, after making *India 58*: "With *India 58*, I wanted to give the feeling of a world. I would like the spectator to come out of the screening with that feeling. And it would be up to him to judge whether it was important, whether it was urgent to show it to the public or not. The public has to come out of the theater with the same feeling that I had in India. In other words, he would have to discover that a world is there before his eyes, and it is our world." And he also wrote: "Editing is not essential anymore. Things are simply there, and especially in this film. Why manipulate them?"

LM: Ah! I am absolutely in agreement with him, and I could repeat his declaration for myself. I love Rossellini's cinema, and I projected *India 58* for myself right before leaving to shoot in India. That said, our films are very different, because we didn't take the same approach to the subject. He stayed there, and he made the film in normal shooting conditions, with spotlights and a real crew. He still "constructed" a film, choosing a certain number of episodes and characters which seemed to him to be representative of the India of today. It's a film that makes me think more about Rossellini than about India. Whereas we just arrived in India—I had just a cameraman and a sound engineer, we took out our equipment, and we started filming. We included everything: things that astonished us, things that were difficult for us, and even things that seemed to us to be unfilmable or unusable. On the other hand, Rossellini gives a bit of an ideal image of India, and at the same time a bit of an official image, because he was attached to the idea of showing that India was modernizing while respecting its traditional values. In a sense, it's a very reassuring film. As for me, that was not at all what I felt in India. I had the impression of two forces that met in a very indecisive battle with a very short deadline: modernization and tradition. And I never saw a satisfying synthesis between the material advantages of Western civilization and the cultural and spiritual values of India.

Interview with Louis Malle

Robert Grelier / 1969

From *Image et Son—La Revue du cinéma*, no. 228 (May 1969): 81–89. Translated from the French by CB.

Robert Grelier: After the prestigious fiction films you have directed up to now, you have just modified your itinerary once again by directing *Calcutta*, but this time taking a completely different path from the previous films, since you chose to make a documentary. Why?

Louis Malle: I'm a director for whom it is always difficult to place a label on each of my films, or on the ensemble of my work, because each time I have always tried to renew myself by constantly changing in terms of genre and theme. I am in favor of experiments, and at several points I have shot films in 16mm that I never edited, considering them to be imperfect. Among them is a film set in Algeria in 1962. Don't forget that I started as a documentarist, since I was a collaborator of Cousteau for three years, and since then I have never completely abandoned the genre. I made a film about the Tour de France (*Vive le Tour*), a short film made for television about Thailand, and another short film for television, which I consider to be a draft version of the film you have just seen on Calcutta. But the most important thing for me is that, since 1967, I have had a strong desire to change the focus. It is, in fact, more a need for a change in life than in cinema. Since *The Thief of Paris*, I have had a physical need to go back into the world, into reality. Fiction films, with actors, interest me less and less. I no longer feel the pleasure in making them that I did a while ago. The cinema, which had always been a source of amusement for me, had become a boring routine. I had to get myself out of it, or I would have exploded from the sheer facts about my origins, my education, and my social milieu. I was in the process of becoming a pillar of society; I could feel it very clearly.

RG: Was this a precursor to the events of May 1968? No one would have blamed you at that time for having a sudden awakening; they would have believed that it was as good opportunity for you.

LM: This bad feeling that I have just explained to you was something I felt well before May '68. I returned from India on May 3. On the plane I had read newspapers that led one to believe that important events were going to take place, but no one knew exactly what they were going to be. We thought that it would be different from what had happened up to then, but we didn't know exactly what that was. On that evening of May 3, I got clubbed by the police. I was there by chance, but that put me in contact with a reality that I had not been able to suspect, and that only confirmed my need for change.

I wanted to take this dive into the real with something that was new to me, and India was the ideal terrain for that experience. Our position in the beginning was to be interested first and foremost in living beings, before being interested in temples, in the stones: I leave that to tourists. When I asked for an advance from the Centre National du Cinéma (CNC), I was only able to write two pages of text, not knowing anything about what I was going to find, since the trip of a few weeks that I had made a few months earlier had not given me the elements I needed. The only thing that I could point to in this synopsis was that my project was going to be a journal of a trip that I had a great need of taking, a little bit like writers who, in their lives, have experienced this same necessity at a certain moment in their existence. It was, in a way, a method for looking at myself, different from one I would have known about until then. It was a kind of game of mirrors that I made for myself. This kind of cleansing that I gave myself was very healthy, and because of this confrontation with the reality of a country that is so different from the one I had known, a new man was born: the one I am today. I'm not saying that I won't make more fiction films with actors, but what I would like to say is that they will be very different from what I could have made up to now.

I would have a lot to say about the so-called spirituality of Westerners who go to lose themselves in India, to try to rediscover what they could not find here, but my project wasn't that, because there is a terrible temptation to lose yourself in this labyrinth, and I have to say that I would be quite ferocious with these Westerners, because I don't believe in the synthesis of cultures. It is a flagrant contradiction. You don't go through one to get to the other. It's not possible, and I don't believe in it. In the same way, the Anglo-Indians are very uncomfortable. They are sitting on two chairs, and they don't know which one of them to adopt for living in. For *Calcutta*, I refused to give myself any veil of fiction, and I made myself naked; at its heart, it is a very personal film. At least, I tried to make the film in that way.

RG: What do you envision for the distribution of *Calcutta*? Because you have declared at several points that it is not possible to distribute this film as you would another film, as you did with your previous films—in other words, like an ordinary consumer product.

LM: *Calcutta* is not a spectacle film. I don't have a solution for the distribution. The film is made in the absolute logic of a system in which we live. You only have to look at the posthumous fate of Che Guevara: it is completely exemplary. There is a recuperation at every level. The other day, I was at the CNC on Rue de Lubeck, and I saw, through the window, two young girls of fifteen, middle-class teenagers, who were both dancing. I couldn't hear the music, but what I was able to distinguish clearly was that the walls of their room were completely covered with posters of Che! I counted at least twelve of them. Everywhere there is recuperation. . . . The bourgeoisie can easily allow itself to distribute Lenin and Marx on a massive scale because their books become a source of profit. For *Calcutta*, something similar could happen, but even supposing that I could make money from it—which I doubt, given the stage we are at with the representatives of distribution companies—I have taken the moral stand of not trying to make a profit on the lives of the Indian people. I could easily send checks to Mother Theresa's organization, or to the charitable associations that take care of lepers, or to the Indian government, but what purpose would that serve? I would prefer to send it to the people who want to change the social order, but who are so few and so ineffective that, even then, the money would not be of much use. I wouldn't send money to the Indian government, because when you see what the level of corruption is within it, that money would only serve to pay for a few more cases of wine.

RG: Have you seen *The Hour of the Furnaces* by Ferdinand Solanas? For those of us who had just seen the two films, it seemed that the only response to your film was to watch a screening of the Argentinian film. Not that the solutions proposed by it could be immediately, easily, or identically applicable to India, but the film demonstrates that the only possible solution to changing the structures of a developing country—to use that euphemism—is armed struggle.

LM: Alas, I haven't seen the film yet, and many of my friends have spoken to me enthusiastically about it; but I think that *The Hour of the Furnaces* is a film that speaks to militants, whereas mine stops short of that and does not seek to create a political conscience based on human facts.

The distribution of *Calcutta* is creating a lot of difficulties for me. It seems to me incompatible to present the film in ordinary theaters, asking for an entrance fee of eleven francs. That seems indecent to me. The solution that I envision would be to ask viewers to pay only a price of five francs, for example, so that the maximum number of people could see the film, but that is hardly possible to do nowadays. The best solution of all, and the one I would wish for, is to make it so the film could be seen for free! Someone just proposed to me that it could be screened with the aid of the Worldwide Movement Against Hunger, with part of the ticket price going to India. I can't accept this proposition either, because it would be going against what I just said. So, what should I do?

RG: What about television?

LM: Assuming that they would agree to show the film in its entirety—which I doubt—I am worried about the receptivity of television. Cinema has, after all, a different impact: it is a more effective medium. In the United States, there is a whole system of universities, which favors using that means of distribution, but, even there, we would only reach one category of spectators. There is a lot of work to be done on the level of structures of distribution, don't you think?

RG: After the screening of *Calcutta*, we said to ourselves, "This is terrible! But what can we do about it?" We are taken over by an immeasurable sense of impotence when faced with what remains to be accomplished in that country, which neither charity nor aid from developed countries can resolve. The problems are both innumerable and immense.

LM: I wanted to put the quote from Frantz Fanon at the end of the film: "The national liberation of colonized countries unveils their real state and makes it more unacceptable. The fundamental confrontation which seems to be that which exists between colonialism and anti-colonialism, or even between capitalism and socialism, loses its importance. What is important, today, is the necessity of a redistribution of wealth. Humanity, under the threat of being shaken to its roots, needs to respond to this question." But Fanon is too aggressive, and spectators would be scared. Fanon thinks that the people who were exploited by colonialism and capitalism have the right not only to claim the things they have the rights to in the present day, but also to take back what was stolen from them over the centuries. And, consequently, that doesn't correspond completely with the film, so I didn't know exactly how to end it. Some leftist friends of mine were indignant when they saw the film, because I don't propose anything; I don't go far enough. I don't demystify religion enough. But I'm not the one who has to go further: it is up to India to do that. We can't do the work for them. You know, the aid given by developed countries to developing countries—as we now call them—is in constant regression, and that contributes to a perpetual ambiguity. We never stop saying to the Indian people that the solution can only be found in a radical change in social structures, but—here is the problem—there is both religion, which has an unimaginable importance, and the caste system, which, despite its official abolition, is nonetheless very trenchant. It is the caste system that gives the direction to society and that regulates the social order. I read in a provincial newspaper that in one region they are continuing to live as if outside of time. They don't realize that the English have left, and a man of a certain untouchable caste—the lowest one—was lynched because he wore sandals and these men have to go barefoot! Only either a revolution or a bloody dictatorship could, with a lot of hard work, change the order of things.

RG: In India, is religion the real opium of the people?

LM: Religion is the element that guides the Indian at every moment of his existence. It is what guides his way of life and what makes him reject reality. During his whole life, he is waiting for death, because the passage through life is not a very important one, and he does not pay much attention to it. I don't know any other countries in the world, even Muslim countries, where religion is as much of a way of life, or where religion is so connected to a way of thinking and to people's behavior. It is, in my opinion, the country that will resist communism for the longest time. The communists, who, after independence, chose the most intense struggle, relying on the peasant masses which make up 95 percent of the population, had to give up and change their approach by becoming integrated into the parliamentary system as well as the caste system, even though those two systems are the only ones which fought against communism in a powerful way. Beyond the fact that they are divided into communists on the left and communists on the right, they are sometimes forced, in certain sectors, to make alliances between castes in order to win seats in the parliament. They are becoming integrated into the system, because it is very difficult to function outside of it. I don't blame them: we have to understand things as they are.

This religion is much more than the opium of the people, because in India it has two meanings. It pacifies suffering, and it isolates people from reality. What do Indians do on Sunday? They pray for hours on end! Religion is not a way of exercising power, as can happen in Western countries. In India, it is useless in that sense; on the contrary, it unites people who have been divided by the castes. You can't use the "opium of the people" idea in the sense of oppression, as the author of the maxim meant it, because it is never linked with power. It has many more implications in daily life.

RG: You not only encountered the terrifying problem of religion in India, but also another one which seems just as important: charlatanism.

LM: In every religion, it is always difficult to decide how much of it comes from sincerity, and that is even more true in India, where the number of sects in unimaginable. Every one of them has its followers. You can create an infinite number of sects without destroying the "religiosity" of them in their ensemble. The man in the film who had not slept or sat down for seven years and who has the moral and financial support of dozens of followers is a characteristic example of the mindset of a large part of the Indian population. The number of people who withdraw from society to live as parasites is quite considerable. Besides that, for any Indian, beggars are not considered parasites, whether it is a question of those who are beggars because of constraints (unemployment or sickness), or those who have chosen this existence.

RG: With *Calcutta*, you have succeeded in making a film as synthesis, going from the microcosm of a city to introduce us to India in its entirety. Also, your refusal to provide commentary during a whole section at the beginning of the film and your method of intervention—which goes toward a crescendo of the film's diverse elements—suggest a new way of approaching the documentary.

LM: What you say gives me great pleasure, but I don't claim to have made a film as synthesis, because I didn't know Calcutta after three weeks of shooting, and I knew India even less after several months. There is nothing exhaustive about the film. I tried to include everything that one could find in a city, and above all what one could find with a fresh gaze. That, it seems to me, is the most important thing. All the contradictions that exist in this city, and in this world, can be found in the film, as well as those which have to do with both resisting the modern world and seeking to be integrated into it. The most visual example is the construction of that twenty-five-story building. With my editor Suzanne Baron, in whom I have found a very valuable collaborator, I wanted to create a spiral form of montage, where we see the additions to the building over time, each time adding a new dimension to what we had shown in the previous shot.

RG: In effect, it is not that the first part of the film seems like an introduction and the second part as complementary to it, but instead that there is a series of elements that comprise a whole. At no moment do we have the impression of there being repetitions, unneeded images, or pleonasms: everything is complementary to everything else, in a process that one could call dialectic.

LM: What is quite funny is that the editing of the film follows the chronological order of the shooting, without our having wanted that to be the case. The images of the crowd were also, for us, a discovery of the city, and they were put in during the editing as if they are an entry into the city that is experienced by the spectator himself. Those scenes are at the border of becoming picturesque, but they are never folkloric. There is no folklore in India; it would be useless because there is no tourism. It's not like Mexico, which is visited every year by millions of North American tourists and which is a country that reinvents its folklore for them. Folklore is something that is a veneer, artificial, a vulgarization of traditional forms. I didn't want to betray India in that way. Also, I didn't want to put in any commentary, because I was afraid of breaking up the image, or of covering over the sound, which is very important. But I was forced to provide a few explanations. During the sound mixing, I took out a few sentences that were pleonasms and that didn't fit in with the dimension of the film that you are talking about.

RG: This absence of commentary during a long section at the beginning of the film plunges us into a certain sense of confusion.

LM: That's exactly right. There are already several people who have seen the film who have had this same impression. It is a confusion that borders on fear. We wanted to make the spectator penetrate gradually into this universe that we had discovered over the time we were shooting. The images of the teeming crowd are not just there for no reason: they were put there because they convey our own impression, and that of any foreigner who arrives in Calcutta. When you think that by the year 2000, if the current rate of growth continues, the population will reach twenty million. . . . We decided to make the commentary enter the film only through translation, because I really didn't want to speak: the image was so clear that any voiceover seemed superfluous. It is true that we wanted to have a *mise en scene* that was geared toward the spectator, not in order to move or enchant him, but more precisely in order to make him more conscious when presented with this situation, with this world about which we know so little.

RG: In the same way, you don't give us any ending—that is, any "happy ending"—because there could, quite simply, not be one. At one moment, you stay with the shot of a sickly child from the slums, and we think you are going to end the film on that image, which also looks strangely like the poster for the fight against hunger. But then, no, you don't allow yourself to be tempted by this image, which we would be able to identify as a call for public charity.

LM: Exactly. There cannot be an ending to his film, and a while ago I spoke to you about that quote from Frantz Fanon that I had thought of putting there, along with other quotes, but all of them seemed to be betrayals. I think that, finally, there was no ending that I could propose, especially since people other than me have not yet found a solution to the problem.

RG: Was this the first time you have worked with a camera with synchronous sound?

LM: In a quite naïve way, I was wild with happiness to be able to work with a camera with synchronous sound, because for me it is a marvelous tool. Without actors, without lighting, without a screenplay to follow, I had the impression of complete freedom. There was a kind of effacement of the auteur which seduced me. I discovered, in the course of the shooting, that sense of enthusiasm that I had lost, as I explained to you at the beginning of the interview.

RG: The film is still a very personal film, where the auteur is involved at every moment, and where it is a question—at the most basic level—of the choice of this city as a place to shoot a film. And then there is the choice of individual shots, and then—perhaps even more of a determining factor—there are the choices made in the editing. Besides all of that, we feel, in this film, a determination not to leave anything to chance, and, in our opinion, the synthesis could not have taken place without the choices that were made.

LM: Of course, I agree with you about this, but I would like to say that I made a choice in the *refusal* of a *mise en scene*. I never wanted to redo shots where there were people looking at the camera. In the beginning, the cameraman Etienne

Becker was very bothered by this aspect of the shoot, by the fact that you could not prevent it from happening every time you shot. If we had tried to prevent it from happening, it would have been against the spirit in which we wanted to work. We just dealt with it, and now we actually think that these gazes toward the camera lens lend a certain feeling of authenticity. We were being watched for two reasons: first because we were Westerners, and secondly because we had a camera, and because of that we could not go unnoticed. So we had to make use of the situation rather than eliminate it, which was sometimes quite difficult!

What we wanted to achieve was a complete stripping down, which would lead to a wiping away of *mise en scene*, and it was only the synchronous sound camera that allowed us to do that. We were much more available for shooting than on an ordinary film set, because we didn't have to be preoccupied with any problems other than those of the eyes and ears. All three of us—myself, the cameraman, and the sound recorder—were in agreement from the start about what we had to do. I could never have made this film five years ago: I was too deeply soaked in the *mise en scene* and the dramaturgy of fiction filmmaking.

RG: Often, we see that the shots have not been refined to the point of making them lose their effectiveness. For example, if a child starts running in a field, or if someone makes a gesture, that is not a reason for a cut to be made.

LM: That's exactly right. Becker filmed while watching with both his eyes open, and he did not hesitate to look for the event outside the frame in order to capture the most he could, but we never wanted a fortuitous gesture to interrupt the continuity of our shooting, and, even in the editing, we always tried to preserve this aspect of things. What every cameraman tries to do is to create a good *mise en scene*, to look for the best framing, and to create the composition that would allow for a best final edit. So I had to prevent him from doing all that, and I played—at least at the beginning of the shoot—the role of the director who rejects a *mise en scene*.

RG: And now, how long do we have to wait for a film about France, one that would be made with the same visual acuity and the same rigor?

LM: It is always easier to make a film about other people than about yourself. It would be very difficult to make the equivalent film about Paris, because at this point in time there would be far too many details that I would not be able to avoid. Whereas, in a foreign country, I am forced to go toward what is most essential, to look with other eyes than those that are used to living in the same place. Just see how quickly we habituate ourselves to what is around us, to the faces and the objects which we see every day. What I would wish for is that an Indian filmmaker would come and make a film in a country like Italy or France, and would give his point of view, from his culture, like I myself did in India. A political film about France would be necessarily polemical, and that seems like it would be very difficult if you did it in a city like Paris. But I think that a film about France after ten years of Gaullism would be great.

RG: The only attempt to make a film in this sense was the film made by Chris Marker in 1962, *Le Joli mai*, which was a work that was trying to approach a certain contemporary reality.

LM: What you would have to do is go into a city and shoot everything that has to do with that city in a very defined context: that of our present time. I would already be someone who was an outsider there, and I could therefore remain exterior to current events, electoral quarrels, business negotiations, intrigues, et cetera. So you can imagine how a foreigner, who is spending a bit of time in France, would have clearer ideas about France than we do about our own country. It was this clarity, this gaze, that I was seeking, and that I required. Believe me, I don't run away from my responsibilities, but if I were to make a film about France I would really like to be able to get a result similar to the one I achieved in *Calcutta*. Usually I don't like the films that I just made, and this is the first time that I have a real infatuation with one of my films.

RG: Despite the shocking images that you present us with, like those of the lepers with faces and hands that have been ravaged by the illness, *Calcutta* still displays a great modesty on your part. You never dwell on images in order to make them irritating. You show them because it is necessary and indispensable, but as opposed to Bunuel in *Land without Bread*, you don't create shocking images intended to upset the spectator.

LM: I didn't allow myself to engage in an act of cultural rape via images. I never wanted to intrude on people—and that includes their faces and their bodies as well as their private lives. My goal was not to work on that level. I think that my engagement was more consequential in this refusal than it would have been if I had penetrated a bit more into the horror of things. On our arrival in Calcutta, we came across a dead man in the street; he had been there for hours, and his face was covered with flies. I did not feel that I had the right to film him, because I thought that would be indecent. Perhaps I sinned through an excess of modesty. If this same situation had presented itself in Bombay at the end of our stay, I might have done it. But would I have left it in the final cut? I don't think so. In any event, I don't regret what I did.

RG: This modesty can be seen very clearly in the image of the child with the deformed face who is playing the drum and whom you show us only in profile.

LM: Becker asked me, at that moment, if he should film his face. I told him that he shouldn't, and he himself didn't want to do it. He was asking me in order to justify his own reaction rather than in order to respond to a professional need. There was an odious aspect to filming these people, this misery, which bothered us, especially at the beginning, so that it was useless to amplify it further through the creation of shock images.

RG: Is India the dream country for Gualtiero Jacopetti?[1]

LM: There is an inexhaustible source of human horrors which he could very well develop through the appropriate editing; but as far as we were concerned, we think that we made a film that is opposed to Jacopetti's vision of the world. My second feature film on India, which is four hours long and that I am in the process of finishing, should further reinforce the image of what I found in that country.

Note

1. Gualtiero Jacopetti (1919–2011), was an Italian documentary filmmaker known for his "shockumentaries," also known as "mondo films" after the success of his most famous film, *Mondo Cane* (1962).

Interview with Louis Malle

Guy Braucourt / 1971

From *Cinéma*, no. 157 (June 1971): 106–109. Translated from the French by CB.

Guy Braucourt: The last time we were together, it was to discuss *Calcutta* and *Phantom India* (broadcast on television), at a time when you were talking about renouncing "classical" cinema, and when you saw the notion of auteurist film as something you had moved past, preferring a "direct contact with reality." And we are together again to talk about a fiction film with actors, an example of auteurist cinema that is completely classical.

Louis Malle: If we mean by "classical cinema" a cinema in which the form is integrated with the content, I have never made anything other than that, even with *Zazie*, which was judged to be too baroque at the time, and even with my films about India, which are certainly the most classical of all. But what I wanted to express at the time *Calcutta* was coming out was the need to put an end to a kind of cinema that is made according to the star system, with a literary adaptation, a collaboration on the screenplay, big stars, and large and paralyzing budgets. I was talking about the need to reach a much freer and more direct form of expression, with a reduction of technical and economic structures. And my biggest hesitation about making *Murmur of the Heart* came from the necessity of reconstituting the historical period—1954—which always presents major logistical problems. That said, there is, I realize, a contradiction in the statements made by filmmakers, who, if they have a modicum of lucidity, try to progress, to evolve, while at the same time being aware that it is not possible to decide to make only this or that kind of cinema. And it is interesting to see for oneself, through this desire to change, what still remains.

GB: Would *Murmur of the Heart* have existed, or existed in the same way, if you hadn't taken that voyage to India?

LM: Certainly not! I needed the complete rupture of that trip to help me break through a certain number of blockages in myself (which you could call modesty, holding back, or self-censorship) which prevented me from saying things fully, and which forced me to take roundabout routes like using screenplays written by other people and allegorical subjects: in other words, to say things only by proxy. And for the first time in my career, something really spontaneous happened to me, something that did not require an effort to think about it or to construct it, that didn't even come to me through the filter of conscious thought, but that suddenly gushed up as I was working on a project having to do with utopia, where I was describing an ideal imaginary society that I had been thinking about for several years. But I never could have made this film on adolescence, or written this script in a single draft, in the way Truffaut did with *The 400 Blows*, at the beginning of my career, because I lacked a certain number of endowments like simplicity, innocence, and freedom, and I only acquired them over time.

Also, even if it seems like I am going back to the same cinema as before *Calcutta* with *Murmur of the Heart*, I have the impression that I am conducting myself with much more freedom. It's less a question of technique, which has never really interested me, than one of relationships between people—relationships which for me constitute the essential fact of this profession. Making a direct cinema film in India meant coming face to face with thousands of people with whom you have to establish a dialogue; and having to improvise like that, having to grab things in real time, gave me a greater flexibility, a greater facility with my contacts with the crew and the cast, with children in particular, who, not being professional actors, gave me less problems than the adults. Especially since they behaved more like assistant directors on the set than like actors, since they were more interested in cinematic technique than in dramatic art. It was impossible for me to take a position of authority with them—as one can with professional actors, who are often expecting you to brutalize them, either because they need to be pushed harder, or just out of habit—because they were only good when it was fun for them. In that sense, it is very different from my previous films, with less of a direction of the actors than a sort of creative collaboration, which was established on the basis of brotherly relations. And that corresponds better to my temperament, which is not at all that of a "trainer."

GB: On the level of technique, two elements in particular hold our attention: the way the soundtrack prolongs sequences—connecting them with each other—and the use of jazz.

LM: It so happens that I'm not very fond of sequences of images that become a kind of habit, a formal laziness, and, in addition, destroy the film, because they force you to keep going back to similar images. I wanted to create a rhythm that was constructed around the sequence of sounds, and that could give a bit of the feeling of a film of someone's memory, with memories going by one after another and forming an allusive chain. As for jazz: it is at once a kind of music in which I immersed myself during my whole adolescence, and a style of music which, at the time—the 1940s for me, who was fifteen years old in 1947, and for the boy who is this same age in 1954—was part of the generational conflict, since my parents hated what they called "that music of the savages." There is, as well, an affinity in sensibility between the boy and the music of Charlie Parker, and between the theme of adolescence and the musical themes of Parker's recordings from the end of his life. It's a bit like in *Le Feu follet*, where there is an affinity between the protagonist and the music of Erik Satie. For me, the use of this most wonderful representative of modern jazz (modern for the 1950s, of course) is justified in an obvious way. But I was afraid for a while that, for a portrait of this bourgeois family milieu of that period, jazz would seem too ironic a reference.

GB: Why exactly 1954, which is neither the date of your adolescence nor the time in which we are living now?

LM: Because 1954 seems to me like a turning point between the postwar years in which France took a long time to get past the war, and our era of revolt, which put an end to a certain number of things. Nineteen fifty-four was, on the one hand, Dien Bien Phu, and the sign that our hegemony and the colonial empire were falling apart, and, on the other hand, a time when the old order still reigned, despite the hope that Pierre Mendès France brought. It was a time when the adolescent revolt could only be that of a minority which was striking a few blows at the order that had been established and that was still in place. It would therefore have been impossible to give the same resonance, the same weight to the subject, if it had been set in the 1960s, when the revolt had become a movement with a more generalized base, a movement encountering a world whose sexual and political taboos were starting to break down. The youth of today—and this is really their tragedy—find themselves in front of a great void, while the young people at the time of the film, or in my own, were colliding with a very rigid wall: it was this resistance that interested me in the evocation of the life passage that is so crucial to adolescence.

GB: A resistance that incest ends up breaking down.

LM: Yes, as an act that comes as a natural ending to a love story, a bit in the same way that the spectator watches the film as it progresses. In other words, according to a kind of convergence, the relationship between the mother and her son becomes more and more intimate, in much the same way as in *Les Amants*, which also consisted of bringing two human beings from a certain place to another place, and thus of passing through an acme in their relationship. That's where the love scenes in both films come from, and showing them was necessary in order to underline the importance of what happens to these two couples. And it would have been hypocrisy on my part to want either to avoid them or to hide them by having a panoramic camera movement to the window! These kinds of passionate relationships often exist between a mother and her son, but because these relationships are generally suppressed, they go through all the emotional stages except for that of the act of love. The question is: what, in these situations, is more abnormal? And another question is: if the incest taboo helps to maintain the structures of a rigid society, at the moment that these structures start to collapse, or have collapsed as is the case today, why doesn't this taboo, which has become outdated, disappear? Whatever the answers that people give to these questions, I tried to demystify the incest taboo by de-dramatizing the context, which is treated in a tone of comedy, especially the part of the film that follows the incest, and most notably the shot of everyone bursting into laughter with which the film ends. Any notion of guilt is thus erased, which is very different from what happens in Visconti's *The Damned*, where the act in some ways comes as a crowning of a whole series of crimes, and appears as the culmination of the depiction of a society of crazy people. In addition, the act of incest is condemned by Visconti as part of an ancient Judeo-Christian morality, and his film is, in this sense, very moral, with the incest being less upsetting because it didn't pose as many questions.

Interview with Louis Malle

Robert Grelier / 1971

From *Image et Son—La Revue du cinéma*, no. 254 (November 1971): 69–78. Translated from the French by CB.

Robert Grelier: In 1969, you told us that fiction films with actors interested you less and less. You said you took none of the pleasure from them that you had before. The kind of cinema that had been a source of amusement for you had become a boring routine. And, today, you have just made a fiction film with actors. Are you reneging?

Louis Malle: No, I'm not reneging at all. When I said that, I was really asking myself the question of whether I was going to go back to fiction cinema. And for a long time—in other words, almost until last summer—I was deciding between different projects which were not really fiction films. Also, I didn't really want to be back on a shoot with actors. I wrote the story of *Murmur of the Heart*, and that story required that it be a fiction film. The problem wasn't one of knowing if I was going to use professional actors or not: there are actually a large portion of the actors in the film that are not professionals, but that didn't change anything essential about the film. I asked myself whether I could find a technique for shooting the film that was less heavy and less cluttered than the one that is used in traditional cinema. Given the genre of the film—which is a film set in another historical period—it became almost impossible to do that. For example, I had thought of making it in 16mm, but that would have been absurd, because it would have been a kind of aestheticism. I therefore shot it with the same amount of technical means as for the kinds of low-budget films that they used to make, but this created a lot of difficulties.

RG: After *Calcutta*, you gave us the impression that there had been a complete change of orientation on your part.

LM: I think that this is a false problem. *Calcutta* and the other seven films made for television, *Phantom India*, are really films made in the first person. It was, in the end, no doubt, a very personal experience. In any case, I don't give myself interdictions. I can want at one moment to make one thing, and still be allowed to make a different kind of cinema at another moment. One characteristic trait of my work has always been that I go from one extreme to another, and now it is very possible that I will go back to another project in direct cinema. I don't see any problem with alternating the two forms of cinema, or even with trying to make them come gradually closer to each other. I know that it is a bit artificial to imagine that they are two completely different kinds of cinema. *Calcutta* was a very subjective film, in which I tried to be objective, but I think that it is perhaps one of my most personal films. What interests me now is having the freedom to make a more improvised cinema, not hesitating to take on a project of strict documentary but letting fiction enter the reality. This is something that has been attempted a few times, but it is certainly very difficult to achieve, if only for technical reasons. I imagine that it must be possible to conceive of a film about Calcutta in which I could introduce certain elements of fiction. There are, after all, unconscious choices in a documentary that are a certain form of fiction. I remember that *Le Monde* published an indignant letter from an Indian reader, whose identity I later found out, since there are not a lot of Indians in Paris. It was a woman who had, for one thing, never set foot in Calcutta. This person explained that the film did not correspond with reality, and that I had been raving about my own fantasies. It was an absurd critique, because it didn't really deny the evidence, which is what many Indians do, especially when they live abroad, out of chauvinism, or just out of ignorance. But that said, what she had written was partly true. I can't deny—and I have always said—that even the title of the film wasn't very accurate: I should have called it *Three Weeks in Calcutta*. As for the series of films I made about India, *Phantom India*: when it was being reviewed by the Centre Nationale du Cinéma, they suggested calling it *Louis Malle's India*. I asked them if that wasn't pretentious. On the contrary, they thought that it was a way of presenting the project that sounded less ambitious; in other words, that it would be the reflections of a filmmaker who had just spent a certain amount of time in India, and who was conveying what he had seen, what he had felt. In fact, the border between documentary and fiction film is very imprecise, very ambiguous.

RG: We didn't want to put a label on your film in any sense, because you are the filmmaker on whom it is the most difficult to put labels. It was more that we thought we saw a change in your intentions. Also, if you will allow it, we would like to ask again about what you said at the time: "I'm not saying that I won't go back to making fiction films again, but I can say that they will be very different from what I would have been able to make up to now." We would like to know what the differences are between *Murmur of the Heart* and the films you made before *Calcutta*.

LM: That is very hard to explain. I felt it both while shooting it and while editing it. As seems apparent, though, it is a form of cinema that is not very different from the one I used in my previous films. But that said, *Calcutta* was not a very different film either.

RG: The difference that we see in *Murmur of the Heart* is mostly in a new way of approaching people. There is, among other things, a certain intimacy which exists in this film and that had not appeared in your earlier films. We don't have the impression of seeing actors playing roles, and, to be more precise, we notice that a certain gaze has been thrown on people who are in the process of living out their own stories.

LM: It was a question, at first, of a reconstruction that we did by establishing the background of a provincial bourgeois family. I cast actors and put them in a situation, but from that moment on I allowed them a lot more freedom. Even in the technical work, I pushed myself to get to a flexibility that allowed me to film them both as I had placed them in the situation and in a way that could surprise them. This was, actually, a contrast with my earlier films, where there was still a lot of distance, and something cold in the tone. What strikes a lot of people about this film—without trying to analyze it—is that it is the warmest, most natural, and most alive of my films. I certainly owe that to my work on *Calcutta*, to the rupture it represented, to the return to reality. This is a film that is much more anchored in life than some of my previous films. I had the impression of having a much more direct approach to people. And a greater communication with the actors. It is certainly a film where I allowed the actors to have more freedom, and I really thrived on that, because I had placed them in a certain climate. It is also a film where the actors brought a lot to the screenplay: it was really a collective creation. They added a lot of things to the film—not in the written text, of course, but in terms of bringing a warmth, a sincerity to it. If I had made this film five years ago, for example, it would certainly have been stiffer and less effusive. There would not have been this freedom which has struck many viewers.

RG: You were speaking a moment ago about "cold" films, and if we think of a film like *Vie privée*, that's certainly true, despite a theme which should have lent itself to a great warmth. Even in a film like *Les Amants*, which goes in substantially the same direction as *Murmur of the Heart*, there was a pulling back in terms of the warmth of communication when compared with this last film.

LM: In fact, *Les Amants* is a film that didn't satisfy me at all, because I had the impression that there was a pane of glass between me and the actors. However, and very fortunately, there was something extraordinary in what Jeanne Moreau constructed that made it all work. The work of the other actors stayed on the level of theoretical interpretation. The film that viewers have generally preferred is *Le Feu follet*, despite its rather icy tone, because that tone worked very well with the subject. *Le Feu follet* was the story of a man who was not able to communicate, which was my own problem at that time. For me, *Murmur of the Heart* is a step forward, and I am conscious of the fact that I owe a great deal to the change in my way of seeing that I acquired on *Calcutta*. . . . What I am moving toward now is being able to get the most active images, which, I must say, requires a considerable flexibility when compared with traditional fiction filmmaking. I will give you an example. If a scene looks monstrous in 35mm, it's because we don't have a very light 35mm camera with synchronous sound. There is no 35mm equivalent to the Éclair 16mm. Arriflex has just produced a 35mm camera, but it is not on the market yet. As a result, we are still working with the same voluminous, heavy equipment as before the war. I didn't want the movements of the camera to show, and I didn't want to constantly shoot handheld. That kind of aestheticism doesn't suit me; it's not my method of working. I had to be very careful that the film I made based on this screenplay—which was very spontaneous and written in a kind of burst of energy—did not become stiff. I had to work hard to reinvent the sense of spontaneity.

RG: There is a scene where we actually do have this feeling of heaviness: it is the scene of the July 14th celebration. The gaze is very distant, very far away, as if the characters were seen through a telephoto lens!

LM: It's interesting that you say that. In fact, that was the only scene in the film that was rushed. We had foreseen two nights of shooting for the scene, which was a long scene: I actually had to cut a lot of it out in the editing. And it happened that the first night we hardly shot anything, because the electrical equipment wasn't working. On the second night, I had to do something like twenty-four setups in six hours. I have never worked so fast in my life! Even on *Calcutta* we worked more slowly. That scene was shot completely handheld and in a single take. It's very curious, because it is actually the stiffest scene in the film. There is no doubt that I should have cut it more, but it was an important scene for me, and it was perhaps my only regret in terms of the editing. Most of the text of the scene was improvised. In films that are historical reconstructions, you need to reinvent the spontaneity, to allow it to be born again. That's where the real difficulty of *mise en scene* is. If I had had a budget like the one I had for *The Thief of Paris* and *Vie privée*, I would have probably gone back and reedited some scenes, including the one of July 14th.

RG: Is it a deliberate choice that each of your films presents a provocation with regard to the taboos of our society? For example, the scene of physical love in *Les Amants*, and in this film the scene of incest. At the same time, in both cases, it seems to us that you graft a sort of modesty—one could even say of recuperation—onto these provocations. To take these same two examples: in *Les Amants*, you put this scene in counterpoint to the music of Brahms, which "aestheticizes" it, while in *Murmur of the Heart* you have placed this scene of incest in a very defined context: the action takes place after the July 14th celebration, and the mother is a bit drunk.

LM: I didn't have the intention of shocking people with that scene at all. I simply wanted it to be in the film, because it is important. But beyond that, doing something scandalous would have been contrary to my intentions, because this was meant to show a natural fact that was both something that happened by accident and that inevitably had to happen. What I tried to reproduce in the film was the sense that everything happens normally, as if I were telling the story of a love between two human beings, and it happens that in this particular case it involves a mother and her son. So that when we finally get to that scene, it is much more effective. Even though this schema is in opposition to all their received ideas, viewers accept it. It's only later that they begin to think about it. I have had innumerable reactions of this kind. I am very well aware that if I had made it into a scandalous scene, I might not have been able to do it. I would have created a kind of block, and then I would have created a scandal which would have allowed viewers to reject the scene because they would have seen it as excessive. Whereas, on the contrary, they have the impression that these are really very normal people. The action takes place within a French bourgeois family, and between characters who are above any suspicion on a moral plane. They are neither monsters, nor bizarre people, nor perverts, nor crazy people like in Visconti's *The Damned*. A lot of viewers identify with the character of the mother. There is a kind of Emma Bovary quality in all married women.

At the same time, a lot of people only talk about this scene when they are discussing the film, as if the film was organized around it. Perhaps that is due to everything that preceded the shoot, which included, among other things, the threat of censorship. People try to look for the reasons for that threat, and perhaps they find them in that scene.

For me, it seems difficult to separate that scene from the rest of the film, above all because the incest itself is hardly shown. I shot it as if it was in a dream, without really being conscious of doing that. Deep down, it is the realization of a fantasy, the story of an adolescent who imagines exemplary and marvelous relations with his mother. We find ourselves in the presence of two human beings who go to the limit, and to a place where the Oedipal desire is accomplished, is quenched.

RG: And the mother has an exemplary attitude toward it.

LM: Above all, she doesn't want there to be any regrets. The act has to stay between the two of them, because it is a very simple, very natural act.

RG: The mother accepts it very well, while for the child it still registers as a shock. The mother is in some way the sexual initiator of antiquity.

LM: It is a dreamlike vision of the mother. It is a superb myth, the myth of the mother as sexual initiator, which has also been contested by anthropologists. In any case, it is admitted by everyone that in a social structure of the family where that family structure is the fundamental source of social unity: the birth of sexuality automatically translates into a fixation on the mother. The mother is the first love object, and, even for a lot of psychoanalysts, she is the only real love of our lives. From there comes the idea that the mother assumes this role, and goes to the limit of it. I have to say that I find that very, very beautiful. This taboo has been an iron law in all societies, but it is essentially a biological taboo. I can't very easily accept the theory that it was a cultural taboo, because I don't see any reasonable explanation for it. I don't see what would be so horrible about a mother making love with her son. If in genetic terms the result is disastrous over several generations, one could imagine that this would be the only valid reason for the taboo to be so strong and so imperative, but one could say that with the birth-control pill the problem has been resolved. . . . What I am saying might seem like a joke. But we find ourselves in a society where this danger should no longer exist. We continue to live in a system of taboos, a scale of moral values, that doesn't correspond with the technical or scientific reality of our civilization anymore. There are certain elements like that which seem to some people to be insurmountable: for example, for certain Catholics, the idea of priests marrying is a traumatizing idea. It is a concept that would never come into their minds, even though priests were married during a long period in the history of the church, not to mention that in the protestant clergy ministers are married. I think about people in my family who are very strict Catholics, and this idea of priests marrying would seem monstrous to them, just as monstrous as incest, whereas the decision not to allow priests to marry was—at the time it was made—a political one.

The press have aberrant positions on the subject. In a magazine like *Elle*, they don't know how to write about it. They want to talk about it because it is important, but they don't want to shock their readers. I just appeared on a television show hosted by Michel Polac, "Post-Scriptum," where I was with Alberto Moravia, and we were talking about the Oedipus complex and the trauma of the mother. And we were discussing things we had thought we could talk about freely, because the Oedipus complex is something we study in high school. And afterwards, the television viewers were absolutely mad with rage. It wasn't us, but Freud, who seemed monstrous to them. The first reactions Freud got when he began to write—he had the most vulgar epithets applied to him and was almost kicked out of the medical societies—can still be found today. Nevertheless, we have to try to liberate people.

RG: It seems that you received hundreds of insulting letters about this.

LM: Yes, hundreds of insulting letters. When the censorship issues began to calm down, other people began to maneuver. Even a person like Claude Mauriac took incredible positions.[1] Members of the government were affected by it. On this television show, we had obviously talked about politics, but the principle of television is that you only talk about politics on political programs: cinema is just cinema. We don't have the right to talk about politics, because we have to remain artists. This the most complete hypocrisy on the part of this government and the current administration of the ORTF (National Bureau of Television and Radio). Also, they are now in the process of shutting down Polac's show. I am very much a follower of Wilhelm Reich. I don't always agree with what he says, but I do find that we need a revolution: we have to liberate society, because we are constantly locked up inside a form of repression. The traditional patriarchal family is absolutely maladapted to the modern world. The new generation is very aware of this. Incest is a false problem. If there wasn't this very strong sexual repression of adolescents, they would be able to leave the family much earlier. Instead of establishing this fixation on the mother, they could satisfy their natural sexual needs, which begin when they are very young. In point of fact, in our society we agree that a boy has the right to make love at the age of seventeen or eighteen, whereas he doesn't stop thinking about it from the age of fourteen on. This terrible repression is the cause of trauma, and I am persuaded that Reich is correct when he says that the Oedipus complex would be partially resolved, or at least undramatized, if we allowed children to have complete sexual freedom from the onset of puberty on.

RG: The family that you chose is one that is—one could say—irreproachable; it even expresses a certain ideal type of the bourgeois family.

LM: This family is without any doubt a family that would have appeared quite modern at the time. That said, there have always been families in which the father and the mother had a certain freedom within the context of a great hypocrisy—in other words, while continuing to play the social game. Bourgeois society had created spaces that were safety valves allowing them freedom. We can easily understand from the film that the father has little adventures, that the mother has a lover, and that the children are very free. But it is still a very strong family unit: in other words, its members are very often together.

Let's just say that I don't choose Mauriac's extreme vision of the bourgeois family: Christian, tortured, and miserable. That schema doesn't correspond in any way to my memories. It's no coincidence that the father reads *L'Express*. He is the kind of liberal bourgeois who is trapped in his own contradictions. I have very precise examples of this in my family, even though the description of this particular family doesn't correspond to my own, because my parents were fairly free. But I know that at the homes of some of my cousins, summers were a hell: some of them are still traumatized by it. It's like having a religious education: it can traumatize you, but it can just as easily release a revolt which can be very healthy.

RG: How much of the film is autobiographical? Should we see it as an autobiographical film that has been tweaked, as if you have accounts to be settled with a certain class, or as if you wanted to get revenge on something in your past?

LM: It's obvious that it's a transposition of my life. I started by setting it in a different time and changing the setting and the characters. The milieu is not exactly the same as the one I grew up in. The characters in the film are people whom I know very well, whose lives I have seen, but there was an imaginative process involving my memories, which enriches them. I also spent some time pulling together the various elements of the story. It's more of a collective autobiography. Personally, I don't feel so much like it was a settling of accounts. I wanted to convey this passage into adolescence, this key moment, and I experienced it in a world that I know very well, or at least about which I understand all the emotional references. It was only in that way that I was able to go to the furthest possible point in the depiction of this world, but it wasn't the ridiculous or hypocritical aspect of that world that interested me. *Murmur of the Heart* is more of a comic take on things. I am persuaded that seven or eight years ago I would have made a much more aggressive film.

RG: Why did you set the story in 1954?

LM: Because I didn't want to talk about the immediate postwar period. I wanted this slight transposition without having to explain to myself why! That allowed me to separate it a bit from my memories. And the other reason why I chose 1954 was because it was a year that I remember very well. It was the year of Dien Bien Phu, and the year of Mendès-France. And it was also because I believe that this year was very important to postwar France. The defeat at Dien Bien Phu was very serious and very humiliating for France. There was the discovery, all of a sudden, that a world of traditional values was falling apart. For the first time, French generals could be ridiculed by a Vietnamese general! And it was the moment when we had a government on the left in France.

RG: In all of your films, there is this connection with the historical context.

LM: That was very easy for me, because when I started to write this story there were a thousand details that came back to me. If there had been nothing more than the mother-son relationship, I could clearly have set the film in any historical context, but it was very important to really make people understand who Laurent was, what the baggage was that he was starting life with.

RG: You develop your film through a description of several characters and their environment. The film is not at all subjective: it is an eye that is watching Laurent live his life.

LM: It is simultaneously the world seen by him and a description of the world that is imposed on him. We see him evolve in this world, but he is controlled by an invisible spider's web. At times it is very subjective, and at other times it is like a behavioral study.

RG: *Murmur of the Heart*, which tells the story of the growth of an illness which you never or almost never show, should be a very hard, sad, pessimistic film, yet in reality you make it a kind of farce: an optimistic, healthy work. Beyond that, the ending is quite revelatory.

LM: It is obvious that we could have made the same subject into a dark drama, but the complicity of the three brothers gives it a demystifying and ironic tone. We needed to present all of that: the elation that belongs to adolescence.

RG: Why did you publish the screenplay of the film?

LM: Because Gallimard asked for it, and because I was afraid that I would have troubles. I was afraid that the film would be censored, and I was expecting the worst, given that there were so many stupid comments made about the screenplay. The publication presented a further argument against banning the film.

The publication of the screenplay was especially interesting for viewers who are interested in film, and who want to know more about the way in which a film is made on the basis of an intermediary text that doesn't exist as a literary work, but only as a reference to the film.

RG: Can you say what happened to the screenplay you were writing on utopia?

LM: It's not exactly a screenplay. I started a first draft with Pierre Kast, but it was more precisely a work of investigation and research, which was also fascinating but which we were not necessarily intending for the cinema. After having read through all the publications on the subject, our goal was to do research on what is hiding the notion of utopia today, and what it represents for people. For a while, I had an English producer who was interested in the subject, and we spent a weekend shut up in a house with twenty young Englishmen who were fairly brilliant people in all kinds of disciplines: musicians, engineers, sociologists, et cetera. I asked them what utopia represented for them, and how they imagined an ideal society. Their answers were fantastic. I posed these same questions to physicians and sociologists at a symposium in Stockholm. It was a very interesting experience, but for the moment—given that it is extremely difficult to define the terms of an ideal society—I have the impression that it is a sterile quest. Right now, this theme interests me more in terms of a personal way of living than as something to make a film about. That said, it is possible that one day I will find a method of filming it very simply. The solution might be to make a film as reportage; for example, it could document the life in one of the experimental communes that exist in the United States and that are starting to exist in France. So that people could see how they function, what problems arise, and on what basis they are trying to change the fundamental relations in our society, as well as the reasons for our society's failure—because there have been a lot of failures! In fact, the film—as Kast and I wanted to make it—was itself a utopia.

Note

1. Claude Mauriac (1914–1996), the son of the novelist François Mauriac, was the personal secretary to Charles de Gaulle, and later a film critic for the conservative-leaning newspaper *Le Figaro*.

Interview with Louis Malle

Gilles Jacob / 1974

From *Positif*, no. 157 (March 1974): 28–35. Reprinted by permission. Translated from the French by CB.

Gilles Jacob: Louis Malle, did the screenplay for *Lacombe, Lucien* come to you as easily as that of *Murmur of the Heart*?

Louis Malle: It was a longer and more complicated journey. I was in Mexico, two years ago, and I was very interested in the story of secret paramilitary groups organized by the Mexico City police, or by elements of the far right who were in the shadow of power; that story has never really been brought into the light, and for good reason. Nevertheless, it is clear that they had signed up boys of between eighteen and twenty years old, who almost all came from the slums of Mexico City. In general, they had problems with the police, so they just gave them their marching orders and took them. They received a very intense training: karate, close combat, shooting practice, et cetera. When there were demonstrations, even if the police were not getting involved, they would mix in with the students, dressed in civilian clothing, and armed with long sticks or machine guns, depending, and then whatever was going to happen happened. This technique of repression was tested after the events of 1968, which were very violent in Mexico, as you know. At the beginning of the summer of 1971, right at the moment when I arrived, there was a student demonstration, in the course of which these groups which they called "Halcones," falcons, get involved. There were a lot of deaths, because in Mexico they shoot right away. . . . The event made a lot of noise, especially coming after the liberal declarations of the new president, Echeverria, who had just come into office. There were a lot of photos in the newspapers, a wave of protests, the promise of an investigation, et cetera. I got interested in this story. I spent quite a lot of time on it, until the beginning of 1972: I wanted to tell the story of one of these "Halcones," a boy from the *lumpenproletariat* of Mexico City. Next to the airport, there was a slum with a million inhabitants, and with the usual paradoxes: for example, the houses that don't have running water have television. The occupants of these houses are usually immigrants to the city, peasants who have come from every corner of Mexico. I spoke to Bunuel about it, and he made fun of me, saying that I would never make it in Mexico, that it was completely out of the question. He said that even for a Mexican it would be very difficult, and they would never let a foreigner touch it. Of course, he was right. They didn't officially prevent me from doing it, but I understood very quickly that it would be practically impossible.

Then I decided to try to make it in another country. In the spring of 1972, I went to spend some time in Chile, where it would have been very possible and very easy to make it. But Chile and Mexico are like Norway and Sicily: I mean, it's the same continent, but they are completely different. I did a whole tour, going to Columbia and Venezuela, and then, in the end, I gave up the idea. Also, what bothered me a bit in this film—even if it came very close to reportage—is that it was, after all, about a culture and a world which interested me and which I know fairly well, but of which I am not a part. So I let it go, and I came back to France, and I worked on several projects. And then this story was bouncing around in my head, and the idea came to me that in its basic form the same kind of story could have happened to a young Frenchman during the period of the Occupation. Of course, it is also theoretically possible that it could happen today, but it would be very far-fetched. Whereas in 1944, a lot of people found themselves in the militia, just as often fugitives from justice as country squires, just as often workers as former black marketeers. Around Limoges, Bonny and Lafont organized a repressive group composed of Algerians they had found in Pigalle.[1] In the German army, you could find Russians, and even Indians who had been gathered up by Rommel in prison camps and who were motivated to fight against the colonial power, in this case the English. They found themselves in Corrèze, fighting against the *maquis*. In short, it was a crazy mixture. Personally, I wanted to tell the story of a young peasant from the southwest, who was swept up in the series of circumstances and who finds himself in the Gestapo. Of course, there had to be the war, the Resistance, and the repression of the Resistance, in order for these things to happen. But at the same time, it was someone who, in his life, in his relation to society, wanted to explode, as one often wants to do at the age of seventeen. He finds himself suddenly holding a machine gun and a police identity card that gives him all kinds of rights. The story of the film is, among other things, the story of a kid who, for three months, gives himself a good time. There is a sentence of Jean Genet, concerning young members of the militia, which has been bouncing around in my head for a long time: "I had, for three years, the delicate pleasure of seeing France terrorized by boys of sixteen to twenty years old."

So, he works in a small police station that is a branch of the Gestapo, like the one they had, for example, in Cahors, but in this case composed of French people. You may know that they have found certain archives of the Gestapo, and they have found out that in France it functioned 90 percent with local people whom the Germans directed and trained. It was really Frenchmen who made the thing work. There were full-time agents who often gained important reputations, and then, as well, a lot of informers: people who gave information for money, or to get rid of a creditor or an enemy. They found thousands and thousands of anonymous letters. I can imagine the same people, afterwards, writing in favor of the Resistance. . . . So I started from there, and I imagined that my young peasant met a Jewish family which was hiding in this small town, both protected and held for ransom by one of these guys from the Gestapo, a young man, a rogue, we might say. They are rich Parisian Jews: he is a high-end tailor, bourgeois, full of prejudices, but a bit strange. A good part of the narrative revolves around the complicated relationship that is established between the father, the daughter, and the grandmother of this family and the young member of the Gestapo. From that moment on, I felt that I was onto something really interesting, but I felt the need to work with someone. Naturally, I thought of Patrick Modiano, who has written three very beautiful novels which take place during the Occupation. He is fascinated by this period, about which he has an encyclopedic knowledge, which is all the more amazing given that he was born in 1947! There was a very deep alignment of feeling between us, and the screenplay owes an enormous amount to him, in particular where the relations between the bourgeois Jewish Parisian and the peasant from Quercy are concerned.

The difficulty of the film was essentially in finding the boy who would play Lucien; he carries the entire film on his shoulders. In order to find him, we had to do an enormous amount of work. Between all the people who helped me, we must have seen a thousand candidates. Out of that thousand, I interviewed about a hundred and I did screen tests on twenty-five. Of those, I kept five. I did more intensive tests, and I came to choose Pierre Blaise, a young boy from Moissac, who makes his living trimming poplar trees, and who, of course, had never been anywhere near a camera. What amazed me right away was his incredible freedom in front of the camera, in other words in front of us: there was no holding back, fear, posturing, or complex of any sort. In eight days, he understood and assimilated all the technical problems that come up for an actor, without losing his personality. He gives us a correct image of the character, as I had dreamed him up: a mixture of violence, brutality, and innocence. It is not enough to say that he became the character. It was better than that: he *understood* the character. He is an intelligent, complex boy, and all of us learned a lot through working with him. It sounds idiotic to say that, but it's true. If people offer him interesting roles, I believe he will continue to act. That would be a good thing for French cinema, where, as you know, the young male leads are all forty years old!

GJ: You give the impression of giving more and more importance to the atmosphere of the period you are bringing to life.

LM: Don't get the wrong idea: that is not what interests me the most. But I like the fact that my fiction films take place in the past. I have the impression that the timeless aspect of a narrative, of an emotion, of a conflict, comes through better if you don't have your nose pressed up against the event. When we treat a contemporary subject, we lack critical distance, and we allow ourselves to be led by fashions, by details, by side issues: in other words, by things that are not really important. The gaze that one has on something fifteen years back is a freer gaze, one that is finally sharper, and which often brings us back to today, to contemporary reality. In other ways, I find it fascinating to be aware of the period in which I am living, but then I want to really be inside it: let's call it documentary, witnessing, direct cinema—it doesn't matter—but it is a question of entering into a reality without knowing in advance what one will find there. You have to let oneself be guided by what you see; you have to improvise. I have shot like that a good deal, on the spot, trying to record what I felt. At the beginning of 1972, I wanted to shoot in that way in the Amazon. But I had serious problems with the Brazilian government. They were fine with me going into the Amazon, but they wanted me to say exactly what I was going to do there, which was against the very principle of my project. I took a very interesting trip to scout locations, but I couldn't make the film.

Then, I shot for two weeks in an automobile factory, the Citroën plant in Rennes. From that footage, I made a film, *Humain, trop humain*, which hasn't come out yet, but which has existed for a while and which is a hard film to watch. We spent quite a lot of time editing it, asking ourselves a lot of questions. I didn't want there to be a single word of commentary; that seemed useless and out of place. It is almost all in long-held shots, in which we follow the workers in their work. For example, we would stay for three or four hours to be able to see what happens at a particular spot on the assembly line, and then we chose someone whom we would film for a long time. The result is a film that bothers quite a few people, a film that is not easy to define: it's not a course in Marxism, nor a moralizing pamphlet on working conditions. For me, it is a film which leads us to reflect on the fact that a civilization could end up doing that to a segment of its population. It's not meant to go to war with industrial civilization, as we do a bit too easily nowadays. But I wanted to show what it means to build a car, this strange object which everyone in the world uses and without which our civilization would fall apart. In essence, it is very similar in its procedure to the film I made about Calcutta. I don't claim that it is objective, because objectivity does not exist. But the point of view that one expresses while filming is not one that is expressed through ideas or abstract biases: one expresses it more or less consciously through the way one films. I can imagine that other directors, having shot in this same factory, would have shot differently. Starting from the point of shooting in that place, something "happens," which partially escapes us, and it is based on that *something* that the viewers have to take a position. In general, I know that this kind of declaration makes people furious: "What?! But you're an imposter; that's not true; it's *your* film . . ." But I want to show, not demonstrate. This kind of film demands the active participation of the viewer, who has to carry our work further. *Humain, trop humain* makes spectators very uncomfortable, simply because they feel, often for the first time, the physical, muscular, sensorial reality of assembly-line work (the noise of it, for example).

GJ: Don't you feel that French cinema has changed a bit since 1968?

LM: I don't know. Everyone is shouting against French cinema right now. For good reasons, no doubt, but was it really better ten years ago? What is not really taking off in French cinema is the generation that comes after mine. There are some very interesting, very talented people, but no one has really "broken out," other than Joel Santoni. What was very striking in the "New Wave" phenomenon, in the first films of Truffaut and Chabrol, and even in *Hiroshima mon amour*, is that the films attracted an audience immediately. Whereas today, there are often exciting first films, but they are not embraced by the public. For me, both the strength and the weakness of our profession is that it is, despite everything, a spectacle, and you will note that there is, for example, no important director who has not, at one time or another, reached an audience. That is an absolute rule. The exceptions are extremely rare. We could cite Jean Vigo, but he died very young, and today everyone knows his films. Renoir only got a public fairly late, after a lot of great films that were flops, but he got it with *The Grand Illusion*. A fundamental aspect of American cinema—and one which in my opinion is its strength—is that when you talk to a director, even one of the most marginal ones, when they have made a film that didn't do well, they can't help thinking that something in the film didn't work. I find that to be a more sane and positive attitude than that of some of my French friends; when by chance their film is a success, they get a complex, which is a pretty typical attitude of the French intelligentsia.

I believe that it is impossible to establish a relationship between the quality of a film and its commercial success. It's an old rule: there are good films that do well and good films that don't do well, and bad films that do well, et cetera. One can cite examples of all four cases. But it's still important to reach an audience. That is what is perhaps a bit annoying in French film at the moment: one gets the impression that production has been cut in two. As if there were, on the one hand, popular filmmakers like Henri Verneuil and Gérard Oury, and, on the other hand, people who are expressing themselves and making films for their friends. In fact, the cinema that is interesting is the cinema that is in between the two. But when one is between the two, in France, it is considered a bit suspect.

GJ: You, for example?

LM: I have had some enormous flops, like everyone else. *Zazie*, for example. That really astonished me, because I thought it would be a big commercial success, but it didn't affect me that much. On the other hand, the fact that *Murmur of the Heart* was a commercial success made me very happy, whereas in the case of *Les Amants* it really bothered me. There is no doubt that because I have had some failures, I have gotten past this kind of absurd complex.

GJ: But why, in France, do we now see only films made for men, and nothing made for women?

LM: I don't know. I think, for example, that *Murmur of the Heart* was a women's film.

GJ: Yes, of course, we can find four or five exceptions.

LM: You know, it's not only in France. American cinema is also a cinema for men. That said, there is an aspect of French cinema that annoys me a lot, which is what we call "men's films": films starring Lino Ventura, Eddie Constantin, or Marcel Bozzuffi, gangster films, films about masculine friendships—you see what I mean. That kind of cinema, without exception, leaves me cold. In life, I prefer the company of women, and in the cinema as well. There is someone in French cinema who makes films for women, and who really loves women: Truffaut. In France today, we have another variant of the men's film: the big political film. They have been demanding that kind of cinema for long enough! I remember, at the beginning of my career, each time there was a press conference: "Why don't we deal with political subjects in France? Why don't we talk about Algeria? Why do they make films like that in Italy and not in France? Et cetera." To me personally, that has always seemed like a false problem: all films are political. *Love Story* is a political film. It says a lot about the silent majority in America. Whereas certain politically engaged films hammer the nail in so heavily that they don't allow for any serious political reflection. Today, in France, they're making a whole mess of political films. Why? For economic reasons: several of these films have done very well, so the producers want to make political cinema now. It should also be mentioned that censorship has been softened a lot, while remaining completely arbitrary, the domain of princes. And when the prince is named Maurice Druon.[2] . . . It's sad!

GJ: But these films are not politically mature.

LM: Some of them are interesting: I'm thinking of *Etat de siège* (*State of Siege*, 1972) for example. But where is the Francesco Rosi of French cinema? In fact, for me, the most naturally political filmmaker we have in France is Godard. I remember, when I saw *La Chinoise*, I was really astonished, and I called up a friend who was working at the university in Nanterre to ask him the question: "Is that really how things are, among your friends?" A few months later, we saw the answer. Jean-Luc was like a seismograph at the time, always ahead of the event.

GJ: Yes, but you will notice that at that time he wasn't politically engaged.

LM: That's what I mean. He had a very lively sensibility, incredibly sharpened; he "felt" things, without being preoccupied by an ideological system. Don't forget that people reproached him, after *Le Petit soldat*, with having made a fascist film! Given what was going on at the moment when that happened, and even before, it was a particular quality that Jean-Luc had, a unique quality. In fact, it was the vision of a poet more than of a political person, and that made his gaze so piercing, and sometimes so prophetic. Remember *Weekend* and *Les Carabiniers*.

GJ: Who are two or three others who have impressed you?

LM: Polanski often impresses me. I find that, among all the people of my generation, he is the one who is the best director; he directs admirably well. It is a pleasure to watch him take a sequence and to see what he does with it, when it works, because it always works. Certain sequences in *Cul-de-sac*, and almost all of *Rosemary's Baby*: it's admirable. Another person who often impresses me is Chabrol. His project is very clear and very ambitious. He is making a kind of "human comedy" of the postwar era; he shoots a lot, without pause, which I envy! Of course, there are ups and downs in his work, but I watch everything he does attentively and I am sure that with some temporal distance his films will really hold up as a body of work. I said that I envy him because I often regret making relatively few films; because at the end of a shoot one is "in shape," as athletes say. Directing is something like a sport; in other words, you have to find the reflexes, the automatic responses, each time. When I started making *Lacombe, Lucien*, I hadn't made a fiction film since the end of 1970, since *Murmur of the Heart*. In the first weeks, I had the impression of having to learn everything again. In a three-month shoot, it is only after the first two weeks that I really feel comfortable. I understand very well the desire of a director, as soon as he finishes a film, to attack another in the next three months: first of all, because it ends up becoming a need, a drug, and, at the same time, one is really in good shape for it.

GJ: Why don't you make more films?

LM: Because I need to be really excited about a subject. Before making a film, I always work on several things that I give up along the way. I need to experience a kind of falling in love, and then everything happens very fast. But it can be months before that feeling comes. That is why I like to shoot in 16mm, direct cinema, because it is a way of continuing to work.

GJ: But don't you think that there is a problem—I don't know, it depends on the director—but in a period of five years, or ten years, there are people who suddenly have a kind of state of grace, and then it falls away. There are very few great directors, aside from Bunuel, perhaps, who never stop making films throughout their whole lives. There are a number of people who have had a very brilliant career for five years, and then it's over. . . .

LM: In any case, I think that it is a profession that wears you out terribly. During the shoot, my Italian cinematographer Tonino delli Colli, seeing me exhausted one Saturday evening, said to me: "You know, I think that each of a director's films costs him three years of his life." It's true, because there is such a nervous tension, such a responsibility. There is above all this terrifying thing of being supposed to have talent, imagination, and authority, every day from 9 a.m. until 6 p.m., for three months: it's absurd. There are really "without" days, days when one wants to go away. On those days, you have to play the role of the profession, of your experience; you get through it, but sometimes it can be seen on the screen. In any case, I can see it, even in others' films! Beyond the shoot, what is also exhausting is the public relations work: before, during, and after . . . there is no way of cutting through it! Every film is an event that lasts for a year, easily. You can see very well, in the history of cinema, how directors have a state of grace and then become unhinged. It starts to interest them less; it becomes routine; and they do it for the money or in order to continue to exist, but they have lost their "punch." For me, after *Le Voleur*, while shooting the short film *William Wilson* in Italy, without any great desire to do it, I felt the need to stop; I was exhausted, empty; fiction didn't interest me anymore. It seems that in these moments, in complete disarray, one always makes films about stories of doubles, which are a kind of exorcism! Nevertheless, after *William Wilson*, I completely stopped making films for a fairly long time, and I went to India. Diving back into reality, as I had done at the beginning of my career, was great, because it gave me the taste for shooting again, and also, I would say, for living. . . .

GJ: And now, it doesn't bother you anymore?

LM: No, it doesn't bother me, because I have the impression that I have had a second wind; I am trying to find a balance between these two poles of my work: the direct cinema and the fiction films. After *Calcutta*, I said that I could not make more fiction films, which was absurd. Now I want to make a new fiction film fairly quickly. But, for example, if the Brazilians gave me free rein to make my Amazon project, I would go right away: I would leave with a cameraman and a sound engineer, right away, just like that. I have also made changes in my life. There are a lot of things which make it so that I feel much better now. After all, it is banal to go through periods of doubt and crisis . . . and if you are not capable of getting past them, you stay on that road.

GJ: And when you say, "I have changed my life," that has no doubt had an influence on your professional life.

LM: Yes, completely.

GJ: Is it the fact of living in the Lot region?

LM: That is one example. Above all, it is the fact of no longer living in Paris, because Paris is a city that I found fascinating for a certain number of years, and now I have the impression that it is as if I had seen the same play for the thousandth time. There is nothing that astonishes me anymore; I have the feeling that I know everyone. Paris, for me, is a bit like when I go back to the Théatre de la Huchette and see *The Bald Soprano*, which is a play that entranced me when I was a student, and which has continued to run imperturbably for eighteen years. That is a bit what Paris is like for me. It is something that no longer brings me anything. I don't live there anymore, except to work, and work is the same everywhere. But Paris is no longer a source of inspiration for me, a city that I want to discover. When I was younger, I wanted to dive into it. Today, my curiosity is elsewhere.

GJ: You have no desire to shoot films with "stars" anymore?

LM: No, not so much. You know, this film was really a great experience, with complex characters who were very, very difficult to play, and where we had actors who were completely new, or people from the theater who were mostly not familiar with the cinema. It was a fascinating piece of collective work.

GJ: But how did you choose your actors, in *Lacombe, Lucien*, for example? We already talked about the young man, but what about the others?

LM: For the young girl, France Horn, I did the same kind of work. I saw a lot of actresses, and I found Aurore Clément, after a lot of tests, hesitations, and in the end, enthusiasm. As for the theater people, it was a matter of going to the theater and seeing them. I saw a lot of them, and did tests for them as well. To be honest, before shooting the film, I spent two months with a videotape recorder in my hand!

GJ: But why did you use people from the theater?

LM: Because there is a whole part of the film that takes place in the Gestapo offices, with a group of French collaborators who live in a requisitioned hotel. There are five or six of them, bizarre people, and I found it natural to choose theater actors because within fascism of whatever kind there is always something very theatrical. These are characters who are playing a role; they are playing their own lives, and thus it was very logical to use people from the theater. You know, I don't have any *a priori* ideas, any system in this area. I really love mixing amateurs and professionals. What really pleases me in this film—in which the theme and the setting are actually very disorienting—is that the viewer who is not in the business will never see someone come onto the screen about whom he can say, "Oh look, it's Whatsisname!" Don't you find it a bit annoying, in contemporary French cinema, that 90 percent of the films are made with the same five actors and the same three actresses? For me, as a spectator, that bothers me a lot. However, in France, there are a lot of excellent actors whom you never see in the cinema. There is, I believe, a lack of courage and imagination which makes people get stigmatized. That said, I have to admit that I really had cold sweats at the start of shooting the film! Everything depended on the performances, and if Pierre Blaise, for example, who played the lead role, had not been good, there would not have been a film. I spent whole days with him making him work on videotape, but in the end, until the shooting, we had no way of knowing whether he would be good or not. It was an enormous risk, because the paradox of the film is that it still ended up being expensive. It was an intimate subject: we don't see the war, and there are not a lot of big scenes, but we still made it very carefully, with time and means, and it depended entirely on the work of newcomers.

GJ: And do you allow for a margin of improvisation in a film like that?

LM: In certain sequences, yes. The end of the film, for example, was almost completely improvised. It was meant to be like that—an "ad lib" ending—with the understanding that we had shot the film in the order of the screenplay and, in the last days of shooting, we were freewheeling. . . . For the rest of the film, I stayed close to the screenplay, but I never decide on my *mise en scene* in advance: I improvise that based on the actors and the locations, working with the actors. As far as the situations and dialogues are concerned, they turned out to be fairly precise, fairly accurate, so that I didn't feel the need to change much in the shooting, as has happened to me on other films.

GJ: When you write, do you see the film in your head?

LM: Yes and no: seeing the film in your head is dangerous, unless you're working in a studio and can adapt reality to your vision, which was not at all the case here. That said, something interesting happened in this film that had never happened to me before, which is that we found the locations before writing the final version of the screenplay. In particular, for the apartment where the Jewish family lives, where a lot of the film takes place, we found an astonishing location, and we adapted the screenplay to the location: in other words, Patrick Modiano came to see it, and we looked at it really closely, and then we reworked the screenplay in relation to the particulars of the place. A lot of ideas came to us from that location. For such a complex subject, which was also a tense one, I am not a big fan of improvisation. I have had the experience of changing everything during the shoot, and then noticing that an idea that came to me in five minutes, just like that, in the nervousness of the shoot, was not necessarily a good one!

GJ: But do you feed your films with personal observations, with things from your life, or not?

LM: Yes, of course. For this film, there was the Mexican point of departure that I told you about, and then, when I set it in France in 1944, a lot of childhood memories came back to me, and the screenplay was fed by them, even if they were not transcribed literally. For example, at the beginning of 1944 I was in a parochial middle school in Fontainebleau, and there was a young servant boy in the school who had stolen something, I don't really know what, and who was kicked out of the school. Knowing that there were three Jewish children among the students, hidden under false names, he went to the Gestapo in Melun to denounce them. The school was closed, and the director of the school and the three boys were deported. That was the point of departure for my first draft of the screenplay: Lucien was unjustly sent away and went to the Gestapo. And then, I cut that whole beginning out, the character evolved, there was no longer the parochial school, et cetera. In the end, the film begins in an old people's home, and there is nothing left of that traumatic episode from my childhood, but the screenplay was still fed by it. I could cite several other examples of memory as a springboard, if you want: the war in Algeria, for example, which we imposed on the little people of our society, "normal" people who became torturers. There is also the fact that I lived in the Lot for several years and, in passing time there, living there, I ended up telling myself that it would be good to shoot a film there. Places are very important in the film, both in terms of what one sees in them and what one doesn't see.

GJ: Did you write it when you were living in the Lot region?

LM: Yes, part of it. Patrick and I took a lot of walks in the region, in the small towns and villages. For example, this idea of the Jewish family that is hidden at the top of an old, dilapidated hotel in the small town, came to us while we were walking in Figeac. On a little road, we heard a piano playing Schumann, and, pushing open the door of an old hotel, we saw an abandoned garden. All of that is more or less in the film: France Horn, who plays the piano in the apartment right at the top of this hotel, a kind of storeroom that they have rented, with the landlord who tries to extort money from them. There are also chance events that are not really chance. In the house next door to mine, there had been an eighteen-year-old boy, with the last name of Hercule, who was a Gestapo agent who infiltrated the *maquis*, and who gave up dozens of resistants. I didn't know about it until after I wrote the screenplay! Another example: in Figeac, where we shot the exteriors of the film, 800 out of the 10,000 inhabitants were deported.

GJ: After *Lacombe, Lucien*, what are you going to do?

LM: I never know very well what I am going to do after finishing a film. I have a complicated idea, which takes place in the Lot: this time actually in my house! I would like to shoot it quite quickly for a change: there are moments when one feels the need to move fast.

GJ: Shooting a film is quite healthy, basically.

LM: Yes, one is completely cut off from the outside world, but one builds one's own recreated world, a world that ends up really existing, like a shortened life.

At the same time, every end of a film is a death. You have the impression that you have come full circle: it's much more than three months; it's really a piece of your life that ends abruptly. During a shoot, very intense emotional relationships are established between a group of people who are in a restricted space, like a society in a closed circle. It doesn't resemble the real world, but there are very acute, very complete relationships, which bring all the best things life can bring, such as emotions and intellectual stimulation. Our sensitivity and intelligence are strongly stimulated during a shoot, so there is necessarily a terrible drop in tension at the end of filming, at least for the director. Each time, it's as if I came out of a running of the bulls: there is this great emptiness in the stomach, this sense of having no charge left in the battery.

Notes

1. Pierre Bonny and Henri Lafont were French auxiliaries who worked for the Gestapo during World War II. They were both executed as war criminals in December 1944.

2. Maurice Druon was a minor French novelist who served as Minister of Culture from 1973 to 1974.

A Seminar with Louis Malle

American Film Institute / 1975

From AFI's Harold Lloyd Master Seminar with Louis Malle, March 11, 1975. ©1975, used courtesy of American Film Institute.

Question: In *Murmur of the Heart*, how did you find the boy who played the lead, and how did you work with him?

Louis Malle: I put ads in the newspaper, and a lot of young people responded. We had a Sony video camera, and we shot footage of the boys just to have a general feeling about them. After that, when we had made a selection of fifteen or twenty boys, I would give them something to work on—just some lines, nothing to do with the part—and then we did a serious film test. In the case of Benoît Ferreux, who plays the young boy in *Murmur of the Heart*, he came with his brother, and they wanted to work as extras to make a little money. They weren't really interested in playing the lead. I liked the boy very much, and then I found out that he was Jean-Louis Trintignant's nephew!

When I gave him the script, he turned down the part. Then I called Trintignant, and I said, "You better speak to your nephew." But actually, I liked his reaction, because it was honest: he was really afraid of being in the film. In France, we had something called "pre-censorship," which doesn't exist anymore. They wouldn't tell you not to make the film, but they would tell you that if you made it it was going to be banned. In which case, producers are kind of hesitant to make the picture! And that's what happened to my script. I got a very rude letter, which I immediately published in a newspaper, saying that the screenplay was immoral and was going to be banned. And I had no idea of how I was going to shoot the difficult scenes.

Q: Did you rehearse before you shot the film?

LM: Yes, we rehearsed with the whole cast. But not too much, because I don't like rehearsing. We just went through the dialogue, because I wanted to hear the dialogue, especially the dialogue for the kids. We changed it with them. And then we changed it again when we were shooting. I'm very flexible with dialogue.

Q: Were the last scenes with the mother difficult to shoot?

LM: Yes, they were difficult. Lea Massari, who played the mother, was very nervous. The funny thing about the film is that the boy and Lea Massari couldn't stand each other. She thought he wasn't professional enough, and he thought she was a big bore. But it works. He's a great boy, really bright. He's an assistant director now. He wants to be a director, like everyone else.

Q: You're one of the few directors who has constantly gone back and forth between documentaries and dramatic films. Can you talk about how going back and forth between these two modes of filmmaking has affected your career? And has making documentaries had an impact on your fiction films?

LM: I started as an underwater cameraman, and I shot fish. But it was a good training: after three or four years, I knew all about camera, lighting, editing, and sound. Then I went into fiction films, and I made several in a row. And then I decided to stop for one year, and I feel like it was good to do that. That was in 1962, the end of the Algerian War, and I started to make a documentary about Algeria which I never finished. I also made a short documentary about the bicycle race, the Tour de France. It's twenty minutes long, and it's never been shown in the US.

A few years ago, I would have said that making documentaries is a completely different experience from making fiction films, but now I'm not too sure about that. I did an interesting experiment between making *Murmur of the Heart* and *Lacombe, Lucien*. I shot a film on a hundred yards of a sidewalk in Paris, in an area called the Place de la République. It's very near an area called Belleville, which is an area where there are a lot of Algerians, and it's also the Jewish quarter. And they have a kind of love-hate relationship. We spent two weeks on this street with a 16mm camera and a tape recorder. And we would say, "This is a camera and this is a microphone; would you like to talk to us?" And surprisingly, most of them were quite willing to talk. So we had a lot of material, which we edited into a film of about an hour and a half. The film is the extreme of what used to be called *cinéma verité* and which I call *cinéma direct*: just going out into the street and filming people. And it ends up being like a book by Céline or Queneau: it's all about language, and the incredible things people say. And most of these people are like characters out of a novel, so it feels a lot like fiction.

That experience helped me to go into shooting a film like *Lacombe, Lucien*, because I tried to make the film almost like a documentary. And I feel very strongly that, for me at least, the film should not try to explain everything to the audience; it should allow them to participate, and it should show them something which is ambiguous and confusing, and have them bring something to it. Which can be a little difficult, because I think that most of the time audiences prefer to be manipulated. We've seen it in lots of recent American films. They love to be frightened to death!

But it's important to leave something to the audience. I've always had a hard time knowing how to end my films, because I feel like I want to show the lives of certain people for a certain amount of time, and then at some point just stop. I just finished shooting a film with four different endings. Actually, I don't feel it's terribly important how you end a film. It's only important for audiences and distributors. It's like in *Murmur of the Heart*: the ending was improvised. I didn't know what to do, and I finally ended it with the family having a big laugh. Lots of people in France were really furious about that ending.

I love shooting in 16mm. The trouble is that you have a great time shooting, but then you have a terrible time editing it. I got an offer to come and shoot a film here called *Phantom America*, which would be like *Phantom India* but set in the US. But the problem is that it would be a year of shooting and eighteen months of editing.

In editing documentaries, you have to try to rationalize what you shot. First you shoot, and it is very visceral, and then you have to create the structure and the rhythm in the editing. In some of these films, I had to reedit them several times: it's like putting together a musical score. It's interesting, but I've spent too much time in editing rooms in the last few years.

The problem with documentaries is that they're so obviously not commercial that you have a hard time getting people to release them or even show them on television.

Q: Do you plan your films very thoroughly?

LM: That depends. For *Murmur of the Heart*, I thought about the film for some time: for about two years. But I started writing the script without any plan, and I wrote it in four days. But the last film, *Black Moon*, took me six months to write, and I changed it in the shooting. So it depends. When I wrote *Murmur of the Heart*, I was so convinced that you can't write a good script in four days that I showed it to some friends, and they said, "It's good. You should go with that." And then for about a month I tried to make it better, but actually the first draft was the best, and the few places I tried to change went wrong.

I like to improvise. I'm completely prepared to change what I am going to shoot if it's better for the actors. I like the people who work in my films to come with ideas, and that's what I like about filmmaking: it's a collective creation.

I only worked as an assistant once in my life: with Robert Bresson, on *A Man Escapes*. I worked with him on the preparation for the shooting, and on the casting, and also a little on the script. And then I started to work with him on the shoot, but I left after a month, because Bresson really works alone. After a month, I told him, "I feel terrible, but the way you create is so personal that it's impossible to share in it; it's impossible to help you, and it's even impossible to learn anything by watching you. You're so cut off from the rest of the people on the set." And he said, "You're right." He didn't object. But I like to work very closely with other people on the set.

Q: Do you normally shoot in sequence, following the order of the script?

LM: That depends. I like to start with the beginning of the script, and end with the end of the script, especially when I work with non-professionals.

Q: Can you talk about how you cast your films?

LM: Casting is half of it. Even with great directors—geniuses—good casting is so important. I spend a lot of time on casting. On *Lacombe, Lucien*—aside from the tailor, who is a well-known stage actor, and the grandmother, who is a German actress—all of the others are either non-professionals or barely known stage actors. And since there was a problem with accents—the film takes place in a part of the south of France where there is a strong accent—they had to be from that part of the country, which limited the cast.

Q: For the actor who played the main character, was it a conscious decision to go with a non-professional?

LM: Well, it was obvious to me, because he was supposed to be seventeen or eighteen years old, and there is no such thing as a good child actor. I don't know about here, but child actors in France are monsters! And he had to be a boy from that region: it had to show in the way he walks, the way he talks, or, for example, in that scene where he kills the chicken. So it had to be a non-professional. And based on that premise, the rest of the cast also had to be non-professionals. It couldn't have had someone like Michel Piccoli in it. And I was also trying to make the story credible. I always find it difficult in films, especially French films, that they are all made with the same five actors! You see someone opening a door, and you know it's going to be Lino Ventura! So I try to stay away from that. For instance, for the people who played the Gestapo in the film, I wanted stage actors, because there is a very interesting text by Jean Genet where he explains that fascism is very theatrical, and it was interesting to have these people be played by stage actors, and some of them pretty bad stage actors! When I chose them, people told me, "You can't use them: they're terrible actors!" Which was true.

Q: I heard that most of *Lacombe* was shot with a handheld camera. Is that true?

LM: Yes; it doesn't show, does it? I had a very tough, strong cameraman. Actually, about half of the film was handheld. I found out that most of these people, who had no experience of film acting—especially the stage actors—weren't used to having to be in a particular spot for the lighting. So I discussed it with my cameraman, and we decided not to force them to be obsessed with that aspect, and instead to shoot with a handheld camera. That way, if it was a good take, I didn't have to stop and yell "cut" because someone moved slightly. So in terms of getting the best possible performances, it was good. But of course, I was trying to make it look like it *wasn't* handheld.

Q: Can you discuss how you staged the scenes at the tailor's apartment?

LM: The entire film was shot on location: there was no studio shooting. And in this part of France, we were looking for the right places to shoot, and we were very lucky, because there was a huge chateau which is almost completely in ruin, and only one very old man lives there. We were able to use one wing of the chateau, which was perfect. Nothing had been touched for thirty years, and there were piles of old newspapers. I was with Ghislain Uhry, my art director, and when we saw the rooms we said, "This is great." But the problem was that the man wanted to clean it! We convinced him not to touch it, just to leave it as it was. And I used a camera to make still photos of that place, and I showed those photos to the cameraman, and I said, "Tonino, you're going to light it exactly like that, because I want to have that feeling." We had been looking for this location for a long time, and we had even thought about reconstituting it in a studio, but then we found this place.

Q: I'm thinking in particular of the scene where Lucien's mother comes to visit the Jewish family.

LM: I had a big problem on that scene. The woman who plays the mother is a terrible actress. Everyone was telling me that she was fantastic, but she was a very bad actress. That was my main concern, because it was one of the key scenes of the picture—one of the two or three most important scenes—and I was really afraid of having it spoiled by bad acting. So the whole conception of the shots in that scene had to do with trying to get the best performance out of her. One of the principles was to have it be based entirely on reaction shots. We had a lot of material to cover in that scene. Sometimes scenes are made in the editing room, and then other times I don't see any possibility of changing them in the editing. It depends entirely on the actors. I feel that the people on the screen are what is important. I have a great admiration and respect for actors, because at some point they are alone in front of the camera, which is difficult. They are the ones on the screen. So I think my work is really to help them as much as possible and be very flexible. I try to have no principles and to be prepared to change everything if it helps the actors.

And sometimes you have two actors who have to be helped in a completely different way. For example, in *Lacombe*, you had the boy played by Pierre Blaise, and the girl played by Aurore Clément. And the boy was usually at his best on the first take, and the girl was someone who . . . to get the best out of her, you had to do eight takes. I don't mind doing twenty takes, but the problem is to get both of them when they're at their best. What was interesting with Pierre was that after the first two takes he would be bad for the next five. And then I would change something in the dialogue in order to provoke him. I did it when I felt the girl was just about ready. But most of the time it's very difficult to get the best out of different actors on the same take. It's a big problem, and sometimes in the cutting room you don't know what to do, because you have to choose the best take for one actor of the other.

Q: You have talked about how you like to be flexible in your approach, yet it seems that in *Lacombe*, each frame is highly composed, almost like a painting. Can you talk about that?

LM: Well, *Lacombe* was very carefully prepared. First of all, I had to read a lot of documentation about the period. It is a difficult period in France, as you know, so I knew I would have to be very careful. So I spent a lot of time with documentation, which was quite fascinating, especially discussions with ex-collaborators. And then there was the script, which I didn't change very much in the shooting. There was a lot less improvisation than there normally is on my films. Because I knew that it was really—especially for a French audience—like walking on eggshells.

The French are very emotional about this period, very immature. For twenty years, they made us believe that everyone in France was in the Resistance, which is not true. So I had to be careful. There was a big controversy about the film, but there was no detail that they could pin down as not being accurate. I remember that I talked with an historian who was a specialist on the collaboration. I started discussing it with him, and I asked him if I could show him my script, and he said that whatever I wrote it could not be as crazy as what actually happened.

Q: Can you talk about the performance of the actor who played Lucien?

LM: Well, the boy who played that part actually had a complicated relationship to the character he was playing. He was pretending not to relate to the character at all, but actually he could. He was very violent and very tough, and at the same time he had something very childlike about him. But he could be very tough. I remember the first time I saw him he had very long hair, so he looked like every other boy today. And then when we started working with him, I said, "You have the part, but now you have to cut your hair." And he really didn't want to do it. But the first time I saw him with the haircut of the period, all of a sudden I had the feeling that he had become a different person. And then one night, before the shoot, I went out with him. He drank a lot; he got very drunk and he started a fight. He could be very violent.

Q: How did you direct him?

LM: The big problem was keeping him interested, because he would get bored very quickly. After a week of shooting, he wanted to quit, which was a big problem. We ended shooting on a Saturday, and he said, "I want to go back home." And we spent the whole weekend trying to convince him not to quit. And it was like the boy from *Murmur of the Heart*: he felt that he was being manipulated. That is something actors get used to: eventually, they have to accept it. But he didn't accept it at the beginning. He was amazing, because after three days he knew all the technical tricks, like how to move and where to stand: things that it takes stage actors a month to learn, or maybe they never achieve it. Everyone on the set was amazed at how naturally talented he was. And what I found out very quickly was that he hated to be patronized. But we had a very good relationship, because I really admired and respected him, which is something he could feel. He had big problems with some members of the crew who were treating him like a child. I discussed things with him, because he knew a lot more about the part than I did. I come from a different milieu, and a different part of the country.

Before we started shooting scenes, I would ask him his point of view about the dialogue. And many times I would change things because he felt a certain way about them. So it was really a full participation in the film, rather than just playing a part. We had a relationship based on mutual respect, which is the only way when you're dealing with young actors. We've stayed friends: I live in this same part of France now, and we visit each other quite often.

Q: More specifically, what were the kinds of things you had to tell him?

LM: Actually, he made very few mistakes. I would say that out of the large cast that I had in that film, he was one of the ones I had to direct the least. For instance, in the relationship with the Jewish family, he had a rapport with the actor who was playing Horn which was a little bit like the one in the film. He was a little afraid of this man, Holger Lowenadler, who was a professional actor; and at the same time, Lowenadler was a little bit afraid of him. He knew enough to know that it's very dangerous to play alongside non-professionals, because they can give performances that are sometimes more natural. So it was a very strange rapport, especially in the first few days of shooting. But I would say that I had to direct Lowenadler a lot more than I had to direct Pierre. The problem with Lowenadler was that he was a stage actor and had hardly been in films. So I had to rein him in, to keep him from doing stage acting. And sometimes, for reasons that I can't quite understand, the *boy* started overacting. By the end, especially in the scenes with the family, he was trying to rise to the same level as Lowenadler. Which I can understand, but it was really bad for the film.

Usually, I would discuss the scene with him. We would start with technical things and lighting, and then I would do one take, which was more like a rehearsal, and I would watch what he was doing very carefully. And then I would tell him things, or sometimes I wouldn't tell him anything because he got it just right. Sometimes it came right away, just as it was supposed to be.

There were things in the script that I thought wouldn't work, and that I thought I would have to cut. For example, when he's drunk and he comes in the middle of the night to see the tailor, and he opens this little suitcase with all his loot, and gives Horn the watch. And Horn tells him, "You should go to bed." And he turns at the door and says, "*Vive la France.*" And I remember saying to Patrick Modiano, "This will have to be cut, because he will never be able to say that line in a way that works." But it did work. He didn't like the line, but he said he would try it, and it was great. Actually, he was supposed to be drunk, and he *was* drunk when he did that scene!

Louis Malle, An Interview:
From *The Lovers* to *Pretty Baby*

Dan Yakir / 1978

From *Film Quarterly* 31, no. 4 (Summer 1978): 2–10. Reprinted by permission.

Auteurist film critics have sometimes given less than wholehearted approval to the *oeuvre* of Louis Malle, disregarding the stylistic and thematic consistency manifested in his films for over twenty years. His rebellion against the tyranny of genre convention created the impression that each of his films was a new departure that failed to fit into convenient molds. Each Louis Malle film is indeed a new departure—his innovative questioning of the medium rivals that of Bunuel—and his work is much larger than the sum of its parts.

Unlike directors such as Polanski or Forman, who adjusted their considerable talents to the American system to produce successful if less personal films, Malle, in his first American project, *Pretty Baby*, chose to adjust the system to his own creative genius while continuing to explore his lifelong interest in youth and the process of growing up. He has taken an enormous risk with *Pretty Baby*, as he also did with *Murmur of the Heart*. Not only does it deal with a child prostitute and her relationship with an older man, a subject bound to inflame the rage of many, but it is also his most restrained and understated film to date, which may baffle the popcorn addict.

With charm that is never facile and tenderness untainted by sentimentality, Malle examines his adolescent characters before they lose their last vestige of magic, that wondrous look at the world that they can no longer cast as adults. Instead of returning to recapture the bliss of a paradise lost, he embarks on a penetrating search for "a moment of truth, *the* moment of truth in our lives." This moment involves exposure to the absurd and corrupt world of adults.

Dan Yakir: Why your fascination with adolescence and the ritual of entering the adult world?

Louis Malle: I'm fascinated by it through my own experience and what I feel about what's going on today. For most of us, when we are about to become adults and live by the rules of the adult world, we have to leave behind a lot of the freedom, and fantasy, and looseness. There's always a moment when you find out that those rules are not necessarily right.

In previous stages of our civilization—before the industrial society, especially in the twentieth century, where things are going so fast (in twenty years, the world has changed more than during the five centuries in the Middle Ages, so society is much less stable)—in periods of very slow change, children were almost provided with a moment to experiment. In the Middle Ages and the Renaissance—actually, up to the twentieth century—most of the time, if you were the son of a peasant, you would become a peasant yourself, following your father. Artisans would go on tours around the country to learn their trade: society seemed to find it necessary to provide a moment for adolescents to experiment, before they returned to society as members. Today, the cut is much more abrupt and traumatic.

To me, personally, the period of adolescence—between the ages of twelve and fifteen—has been absolutely crucial. There were two central events in my youth, and in my life. One was the war. In 1944, I was eleven. A lot of traumatic things happened to me and I remember it much more vividly than I remember the rest of the forties and even the fifties. I remember the first six months of 1944 practically to this day.

Then I had this heart murmur, so I was taken out of school and had to stay home and work on my own. That's when I started being very much alone, reading a lot—and lots of things happened to me in that period. It was very difficult, because I was supposed to be sick and I didn't know what would become of me—I was not supposed to do any physical activity. I was very sheltered, and I started looking around me. This accident must have accentuated my curiosity. In fact, even in my very first film, I managed to inject into the story a very young couple—the girl was sixteen and the boy was seventeen: he was Georges Poujouly of *Forbidden Games*.[1]

DY: How important to you is the notion of the innocence of children and its loss?

LM: I'm not really sure that children are innocent. From a very early age, practically from birth, they're exposed to a lot of information. If you oppose innocence to a sense of guilt, there's no question that children in our society are tremendously exposed to guilt. It's almost imprinted by their education. When you're a child, you tend to rely much more on firsthand experience, which is acquired through your senses—seeing, touching, smelling. That's what's so great about it. But when you become thirteen or fourteen, education becomes very abstract and you're supposed to get your experience and information from books, which is secondhand: through someone else's experience. This is definitely wrong—it cuts you off from the world, from nature.

DY: I was thinking of innocence as expressed in Jerzy Skolimowski's *Deep End*: a boy discovers the world for the first time by finding sex, and the only thing that can follow is death—everything else would be an anticlimax.

LM: Sex is a terribly important part of growing up. It's obvious. Usually, adults have a tendency to consider children as sexless, which makes it a lot easier for the adults, but we know it's not true. What you find out when you become an adult is corruption—here innocence can be opposed to corruption, and corruption is the importance of money, of social structures, the inability to achieve what one wants and the fact that, for all these reasons, every adult has a double language. You have to compromise all the time, say things you don't really mean, dealing with the obvious hypocrisy in which we live—it's part of the art of living.

DY: This is what Zazie finds out: everything is deceptive and corrupt.

LM: *Zazie* is in many ways a perfect archetype, because it was almost classical in its structure: a little girl coming to the big city, Paris, from the country, for thirty-six hours, and then she goes back. And what happens to her is discovering that not only the world of adults but also modern civilization, the Big City . . . she discovers that everybody, everything, everybody is pretending. They're not what they seem to be. It's part of the game, in comedy, to have people change physical appearances. *Zazie* exposed exactly what I've been trying to do since, but it's very much in the open because in the book it was like that—this man, Gabriel, was changing identity every two reels, appearing in a different costume. His wife was a woman who was also a man, and everybody was upside down. I even managed to shoot scenes where in the same dolly shot we would change objects: a chair was red and the next time the camera passed by it, it was blue. It made it obvious in a very aggressive way that we were in a world which we pretend is one, but which instead is multiple and changing—and we try to deal with that contradiction.

If you're a child, you want the Truth. And we know—and that's the knowledge that takes years to accept—that there's no such thing. It's a matter of consensus: an accepted truth in one society will not be accepted in another. I'm very sensitive to this aspect of living. There's always a moment when you find out that your parents are lying to you—that they all do, even if they try not to. It's the main shock that starts you off.

DY: You have said that *Black Moon* was born out of the last ten minutes of *Lacombe, Lucien*. In what way? Did *Pretty Baby* originate out of *Black Moon*? In *Black Moon*, a daughter breastfeeds her mother, which is also the motif that ends the film. *Pretty Baby* opens with a girl watching her mother give birth.

LM: What I meant to say about the end of *Lacombe, Lucien* is that I had the idea of *Black Moon* around the figure of Therese Giehse, who plays the Jewish grandmother in *Lacombe,* and plays the central character, a sort of Mother Earth, in *Black Moon.* The idea struck me when we shot the end of *Lacombe,* which we shot in sequence. Those three characters lost in the wilderness, with time dissolving—a pause when everything stops and time ceases to be important, a suspended moment. Visually and emotionally, *Black Moon* is a prolongation of the last ten minutes of *Lacombe,* which were a break from the rest of the picture. The fact that they were finally losing themselves is different: it was not really necessary, but I felt I needed it.

Black Moon starts more or less where *Lacombe* stops because, after all, we could very well imagine at the end of *Lacombe* that they find a big house, where there's an old lady in a bed. . . . It was the same archaic landscape. We shot it practically in the same place.

There is also something between *Black Moon* and *Pretty Baby.* In *Black Moon,* I try to make the point—symbolically—about the little girl who is sort of becoming a mother for the mother. In *Pretty Baby,* the relationship between Hattie and Violet is very much a reversal of roles.

DY: What was the function of the role reversals in *Black Moon*?

LM: It was, again, about identities which aren't really clear: people changing physical appearances. They were inside and outside their bodies all the time. And you have this strange couple, who are supposedly brother and sister, but at some point she's more masculine and he more feminine. Consciously or unconsciously, I'm trying to express this fundamental doubt that I have about people actually being what they pretend to be. I show people always searching for something else and sometimes being very unhappy with what they are—this search for identity which seems to be one of the traumas of this society. It was a lot easier to be yourself in a very rigid society like the Indian caste system, where everything—from the moment you were born—was decided for you. You were part of the universe, playing a very specific role vis-à-vis society, your family. . . . All your life was extremely predictable. Today, we're in a much looser society, where people are more in charge of their individual destiny and it's a source of extreme confusion and disorder, because psychologically many of them cannot assume their identity and pretend to be something else.

DY: In *Pretty Baby,* the theme of reality versus appearances is also very strong; apart from the brothel being a factory of illusions, the merchants themselves fall prey to what they manufacture: Hattie believes the earrings she gets from "Highpockets" are hers to keep; the German prostitute tries to lure the old man into marriage so that she could get out, but he never marries her.

LM: The whorehouse is a sort of microcosm of the real world, but a caricature of it, a crude and open reflection of the real world. Politically, the power
structure is very much like in our society, where money is essential. It's all about
money, and men are definitely on top of women; it's about the exploitation of
women. When somebody is rich and powerful, he can do practically what he
wants, and is provided with everything he wants as long as he can pay for it. And
the gigantic hypocrisy, when you have an official red-light district frequented by
politicians—and it's completely accepted . . .

DY: The audience also falls prey to illusion. In the opening scene, we see the
exterior of the house at night, but the rest of the film takes place indoors, so it's
always lit, even at night. For example, when Violet sees her mother give birth, at
first she sighs as if she were having sex, then groans in pain, and finally we find
out she is giving birth.

LM: The opening scene is something I had in mind from the very beginning.
I practically started with the birth scene, which was taken from the Al Rose
book: about one of the whores giving birth in the attic in the middle of the night,
while the sex is going on downstairs. . . . So, I thought if you had this first scene,
starting with a close-up of the little girl watching very attentively and you know
what's going on, you may think the screaming and moaning that comes during
birth is very close to the sounds of an orgasm. The confusion was deliberately
provoked, and it is a good start for the story: this confusion between the process
of life and sexual activity.

Photography is an illusion too. Hattie has to "look like an angel," which she
wasn't. Bellocq himself says he's dealing with magic.

The whole context of the film is an illusion. I took advantage of the fact that
it was set in New Orleans, where voodoo is so important. They live in a strange
world and witness a lot of irrational things. And, of course, Bellocq, "the artist,"
is a man who is trying to track down an illusion. Photography is an illusion;
filmmaking is an illusion. . . . I felt extremely close to the character of Bellocq.
I was very much identified with him and when I directed Keith Carradine, I
deliberately made him behave like a movie director. In the photography session
in Hattie's room, when he tells her those stupid things: "You're beautiful! Perfect!
Don't move! It's going to be great!"

DY: This scene has heavy sexual overtones. Bellocq tells Violet to leave the
room, and then asks Hattie: "Are you ready for me?"

LM: It was meant to be the transposition of a sexual dream, where actual
sex is replaced by. . . . Definitely, for Bellocq, his art is a means to get rid of an
obsession which has to do with sexual fantasy. It's an obvious transposition of
sex into something else, which supposedly creativity is all about.

DY: The only instance where appearance becomes reality is Hattie's marriage. She also keeps her promise to Violet to claim her back. Why do you give her this opportunity that you deny to the others? Nobody else really leaves prostitution. You even said that Violet would probably leave home and, who knows, might even return to the old profession. Why is Hattie so lucky? Or maybe it's a technicality—to leave Violet on her own?

LM: It's a technicality, but at the same time I tried to make the Hattie character so obsessed with the idea of leaving the whorehouse and becoming respectable—she's been trying for years, and when she finally succeeds, the madam says, "Well, you finally nailed one, huh?" Everyone else wants to do so too, but she is maybe more dedicated to her goal.

I took it for granted, because it was in the original story, in the Al Rose book: Violet met one of the johns who eventually became her husband, and from that time on she led a respectable life. So, for me, it was part of the story from the beginning, only I transferred it to the mother.

I had a few things in mind from the very beginning: Bellocq, the birth scene, the scenes with the child in the middle of the whorehouse, the fact that at some point the mother would go.... I considered the possibility that Hattie is thrown out of the house and starts walking in a lower part of Storyville, as a lower-class prostitute, but I dropped it.

DY: Why does Violet single out the "Professor" [the pianist], and then Bellocq to share looks of complicity with? Is it because they're all outsiders, observers rather than participants?

LM: Yes, because if you're Violet, who is raised in a whorehouse and knows very little about the world outside.... Her experience of the world comes from what she sees in the house. She sees men who are like objects—she has no relationship with them because they come for something very precise; they're completely anonymous. The johns, the customers, don't really exist. So, Violet is left with the men in the house with whom she can have a relationship—the two outsiders: the piano player who is Black, as most of them were, who is very lucid, watching the scene with a lot of irony. His presence itself is a comment. During the auction scene, there is a very long shot of him, and you can imagine all kinds of things going through his mind.

Bellocq is also an outsider, and is the one man the girls can relate to because he's different—he's not looking for sex, he's not a john, and he becomes a friend: he's a human being, not someone who's going to "lie on top of you," as one of the girls says.

DY: The theme of observer and participant brings us back to *Black Moon*—Cathryn Harrison is an observer, and so is Zazie.

LM: Oh yes, the character of Cathryn in *Black Moon* is an observer. It's a bit strange: she's watching her own dream, her own illusion. You could easily say it's a world created by her, a daydream she's inventing—watching her own fantasy. But she's drifting. . . .

It has always been essential to me to have the central character as an observer of a situation, whatever the situation may be. In *Pretty Baby*, we see what's going on through Violet's eyes. I even asked Paramount to state it in the advertising campaign: "A world seen through a child's eyes."

DY: *Black Moon* shares with Rivette's *Céline et Julie vont en bateau* references to Lewis Carroll, especially to *Alice in Wonderland*. What interests you in Lewis Carroll?

LM: The obsession with children, with girls, which is totally sublimated, totally transposed—God knows they've been trying to find all kind of sexual perversions in Lewis Carroll, but they don't seem to be able to dig out anything really serious. Technically, it was sort of asexual, and it seems that just talking to girls, taking them for boat trips or photographing them, was enough to satisfy his fantasy. It's very mysterious. There's something opaque about him. This sort of double life he led: being a very respectable clergyman on the one hand and a mathematician and teacher on the other—his odd relationships with girls, how he dealt with their parents. . . . It's very Victorian, very proper: asking the parents' permission to photograph the girls naked . . . and being so prudent and careful about the whole thing! The result is similar to Bellocq's photographs—it's stunning how he managed to capture. . . . Some of these Lewis Carroll photographs are very erotic, because they convey a strong obsession.

DY: Some people see *Alice* as the beginning of the comedy of the absurd. Does it interest you in this sense? *Zazie* can be related to that.

LM: Yes, many times I was tempted to deal with *Alice* in a more obvious way than I have done. The discovery of Lewis Carroll, when I was very young, was very important to me, and I've certainly been influenced by him, but I don't think I'll do justice to my interest in him and his writing just by filming one of his books. There's a very interesting one called *Sylvie and Bruno*. It's a world which is totally double-faced. There are several levels: the real, the dreamworld of these children, and how they invent the people surrounding them in a completely different way. I'm very turned on by this way of looking at the world—that behind reality there's something else, and we're looking for it.

DY: In *Zazie*, *Black Moon*, and *Pretty Baby*, the girls are consistently associated with animals. Why?

LM: It probably has to do with my own interest in the animal world. It also seems to me that children are a lot closer to animals. In the last two centuries, we've managed to isolate ourselves from the animal world, from nature. We've not only cut ourselves from it, but also destroyed it. The more powerful we become technologically, the more we destroy. If things go on at this rate, there'll be nothing left on earth except humans. If there is a capital sin, this must be it.

DY: Why did you use the unicorn in *Black Moon*?

LM: What's so interesting about the myth of the unicorn is that it can be found in almost every culture. So, it must have something very strong about it; it must correspond to a need. It is a fabulous animal, and lots of times it was taken for real. In *Black Moon*, she expresses wisdom. She's supposed to be the equivalent of the old lady—her alter ego, the same person in a different body. Also, in the part of France where I live—which is a very archaic landscape, very wild and untouched—it seems that a unicorn could. . . . She's almost the same color as the landscape, a part of it, so it almost seemed natural that she would appear. When I was writing *Lacombe, Lucien*, I found out there was a local legend about a unicorn kidnapping local girls and raping them. It goes back to the collective unconscious. . . . I was obliged to use the unicorn—I had no choice.

DY: In three key scenes in *Pretty Baby*, Bellocq is seen through glass: when he arrives at the brothel, when he leaves it, and when Violet goes to the house and sees him through the glass door. Is it to bring about a distanciation effect, to leave him a mystery, a reflection that corresponds to the lens of his camera?

LM: In these moments, he's seen by Violet. It's her point of view. The fact that it's through windows or mirrors makes it almost a creation of hers. . . . We don't really see him: we see him "in the eyes of."

There's a big difference between *Pretty Baby* and *Black Moon* in that *Pretty Baby* pretends to be a realistic picture: every rational explanation is provided for what's going on, which is not the case with *Black Moon*. But, finally, it comes back to the same thing: the world of illusion, as you say, the fact that it's seen from a child's eye makes it even more. . . . We could discuss for hours the subjectivity of her *regard* on things.

DY: You mentioned mirrors. In *Pretty Baby*, the German prostitute looks at herself in the mirror as she talks about the old man and we see her reflection. In addition to Violet's make-up session in front of the mirror, there's another scene toward the end where the "Professor" examines himself in the mirror, but we don't see the mirror. Why don't you show it?

LM: I try not to work that way. The more I go on, the more I try to let things happen. It's not something that came out of a reflection—a reflection about a reflection. . . . I feel increasingly free to let things take their course, and I like to be surprised by the way I shoot a scene. When I'm editing, I see the same scene 200 times and I have a lot of time to think about how I did it. Sometimes I surprise myself: I realize I could have done it in an entirely different way, so why did I do it this way? Sometimes I have an explanation, and sometimes I don't.

That's what I said about shooting a documentary: if you put your camera in the street, the way your film is an interpretation. So, it's a mirror game—and it's terribly unconscious, partly because you shoot it very quickly and only later do you try to understand why. I try to do it in my fiction too now, as much as I can. I try to invent a world, I put a camera in front of it, and then I try to shoot it the way I'd shoot a documentary. There's less and less of a difference between documentary and fiction in that sense.

DY: Except in terms of subject matter. You didn't make a documentary about growing up, for example.

LM: I have a son who is six years old, and for the first three years of his life I was filming him constantly. I must tell you, I got to a point where it became difficult. It takes a lot of discipline to do that, so I stopped. But I have piles of 16mm which eventually could be an interesting little documentary. It would be terribly interesting to keep doing it for fifteen years. I've always wanted to do it, and I'm probably getting closer to it: since I have two children now, it's a lot easier . . .

DY: It's interesting to examine *Pretty Baby* through camera movement. It opens with a very slow zoom to the brothel, followed by an almost identical zoom to Violet. There is another zoom toward the whores laughing in the corridor during the game of "sardines." At the breakfast table, at the end, the camera pulls back, taking a distance from Violet and Bellocq.

LM: There first zoom was, of course, on a miniature. I found out in Paris that some crazy jazz musicians spent fifteen years of their lives rebuilding New Orleans in a huge room, so we used it. I tried to give the impression of a bird's-eye view of Storyville, getting closer and closer to what is supposed to be Basin Street. Then, when we get inside, we get closer to Violet with a very slow, almost unnoticed zoom, when she watches the birth: it's a prolongation of the previous shot. I thought it was a good balance.

The breakfast scene is a good one. I used it to show the routine of their life together. It starts with a very irritating moment when she puts a lot of butter on her toast, and then we pull back and discover Bellocq watching her, and then we pull back more and more and see the maid coming in. It's all in one shot. It's a movement which actually replaces a series of shots. The close-up starts almost like an insert, and then you have the entire setting slowly revealed. There was a break in the story—a few months have passed since the picnic scene, since the marriage—and I felt this device also helped indicate the passage of time.

DY: There's a scene where the madam, Nell, washes her feet and a little girl watches and fiddles with her own feet as she will later fiddle with Bellocq's shoelaces. It is very striking visually, though of no visible service to the story.

LM: I thought it would be interesting to establish the presence of the little girl, who is another Violet. From the very beginning, she's initiated into the adult world, and this crazy old woman washing her feet in hot water. . . . I did it insidiously, as I usually try to make my camerawork: there was no separate shot. It was in the movement of the men who bring in the huge piece of meat, and they enter the kitchen, which is when I pan down and discover the old woman wiping her feet with the little girl watching her. It's all part of the same movement, and the pan is almost unnoticed. All these details are significant, but they aren't taken out to be made into something very obvious. If I were to define the way I approach a camera movement, I'd say it's very insidious. My camera movements are not meant to be noticed—they're very much improvised and I try to be as unconscious as possible with the use of the camera.

DY: You mentioned a few images that became the starting point of *Pretty Baby*. How about *Zazie* and *Black Moon*?

LM: *Black Moon* was definitely the old lady in bed—in my bed, in my house. . . . It was a fantasy about a woman being almost immortal and ruling the world from this bed, communicating via a weird radio system. That was the starting point. And also the old convention of the fairy tale: the little girl walking alone in that landscape and entering the empty house. It was a mixture of these two images.

Zazie for me was this tiny little girl in the middle of the Parisian traffic, looking around, and getting in trouble with every possible adult—just her presence was disturbing.

DY: What is the relationship between *Black Moon* and *Phantom India*?

LM: It's very unconscious. I found out later that the whole idea of *Black Moon*—the idea that the world doesn't exist, that reality is a dream, the whole philosophical outlook of the film—is very Indian. It's more precise in the sense that I used this engraving as a sort of leitmotif in the story: there's a vulture, a weeping woman, and a man cutting the vulture's head. And it becomes reality at the point where Joe Dallesandro starts killing the vulture. It's as if it came out of the engraving. The film is completely structured like a myth, and it's a direct reference to the *Ramayana*.

DY: What major literary influences do you acknowledge?

LM: Many different ones. I was under the spell of Montaigne when I was young. I was very impressed by Proust. Recently, I've been interested in Indian literature, the *Bhagavad Gita*. I would certainly mention Lewis Carroll.

DY: Could you attach a book to each of your films in terms of time?

LM: Not really, no. The situation of *The Lovers* is taken from a nineteenth-century short story, "Point de Lendemain," by Vivant Denon, an obscure writer who was a contemporary of Choderlos de Laclos, to whom he is sometimes compared. In those days I was very much in line with Montaigne and eighteenth-century writers like Marivaux. There's certainly something of Marivaux in *The Lovers*. He is a much more important writer than is usually acknowledged. Just by shooting *The Fire Within*, I expressed my interest in Drieu La Rochelle, whose inner contradictions always fascinated me.

Recently I've been freer from literature, I think.

DY: You have revolutionized film music. Using Miles Davis in *Elevator to the Gallows* was completely new. You used Satie in *The Fire Within*, while using no music at all in *The Thief of Paris*. How do you see the use of the soundtrack? Do you see it as an additional layer of meaning, supplementary or contradictory to what goes on on the screen?

LM: I try to use it in many opposite directions. I think it is just as important as the image, if not more so. The problem with the soundtrack is that it involves a contradiction. On the one hand, sound is a lot more abstract than sight. Music is an art form which naturally escapes reality. The great thing about the soundtrack is that you add things, while the camera is a very stupid instrument: it films what you put in front of it. Of course, you can do a lot of things with light, and you can change things a little in printing, but it's very limited. On the other hand, the main purpose of the soundtrack is to bring you the dialogue, which is where the theater, psychology, the "message," and everything that is heavy in film come in. In most films, the soundtrack is merely dialogues with music, which is nothing but pleonasm—accentuating the atmosphere of the situation, usually "psychological" music. This is uninteresting. But there is a lot to invent in the soundtrack. When the sound film appeared, the great thing was to hear what the actors said, and to get away from that has already taken forty years. And it's going to take a lot more.

I put less and less dialogues in my films: I'm a bit reluctant about dialogues, and I don't really trust them to convey what I want. I try to be more ambiguous and more complex than dialogues can express. You could say more with a bell ringing and with an effect that you add to the soundtrack, during sound editing—and I spend much time on it—than by the dialogue.

I try to use music the way visuals are used, as part of the scene. In *Pretty Baby*, jazz was a part of daily life, but I used it very discreetly because I didn't feel the picture needed a score. Sometimes I use music as a comment, and at other times as a counterpoint: against the mood. In *Pretty Baby*, I took advantage of this great music that I love. In the picnic, there's that New Orleans combo playing "After the Fall," a very famous song of the time, and it's very much in the spirit of the scene, but it wasn't written for it. I'd say it's used more as a comment in *Pretty Baby*.

It's different in the case of *Elevator to the Gallows*. It was my first film, and I was completely in love with the music of Miles Davis. It's a very interesting film, but I find some moments almost embarrassing. Miles Davis made it into something better than it actually was. It gave the picture a style, a tempo, and a climax that it didn't have. It's practically the only time. . . . Yes, the other exception would be the use of the Brahms sextet in *The Lovers*. It's used in a conventional way because it brings a romantic mood into the love scene in that long, slow night shared by Jeanne Moreau and Jean-Marc Bory. It was beautiful, but its use was almost manipulative. It was certainly trying to convey certain emotions.

The use of Satie in *The Fire Within* was much more discreet, more like a counterpoint. These little piano pieces create a very melancholic atmosphere, but, at the same time, there's definitely something ironical about it. It was a sort of distanciation from what was going on on the screen.

When I've been successful in using music in my films, it's always been music that I've been listening to while writing the script or shooting the film. So, naturally, it entered the picture and became part of the structure. I always use music that I'm very familiar with and that corresponds to my mood, because I take for granted that my mood is in my films. I was very much into the "Gymnopédies" and "Gnossiennes" by Satie that I used in *The Fire Within*.

If I used Wagner in *Black Moon*, it's because I became interested in him fairly recently. I used to be very much against his music because of my family background—my grandfather was a Wagner scholar. I used to think his music was boring. But I listened to a lot of Wagner when I wrote the script of *Black Moon*, so it entered the picture.

DY: Can a film be structured musically?

LM: Yes, but audiences don't like it. I think *Black Moon* was structured musically: there are a number of musical figures that I use in the script, like the principle of recurrence, which has a contrapuntal value—you expose a theme and then return to it. The way the themes are exposed and re-exposed in different ways, the way they are repeated or reversed, the use of leitmotifs—how the same sound, image, or movement come back.

It has not been very well received, I guess because they're not used to it. When they listen to music, I suppose they close their eyes and concentrate. When you're listening to a fugue, you're capable of following more or less what the composer intended, but in film they still want to follow the plot—which is more related to the theater than to anything else, in terms of dramatic rules. It's difficult to offer something different.

Note

1. Georges Poujouly played the young boy in René Clément's 1952 film *Les Jeux interdits* (*Forbidden Games*). The character of Louis in Malle's *Elevator to the Gallows* is also played by Poujouly.

"Creating a Reality That Doesn't Exist": An Interview with Louis Malle

Andrew Horton / 1979

From *Literature/Film Quarterly* 7, no. 2 (1979): 86–98. Reprinted by permission.

Louis Malle's *Pretty Baby*, the story of a twelve-year-old prostitute and a withdrawn French photographer in a New Orleans whorehouse in 1917, is the latest film in a distinguished and varied career that began in 1956 when the then very young French director worked with Jacques Cousteau to make *The Silent World*. His films since then include *Ascenseur pour l'échafaud* (*Elevator to the Gallows*, 1957), *The Lovers* (1958), *Zazie dans le métro* (1960), *Vie privée* (*A Very Private Affair*, 1961), *Le Feu follet* (*The Fire Within*, 1963), *Le Voleur* (*The Thief of Paris*, 1967), *Phantom India* (1969), *Calcutta* (1969), *Murmur of the Heart* (1971), *Humain, trop humain* (1974), *Lacombe, Lucien* (1974), and *Black Moon* (1975).

The interview took place in Mr. Malle's office in the Paramount Pictures offices in New York, on April 23, 1978.

Andrew Horton: A number of your films focus on youth: *Zazie dans le métro, Le Souffle au coeur, Lacombe, Lucien, Black Moon, Pretty Baby*. Why?

Louis Malle: I don't know, really. Maybe I should do something else now. It's getting a bit obsessive! I'm not doing it on purpose. It is true, however. And even *Black Moon* was a sort of variation on the theme of the rites of passage. You could even say this about some of my earlier films in the sixties, such as *Le Feu follet*, which finally is about a man who commits suicide because he refuses to become an adult.

Probably I was terribly impressed myself at that age with the difficulties and trauma of entering the world of adults. This is sort of the moment of truth. It is *the* one of a lifetime. And I see a lot of children at that age have a moment of total lucidity. But the moment you become part of this world of adults, you are just one of them. You start cheating and lying: there is a vast difference between what we say and what we do. All of this compromise. *Lacombe, Lucien* was very obviously about such corruption.

AH: In *Lacombe, Lucien*, we see a progression in the young peasant boy's corruption as he moves from killing birds, chickens, and rabbits to killing people as a Nazi collaborator. But in *Pretty Baby*, Violet seems to already be *there*: as one reviewer put it, she has no innocence to lose. Is this correct?

LM: I'm not sure about that, because innocence is not so easy to explain. One of the things that impressed me about the Al Rose book, *Storyville*, was that in an interview a woman said that when she was five years old she knew everything there was to know. This is terrifying, but still I don't really believe that innocence is just the lack of information. Violet is a part of the world around her, but she is still very much a child. What makes the character so interesting is that she is graduating into corruption at a very early age, but at the same time I have a strong suspicion that she has managed to save a lot of values of what it is to be a child.

It seems to me the more I get into the things I really care about—and the theme of *Pretty Baby* I really cared about for a long time—the more there are contradictions and unanswered questions. But the reason I got interested in the whole situation is because I don't have the answers.

And I certainly don't believe that it is by making a picture that you find answers. The first time I felt very concerned about something, and I felt that the only way to cope with it was to make a movie, was when I made *Le Feu follet*. I was worried about the question of suicide, since the story more or less happened to a friend of mine. I was very emotional about it and the picture, once it was shot and shown, was more sentimental than the films I make today. It looks like I have been cleaning up my act a little bit concerning this!

But I didn't find the "answers" with *Le Feu follet*. I remember that I did not want it to open because it was a little too personal. There were a lot of very confusing things about the film. And I also made those documentaries of India, which were something like seven hours long, to prove that I did not understand anything about India!

AH: You seem to emphasize, as witnessed by your documentaries for Cousteau and about India, a "documentary" approach to your subjects, yet the result is to uncover the unusual or "fictional." Could you comment on the relationship between documentary and fiction in your work?

LM: I don't mean to say that documentary and fiction are the same, but as I have found out more about both aspects of filmmaking I have realized that you could, for instance, speak about the fictional aspects of documentary. And I believe strongly that documentary filmmakers who pretend to be objective are just dishonest. It's absolute bullshit. You're much more subjective and personal in documentaries because you are supposedly just filming what you see that you didn't create. But obviously the way you film shapes what you get.

There is more said, for instance, in *Pretty Baby* in the way the picture is filmed than in its content or in the script. Because I think what is disturbing to many people about the film is—and I don't mean to say it is my best film because it is not, but it is advancing in a direction I am interested in—what is disturbing is that I try to address the *sense*, rather than the intellect. I want, through visuals and sound, to create a world that is *almost* tactile. I feel this very strongly. In *Pretty Baby* there is something very seductive and corruptive in the way the film is narrated. And it is probably most shocking for people in this country that sin is presented as absolutely exquisite. Which it is!

AH: You have worked with Robert Bresson as assistant director on *Un condamné à mort s'est échappé* [*A Man Escaped*]. Is he an influence on your work? I am thinking particularly of *Mouchette*.

LM: It's interesting that you mention *Mouchette*. I'm still an enormous admirer of Bresson, and I think I'm the only filmmaker he cares to see, and we've kept up a very good relationship. Bresson is supposed to be a very austere filmmaker, but I feel that *Mouchette* is a very *sensual* film. The end of the film, where she is rolling down the hill to her death, made me cry. I literally cried, and I very rarely cry when filmmakers want me to cry. And *Balthazar* was also very much about an experience of the senses. That's what I admire about Bresson: that he has managed to create these sensual moments. When I worked with him on *A Man Escaped*, Bresson was interested in me because I came from documentaries. He asked me to take care of all of the details such as the spoon with which the prisoner was digging—all of these details which had to do with the escape. I was very impressed with all of his close-ups of such details and with his concern to show a sense of touch.

The soundtrack for the film was also remarkable. I saw it again recently and it is extraordinary. He manages to create a world of sensation that he conveys. In that sense I feel very close to him.

AH: The same seems true of your work. While one is at first struck by your distinct visual style, it seems you have also paid, especially in *Pretty Baby*, close attention to your soundtrack. There is something always happening—off-screen songs, children talking, cars passing—even if nothing is happening on screen.

LM: We spent a lot of time on the soundtrack in this picture. The paradox is that we shot in New Orleans, and you don't see anything of New Orleans! We found this incredible house in the city which no set could have done justice to. In a way, the house was more important—along with Brooke Shields—than the script! But the soundtrack was meant to suggest the world outside the house, since they are like prisoners.

I worked with my editor, Suzanne Baron, whom I usually work with, and we felt we should evoke the outside world as if we were in a cell. And there was also a lot of use of the sound as counterpoint: the sound of children, for instance. Sound was very important also to give a distance. One scene in particular I am very proud of because I think it is one of the most interesting things in the film. In one scene, Bellocq is photographing Hattie in the room during the afternoon and the piano is playing in the background. The music disappears and then comes back. Floyd is supposedly rehearsing a Jelly Roll Morton song, "King Porter's Stomp," and it stops and goes, and it works incredibly well with the scene. I remember that Jerry Wexler, our musical supervisor, was against this idea, wanting us to play the song straight through. But I said, "No!" It's much more interesting to have him stop and play. And it gives distance.

AH: Could you comment on the importance of music in your films, since each film features some particular kind of music: in *Lacombe, Lucien*, for instance, you have the opening scene set to a bouncy tune by Django Reinhardt.

LM: First, I must say that I am very shocked by the way music is usually used in films. It's one of the most efficient ways to manipulate audiences, as you know: a kind of Pavlovian response. And it works so well it is frightening! Myself, I am not prejudiced against scores, but in recent years I have been working with *source* music. And so the music is already a part of the scene. But I try to use it more as a counterpoint—not to reinforce the situation, but to work against a situation. But basically music is important in my films because it is important in my life.

For instance, the music in *Le Feu follet* came as an absolutely natural thing. I was in that kind of a mood, that kind of situation, and that was when I was listening to Erik Satie. And so, very naturally, this music entered the film and became the score. In my first film, which has the ridiculous English title *Frantic*, with Jeanne Moreau, I used Miles Davis. When we were shooting the film we were all crazy about Miles Davis, and I was in the middle of sound editing without knowing what to use. I was thinking perhaps of using some records. But then I found out that Miles Davis was going to be in Paris to play in a club. Then I spent five or six days trying to convince him to come and see the picture and to accept to do what he finally did, which was to improvise! We finally ended up in a sound studio for one night where I showed the film to him several times and then he made up a remarkable score. It really made the picture look much better than it was.

That's the way I've always worked, though some of my films, like *The Thief of Paris*, have no music. Recently I used Charlie Parker in *Murmur of the Heart*.

Actually, the film opens with the boy stealing a record from a record shop: it is a Charlie Parker record!

AH: You worked on the screenplay for *Pretty Baby* with Polly Platt. How was your collaboration?

LM: It was a real collaboration. I felt she was a good choice because I wanted a woman for a woman's point of view, and I needed to work with someone who was very much a part of the American cinema tradition. And Polly was very helpful because of her connection with Peter Bogdanovich [former husband] and John Ford. She was indispensable. She was very "American," though I don't know what being an American means, but I felt she helped me respond to that culture. So when I met with her I already had an outline that I had had with me for over a year. Then, first, she did a great job researching the film. With her background in production design, she was very good at that, particularly since it was a period film. We found a number of interesting things: for instance, the unpublished memoirs of a "madam"!

AH: What about Bellocq's photographs? Did you find many of them?

LM: Yes, but what is interesting is that at the time they were made, people did not even know there was a photographer named Bellocq. They had the plates, not the photos, and they did not know whom to attribute them to. Then they sort of invented him! But it's much more complicated than that. The book of his portraits is not accurate, because even though they put together lots of interviews, it is clear that he was not very well remembered! All they really know is that for the last thirty years of his life he worked as a commercial photographer and also, for a while, at a shipping company. . . . They say he was a hydrocephalic and a cripple, and that he was like Toulouse-Lautrec. But I don't think this is a very good comparison, because if you look at the photographs and Lautrec's paintings, you see that they were two different kinds of men. We knew Bellocq best through the photographs. Polly and I spent hours and hours looking at the photographs with magnifying glasses. Actually, a friend who works in a museum in Paris once told me that Bellocq's pictures are fakes, but if you look carefully you see that this cannot be so, because there are too many little stupid details that cannot be faked.

AH: Each of your films successfully evokes an accurate atmosphere and mood of a particular period: turn-of-the-century French society in *The Thief of Paris*, for instance. And yet, one reviewer has said in reference to your work that art has no necessity to be faithful to historical accuracy. Do you feel this remark is correct, or do you find it important to try to be faithful to a sense of history?

LM: I work very hard to be accurate. What do I do, finally? I recreate a world, and then once it is properly recreated, I like to forget about the fact that it is a period. In my way of filming, I don't emphasize the period. I try to film my pictures as if they are something I have just encountered. Maybe this is the influence of documentaries. But, yes, the period has to be as accurate as possible, because then it gives you the freedom not to think about it and to look at the characters just as they are. But this means, of course, that you have a lot of homework to do in order to get to that stage. And I like to do this work. It's interesting and troubling to sort of reinvent the past. It was especially interesting in *Pretty Baby*, because those places were so incredible.

AH: Your vision of a New Orleans whorehouse in 1917 is spoken of by Vincent Canby as a non-romantic kind of "romanticism." You deemphasize sexuality and brutality in order to present "sin" as "exquisite," as you say, or simply quite ordinary. What would you say to those critics who complain that you left out the seedy side of prostitution?

LM: I'm not really quite aware of that. People seem to have been totally taken by the photography. By the way, one amusing aspect of the photography is that Sven Nykvist did not actually film all of the scenes. I just read one critic who writes, "Again, Nykvist takes over for the filming of the picnic scene," but Sven wasn't even there to shoot the picnic scene! That is nice! Sven is such a great artist that he doesn't even have to be near me!

But the photography in this film is not flashy. For instance, Sven practically never used backlighting in the film. Which is unusual, especially for a period film. And the set is remarkable, but it's not the usual image of a whorehouse. Usually you think of colors such as red and gold, which are richer. But we tried to tone down the colors. I don't know. I don't see that the film is so stylized myself. Again, I would say that I didn't really mean to do it in such a way. I guess I could have shown more squalor, but it just didn't happen that way. There are, however, one or two moments when you have a feeling of it. But basically I felt that, dealing with that subject and theme, it might be more disturbing if everything looked so easy and so nice. One American friend saw it before it was finished and said she found the film particularly terrible and beautiful and seductive at the same time. That's what I wanted people to feel. I don't think it would have helped to show more rats. I love to show rats, because I love rats, but they don't need to be in this film.

AH: Let me ask you about Bellocq: he is so elusive as a character, and yet his relationship with Violet is touching.

LM: I must tell you something about the Bellocq Violet relationship. When I was shooting the picture I suddenly felt the little I knew of Bellocq was me. There was a part I could identify with. And I got to identify with him very, very much. Especially as the character was played by Keith Carradine, but, of course, it does both ways because I also felt close to Keith. There was something in him

I responded to, and I had been considering lots of other actors. We were very much like brothers. We had a kind of intimate communication. And I felt in the middle of shooting, especially during those difficult scenes in Bellocq's house where Violet is supposed to come and stay with him—I started asking myself, if I had been Bellocq and considering that Bellocq was not terribly interested in sex, you could very well imagine a relationship without sex. Which probably would have been my attitude. After all, this child is a child. That would definitely be my interpretation.

If you used your imagination, you could imagine a lot of things taking place between them. But obviously this big sexual fantasy, this hang-up, of the child molesters who enjoy child prostitution or child pornography has to do with the fantasy of incest and perhaps also the fantasy of rape. It's about penetration; it's brutal. And it's repressed. But it seems to be such a strong fantasy that I think that's why it's so big today in this country, for instance. But you can also imagine another kind of relationship between a child and an adult, one like Violet's and Bellocq's.

And in this relation I must tell you I thought a lot about Lewis Carroll. He was a fascinating man who used to photograph nude little girls, pictures that have been published. He was a clergyman, but I have no idea what was going through his mind! Yet he never *did* anything. He was just interested in little girls, and so he wrote *Alice in Wonderland*. But his photographs are remarkable.

The fascination with children is something I certainly share. You could say that the human body starts decaying at the age of sixteen. There is nothing more moving and beautiful than the body of a child. It's one of the things I find fascinating with my own children, for instance. I always feel like hugging them and touching them because they are so. . . . But I have so many troubles with such a film because people talk about nudity. For me, nudity is not taboo, because it is not obscene. But a lot of people bring in their own fantasies, and that's why they get so emotional and outraged. I see it completely differently.

AH: You have two artists in the film. Floyd has his music, which is background for the business and life of the house. He's a professional who moves on to Chicago when the house closes, yet he is also human, as witnessed by his reactions to Violet's tribulations. Bellocq, with his photographs, intrudes into the house and, ultimately, into Violet's life, bringing art and life together in an unusual way. Do these two examples reflect your views of art and reality?

LM: The scene where Bellocq brings a picture of Hattie, which the other girls gather around and admire and notice for the first time how beautiful they can be, is a strong comment on my work. That scene was *my* scene. The girls are surprised: they have to see a photograph in order to understand that Hattie is beautiful. And then at the end of the scene they ask him, "How did you do that?" and he says, "Magic! It only takes one second!" [It's] a good line. You know, I showed the picture to Susan Sontag when she was just finishing her book on photography, and she was fascinated by that line. That scene is essential to an understanding of what art is about: creating a reality that doesn't exist. And that would be my answer to many critics, because, of course, *Pretty Baby* is about a world that doesn't exist. Yet it is very realistic in a way. I think I'm very much of a realist, but there is, on the other hand, a certain interpretation of reality that is somewhat stylized; but I create style in a way that is a little bit "wicked"!

AH: Perhaps your term "wicked" embraces your sly sense of humor. You have, after all, been compared to some degree with Luis Bunuel and the way he presents a "realistic" picture that can at any moment become humorous, absurd, surreal.

LM: I love Bunuel! I love the filmmaker and the man. But Bunuel is often made into something that he is not. I find his so-called "surrealism" is his least interesting feature. The secret of Bunuel is his childhood, that he came from a middle-class Spanish family. Probably his best film is *Tristana*, which is an adaptation of the novel by Benito Perez Galdos, a kind of Spanish Dickens. This film is the real Bunuel, into which he puts a lot of humor and self-parody. He is very, very funny. I like his irony, and I like his style, and I feel very, very close to him in that way. He's austere, and his technique is to have the most outrageous situations in his script and to film them in the most *realistic* way, and it works wonders! It's astonishing! Those who try to imitate Bunuel don't understand that *style* is what the person is about. People make the mistake that something is Bunuelian because it is bizarre. But the opposite is true.

I'm often amazed that people will tell you a lot about character and theme and motivation in a film, but they don't realize that it's the way a picture is filmed that is much more important. Perhaps they are unconsciously aware of it. Because if someone else took the script of *Pretty Baby*, they would have done an entirely different film.

AH: You seem to work quite often with non-professional actors such as Brooke Shields in *Pretty Baby* and Pierre Blaise in *Lacombe, Lucien*, and to keep you actors off balance while shooting by changing scenes or tactics at the last moment. Is this an effort to maintain spontaneity and sincerity?

LM: It's an effort to fight the essential weakness of filmmaking, which is that it is so slow and technically so heavy. And you lose that innocence very quickly. I try to "reinvent" it. Everything is so slow. And don't forget that a filmmaker has to make a film three or four times: you have to write the script, then shoot it, then edit it, and then when it opens there's the fact that you have to talk about it! So, to keep a freshness, especially for the actors, you have to find new ways.

AH: I'm interested in how much altering and improvising you do in a film. For instance, the effective auctioning scene during which we momentarily see the reaction shots of the men gathered around watching, especially Floyd, with a mixture of sadness and nostalgia. Was that in the script?

LM: No. Actually, the script was a lot more complicated, and I cut out some during the shooting and even more during the editing. The reaction shots are something I added as a sort of introduction to the scene. And I added the long close-up of Floyd, which becomes an important moment. That scene is quite different from the way it appeared in the script. For instance, I had Brooke look straight into the camera, because I wanted the audience to be *involved*, to be a part of the action. I like for the audience to be self-conscious of themselves as *voyeurs*, because they are! After all, they have paid to see someone else's dream! That's what cinema is: in the dark, isolated, it becomes a voyeuristic medium. Which is not true in theater, where another kind of ritual communication is important. But film leaves you alone in the dark with your own fantasies.

I've always had the theory that the spectator is a very important part of the film. The same film viewed by two different viewers is not the same film. The spectator is a creative part of the process.

AH: Was the ending of the film a problem when you were writing/shooting? We see clearly that she is a child as she tries to get Bellocq to come off to St. Louis with her and her "parents," and yet she is heading from a whorehouse and a child marriage into a pure bourgeois life.

LM: I thought it was very ironic in a way to have what was supposedly, from a moralistic point of view, a "happy ending." But in fact it is completely heartbreaking. I've always had a problem with ending my films, because my films are about certain extreme situations in which the characters are more important than the outcome. In *Lacombe, Lucien*, for instance, this totally obscure peasant with no past and no future, who for accidental reasons for three months has a life where he is in a position that should not have happened to him—to be a Nazi—but it lasts for three months, and what happens to him is very incidental.

In *Pretty Baby*, I was interested in Storyville and Violet because it is obviously the *end* of something. For most of the characters, it is the end of an era, and for Violet it is a time to become an adult. She might become respectable and bourgeois as in the true story, or she could become a prostitute again. But either way, it doesn't make the characters different.

AH: What happened to the "real" Violet?

LM: The original story is with a sort of old housewife with grandchildren in the suburbs of New Orleans, and she told how she was born in a whorehouse on Basin Street and started working at twelve. And then at sixteen or seventeen she married one of her customers and became very respectable.

AH: Your attitude toward society—that is, bourgeois society—seems to be similar to Buñuel's in many ways. On the one hand, you point up the shortcomings of that society, yet on the other hand you seem to have a certain affection or at least acceptance of it with all its faults.

LM: There's a beautiful line in *The Thief of Paris* that says something to the effect that the thief is the moon of the honest man, meaning he is the fantasy or other half of the same person. But, of course, the whole idea of that film was that the thief and the honest man become incorporated when he—Belmondo— became a *successful* thief, so thus quite bourgeois.

I feel a lot like that as a filmmaker. I probably started making films out of rebellion, protesting the system of values, but the moment you become successful there are lots of temptations to join the Establishment. It was after *The Thief of Paris* that I went to India, because I felt the danger of such a situation. I've reached a point now where it doesn't worry me much. I know that we live in a world of compromise, and filmmaking especially has a lot to do with compromise, but I consider myself as one of a very small group of directors who have not been compromising very much. Like Bunuel, like Bresson.

At the same time, you know the price you have to pay. Sometimes you have to be polite to people you want to throw out the window. But that's not terribly important. What's important is what you do with your film. And I don't compromise as far as the films themselves are concerned.

And it's important to be able to drop out at any moment, which I might very well do now, for instance. Especially since *Pretty Baby* is doing well. That's my reaction to success!

AH: You have been classified by some as part of the French New Wave, but in earlier interviews you have disowned such a classification. How do you see it now?

LM: I never knew exactly what it meant. There was the whole group at *Cahiers du cinéma*, and I was not part of *that*. In that sense, I am not technically part of the group of Truffaut, Godard, Rivette, Chabrol, and Rohmer. But we all had something in common, for we were a generation that learned everything through seeing films. We were all complete film freaks. But I myself also learned from music and art and other interests. While someone like Truffaut was and has remained a film maniac. Any town he would go to he would check the papers to see what film he could see that night.

AH: *Holocaust* has recently been shown on American television. Mixing melodrama and documentary, it covers the Nazi atrocities. In many ways, however, your film *Lacombe, Lucien* was perhaps even more successful than *Holocaust* in helping audiences understand how an individual could become a fascist killer. Do you view your film as a *political* film about the Nazi period?

LM: I saw part of *Holocaust,* and I was absolutely shocked. It is probably a good idea to show that this horror existed, but the way that it was shown was so heavy and simplified. Exactly the opposite of *Lacombe, Lucien*. Every film can be considered a political film, but there is a certain political idea built into the film that was very controversial because it suggested that collaboration happened so often. You know, because the old attitude was that collaborators were very few and that they were just monsters. But this is not a very serious approach, of course.

Actually, I could demonstrate fairly convincingly that *Lacombe, Lucien* is a Marxist film. Because it's Marx's idea that the general proletariat could be an objective support of fascism, and of the ruling class, because they are not politically aware and so they become the tools of others in order to survive. And we see this occurring in every guerilla war. When I was in Algeria, I saw a lot of Algerians collaborating with the French. And they were very much from that poor background where they had to do anything to eat.

AH: To what degree was *Lacombe* based on your memories of the war?

LM: The period was very vivid in my memory. I was eleven years old and went to a religious school, and the Gestapo came to the school one morning in January 1944 looking for children hidden under false names. It was a completely traumatic event. They took the children and the head of the school, all of whom had been turned in by a young servant who was working in the kitchen. He had been caught stealing from the school and they threw him out, and for revenge he went to the Nazis. He was just a kid, a little like Lucien. Actually, my first story was like the true story, but it was too close to me, too emotional, so I changed it to what it became.

But I wanted to use that starting scene where he went to the Gestapo and denounced the boys. There was one in my class whose name was Bonnet, which is a very French name, and I remember this little guy from the Gestapo in civilian clothes opening the door and asking for a boy with a name that was very obviously a Jewish name, like Silverstein or something. And we saw our friend standing up and he went around the room and shook hands with every one of us. Let me tell you that this is the kind of experience you don't forget.

Yes, to return to the point, I feel that *Lacombe* is very political, because it implies that evil is not only committed by monsters. It would make life easier if this were so. But again, I have been fascinated with the subject because I have known some of these people. In Algeria, I knew a little fellow who was very nice. He's probably married now and living in the suburbs with two cars, and yet in those days he was torturing people. He was what they called an OR, an Information Officer. But I spend an evening with him and he seems so average, so normal. And that's where the danger comes in, because you begin to understand that everybody could become a fascist. Maybe that's a pessimistic view, but I believe that 90 percent of any population could become fascist.

AH: How do you feel about cinema today? Has television taken over, leaving film as a kind of aristocratic art form?

LM: Well, I would say that the industry seems to be in good shape. But the price they have to pay for this seems to me to be too great! I feel that this religion of the blockbuster is very unhealthy.

Interview with Louis Malle

Jacques Fieschi / 1981

From *Cinématographe*, no. 66 (March 1981): 17–19. Reprinted by permission. Translated from the French by CB.

Suspicious of the siren song of Hollywood after making *Pretty Baby* and *Atlantic City*, Louis Malle lives in the cosmopolitan city of New York, which suits him well. A "star" in France, he sees the field of American filmmaking as a challenge to his own career, and also as a challenge to his independence as a filmmaker.

Question: Based on your American cinematic experience, what advantages do you find in working in America?

Louis Malle: None. . . . The crews are the same all over the world. I wouldn't work without my editor Suzanne Baron, or without my sound engineer Jean-Claude Laureux. The cinematographer is not a problem. I know that American directors demand European cameramen, but that is partly snobbism. I love collaborating with Sven Nykvist, but I made my last two films with people I didn't know. The technique is no better here; the professionalism is no greater. I prefer New York crews to the ones in Los Angeles: out there everyone is a bit slowed down, and here they are fast, funny, and enthusiastic. The difference from Europe is money: there is more of it, that's true. . . . That also leads to stupidity.

Q: What is the money spent on?

LM: On things that are not seen on the screen. For union reasons, limousines and chauffeurs cost more than an assistant cameraman. These are very deeply rooted idiosyncrasies. When you see that *The Blues Brothers* cost 35 million dollars, and *Heaven Can Wait*, a little comedy, cost 14 million, you find that to be terrible, absurd. . . . I made *Atlantic City* for five million dollars, which is a starvation budget here, and I found that to be an enormous amount. In fact, we really spent three million: the rest went into overhead as a tax shelter. And the prices are rising fast: the cost of film stock went up by 40 percent last year. *Pretty Baby*, which cost three million dollars, would cost double that today.

That said, the relationship with money is not any different: there are the same bad habits, the same abusive producers, the same wasted time. For me, the difference is in the fact that in Europe I am a star, whereas here I'm not, and that amuses me. In Europe, directors are stars: we have managed to impose this notion to a ridiculous degree, one has to admit. My French New Wave colleagues are only now recognizing it, even though it was us—them—who invented it. The situation is completely different here. Watch the television programs where they show films from the 1940s and 1950s: they never mention the name of the director. The director still has, in many cases, the status of a somewhat glorified cinematographer. Four times out of five, he is chosen when the project is already moving forward, after the screenplay and after the actors. They are constantly proposing projects for me to make in two months. I turn them down, because none of them pleases me; I would accept them if the subject pleased me, but I don't believe in them. . . . Obviously, the director can discuss the screenplay or suggest an actor. I made *Atlantic City* based on my talks with the screenwriter John Guare: we went there, and we came up with a story based on the town. It was a free and open process, like in France. Here, the screenwriter is very often the most important, but in France also, screenwriters like Jean-Loup Dabadie and Francis Veber are sometimes more important than the directors who work with them, and at Gaumont, the Alain Poiré production unit is an American-style producer. The essential difference is that French law is completely on the side of artists and actors, never on the side of producers. Remember the case brought by Zanuck against Edouard Luntz: Zanuck just had to accept the result. He lost; he was furious, and he appealed the decision twice, but his contract was worthless in the eyes of French law. Here, it is the opposite: the "final cut" that everyone is obsessed with doesn't really mean very much. Cimino had it after *Deer Hunter*, of course, and yet, he had to completely recut *Heaven's Gate*. It was the same thing for Altman with *Popeye*: I know that he had to cut it a lot before it came out. Here, when there is a power dynamic, it is always on the side of money. I have had final cut for my two American films, but if there had been a conflict about *Pretty Baby*, they would have taken away the film. A few years ago, MGM brought out *Vie privée* in the United States, cutting out twenty minutes of the film—and they were the best twenty minutes, even though I don't like the film very much. They found it too slow. . . . When they put movies on television, they cut at every opportunity. George Stevens, just before his death, brought a lawsuit about this against the studios and the television networks, and he lost. It is unthinkable, in France, that a television network would cut a film. . . . Although it has to be said that they are sometimes right to do it. When I made *Zazie*, the people at Pathé were driven crazy by the terrible length of the second half of the film, and I finally cut it, but that was a month before the release! In the United States, those who make films are more conscious of the commercial necessities. They hate their own films when they don't do well commercially, whereas in France a reverse snobbism is at work. If a film does too well, you think that it was shit. . . . And that has nothing to do with it: there is no relationship between the box office and the film's intrinsic quality. The exception is comic films: the flop of *Zazie* really got to me, because it was the proof of the truth that when people don't laugh. . . . The relationship of this job with money is very ambiguous: everyone makes compromises, and there is no completely pure artist.

Q: What is your own attitude in this respect?

LM: My real start was *Les Amants*, which was an enormous success. I didn't leave my home for three months, because I was ashamed: they had taught me at IDHEC that commercial success was scandalous. . . . I have changed: when one of my films does well, I'm happy, because it means that I can make two more. The law of money is just as implacable in France, with a few exceptions like Bresson, but even he is finding it harder to make films. Rohmer, after *Le Signe du lion*, didn't make a film for ten years. Don't forget that all the other filmmakers of the New Wave had big commercial successes: *Les 400 coups* and *Hiroshima mon amour* both made money. Producers threw themselves at us because we were young and cheap. I became a producer of my films right away.

Q: Do you think there is room for a more marginal form of production in America?

LM: For porno and horror films that can be made for $3000, yes. Or for some more artistically ambitious films like David Lynch's first film, which cost $200,000. Advertising is so expensive. . . . They bought a Canadian horror film, *Friday the 13th*, which isn't very good, and they printed 600 copies of it, and they spent one and a half million on advertising, even though the film itself only cost $700,000. It's absurd and disturbing: treating cinema like perfume, where the packaging ends up costing more than the product.

Q: How does it seem to you that French films are being received?

LM: There is a lot of curiosity again. I'm not talking about isolated cases like *Cousin Cousine, Madame Rosa*, and *La Cage aux Folles*. But this year, suddenly, Truffaut and Resnais films are big successes. There was a snobbism in the 1960s, and a total lack of interest in the 1970s. Very important European films never came out here. I was lucky: all my films were released, even if they were sometimes financial catastrophes.

Q: Do you feel, on the ground, an American isolationism?

LM: No. I live in New York, and I go to Los Angeles as little as possible. New York is a cosmopolitan Babylon, where half of the population speaks with an accent. The people I see are not isolationists in any sense. I have always adored the city, ever since my first visit at the age of twenty-three, in 1956. I couldn't live in Kansas City. . . . I am lucky to be just about completely bilingual. I had gotten to the point where I was stalling out in France. It is comfortable for me to be an exile for a while.

Q: Will you make films in France again?

LM: Yes. Everything depends on my personal life. I know why I would like to go back. There are intimately personal things I would like to put on the screen, and I can only do it in France. For the moment, my curiosity is here, but that does not imply any choice, any definitive judgment. I feel that there are certain dangers, of course: I like to make films quickly when a project is ready, and one of the weaknesses of Hollywood is the amount of time that is wasted. You can spend three useless months in talks and then say at the end: "I'm being treated like an idiot." Look at the time Wim Wenders lost in a big fight. It's easier for me to talk to Barry Diller, the chairman of Paramount, than to Francis Coppola. I would never set in foot at Zoetrope, because that mixture of money and artistic conception seems very dangerous to me. With studio people, at least you know what you're dealing with: there are some who are stupid, others who are less so, and some who are quite agreeable, like Diller. I had no problem with Paramount on *Pretty Baby*, and I would have had trouble with an independent producer. In general, the relationship I have with my work hasn't changed in America: I don't feel like I've sold out, but I have adapted.

Q: What are the major difficulties in directing here?

LM: Casting is difficult, because I have a less subtle knowledge of the language. The big problem for the foreign director is language. On *Atlantic City*, I personally cast Burt Lancaster, after some hesitation. I had seen Robert Mitchum, and my first choice had been Walter Matthau. The weakness of *Zabriskie Point*, a film that I find very beautiful but which was rejected here, had to do with a bad adaptation of the screenplay into American language. In *Pretty Baby*, too, there are a few misses: you miss a few clichés that you would immediately eliminate in your own language. What we would call a "southern accent": there are actually twelve of them, from Alabama to New Orleans to Texas. Today, I have these differences in my ear, just like the difference between the accents of Toulouse and Marseille.

Q: Your French career was also founded on large differences between the films you made.

LM: I was in the industry because I had quite a few successes, but without really being integrated into it. I was an entity on the side of the industry, difficult to predict.

Q: It is an American quality, no doubt: that faculty of changing the kinds of subjects you take on.

LM: Perhaps. Hawks, whom I admire a great deal, made films that were very different from each other. I consider myself to be an auteur, because I believe that there is a resonance between my films, but not in the European sense of the auteur, which requires that the director be forced to remake the same film, like variations on a theme. In that way, I feel more comfortable here. I continue to try very dissimilar experiments. My most recent film shows two men talking in a restaurant for an hour and a quarter, and then I came back to documentary, heading for Minnesota with a crew of four technicians. What I refuse to do is films on command, like that film with Sylvester Stallone that John Huston ended up making. The danger in going to Los Angeles is too great: it is a city that has the spirit of corruption, and where one can become paranoid. They are obsessed with values which seem pathetic when you return to New York. The place is so unhealthy that American cinema has remained fairly mediocre: except for *Raging Bull*, which is admirable, and *Elephant Man* and *Ordinary People*, which are interesting, the general level of films is low. Even Altman's *Popeye* is disappointing. This fluctuates: there might be twelve excellent films next year. Someone like Milos Forman is a model of perfect adaptation to American filmmaking: he has the advantage over me in having had the enormous success of *One Flew over the Cuckoo's Nest*. Don't forget that here the fetishism of success goes to the absurd degree: they gave a three-film contract to the person who directed *Grease*. But they have about twenty-five active directors who are talented, which isn't bad.

Q: Would the difference between the United States and France lie in the difference in the amount of coercion versus self-censorship?

LM: In France, I worked in the same mode as Truffaut: I wrote a screenplay or I adapted a book, I had my own production company, and I paid for preproduction myself. Even if I had to endure the rejection of nine distributors, the film would still get made. But in general, it doesn't work like that. You have a producer or you don't, and you wait. A producer like Raymond Danon, Alain Poiré, or Serge Silbermann gets very involved: they propose movie stars; and you ask for the financial support from the *avance sur recettes* system. For *Pretty Baby*, on the other hand, I signed with Paramount on the basis of a twenty-page treatment, and we found the screenwriter Polly Platt together. Six months later they hesitated; they got scared; they thought the subject was too dangerous. They put it in turnaround, making it available to other studios. They finally moved forward, and two months later we started shooting. Jack Nicholson wanted to play Belloc, but they didn't impose him on me, and I was allowed to use Keith Carradine. And my position is still very much lower than that of Kubrick, or Bob Fosse.

Q: One gets the impression that everyone's position is fragile.

LM: It is constantly being revised. I'm not sure that Kubrick will be able to make what he wants after *The Shining*. Of course, when a great artist also brings in a lot of money, all the studios are at his feet, but things can still go wrong. It's much more tied to money here than in other places. But one can still find a crazy guy who builds prefabricated homes in Seattle and who will throw a million dollars into the cinema. . . . There are all kinds of outlying sources of money. I don't know, for example, how Dino de Laurentis finances his American films. An American producer is a very public figure: Bob Evans, who just screened *Marathon Man* in New Orleans, had a full-page interview in a local newspaper. That would be unthinkable in Europe, except for Toscan du Plantier, of course, because he is the patron of French cinema and a smooth talker. . . . Here, they accept the idea that the producer is the auteur. And it is often true.

Q: Here, as well as elsewhere, what do you think is the most important quality of a director?

LM: This is a physically exhausting kind of work, which demands the energy of a manual laborer. It also requires great patience and its corollary, stubbornness: not letting things go. A lot of people can't do it for the simple reason of a lack of muscular tone. Where every minute counts and you are on a shoot for six weeks, you have to have talent from nine to six every day. And who can claim to be able to do that? So you have to do the best you can . . . only my fellow directors would understand. There are days when you don't want to go back to the forty people who are pestering you, who are asking you what to do. When I was younger, I was able to do it. I would get sick, really sick, I would have a fever, and it was still acceptable to the insurance company. I shot for half an hour, and then I got my steam treatment. That happened to me in the middle of a shoot; it made everyone take a break, and it allowed me to step back a bit. But I made my three American films without giving myself that little luxury.

Q: Is violence ever necessary as a director?

LM: No. Sometimes it is healthy to yell. I got angry recently, but I didn't get *really* angry. I get things through persuasion. Things like Clouzot slapping actresses exist, but they are more like folklore. I never slap anyone. You can torture them in another way, without explicitly doing the rest. There arc two kinds of directors: Hitchcock, who always despised his actors, and Renoir, who adored them. I started on the Hitchcock side of things: I came from documentary, and I had directed fish with Captain Cousteau. I was very young, and I was very afraid of actors. In the course of the years, I have noticed that actors are the only thing that matters. I would always sacrifice the camera work, a camera movement, or a piece of dialogue that they don't like, for them. In the beginning, I was in competition with them, in a hostile duel. I was rigid when I made *Elevator to the Gallows*—no one could talk to me about technique—but I didn't know yet that actors themselves are dying with nervousness. When you say "Action," they are in the light, and we are in the shadows: they're the ones who are doing everything.

The camera is terrifying with its glass eye; it is much more difficult for an actor in the cinema than in the theater. You need time to work with them on the nuances. That brings us back to the problem of language: we are often very wrong in Europe about performances in American films, and the Americans admire terrible old dogs that we make. These are all cultural divides that have to be absorbed.

Malle on Malle, Part I

Richard Macksey / 1982

From *Post Script: Essays in Film and the Humanities* 2, no. 1 (Fall 1982): 2–12. Reprinted by permission.

The following exchange took place in Baltimore, Maryland on March 20, 1982, after a screening of *Pretty Baby* and *Lacombe, Lucien*. The questions were from members of the audience, and the conversation was moderated by Richard Macksey of Johns Hopkins University.

Question: How did you first become interested in films?

Louis Malle: I was taken out of school when I was twelve. I had a heart murmur, so I worked at home for two years. That is when I started going to a lot of film societies and seeing lots of films. For some reason, I got interested in films at a very early age. It's almost a cliché example of an early vocation. I was sort of a whiz kid. I passed my baccalaureate, the French equivalent of high school, when I was fifteen, just because I was working faster at home. I went to see my mother when I was thirteen and I said, "I have something to tell you: I want to be a film director." She was so surprised and so shocked that she slapped me, which was great. It was great because it decided my vocation for good.

I suppose that's why I'm very much against permissive education. I think you really need to be hit on the head sometimes. I must say my parents are wonderful people. I started using an 8mm camera. I don't think it was even Super 8. It was just straight 8mm. Then, through a succession of compromises, I convinced them to let me go to the French state film school, provided I passed the entrance examinations, which were very difficult. Three hundred people would show up, and the school would take ten. But by a miracle I got in, and then I started studying films. Of course, the language of film or the practice of filmmaking is certainly not something that you can learn in school. When young people ask me what they should do to get into filmmaking, I always tell them first, "Don't go to film school." That's the ABCs. Of course, it's difficult to find other ways to enter the film industry. What I used to do instead of attending courses was seeing a lot of films with friends. We would just leave the school and go see films. Then at some point Jacques Cousteau came to the director of the school and asked if one of the students would like to join his crew on the *Calypso*, Cousteau's oceanographic ship. The only requirement was that the student had to be a good swimmer, and I was an excellent swimmer. I got the job and was supposed to stay three months, and I stayed four years. I never went back to that school. Of course, I was not supposed to get a diploma, but when I became a full-time director a few years later, they sort of forced me to take it, because it was good for the prestige of the school to put me down as an ex-student. They gave me my diploma, which I certainly didn't deserve. I started working with Cousteau when I was nineteen. I worked for four years with him, and it was a complete one-man show. I remember, for instance, that in the Persian Gulf I had to do a short documentary about what Cousteau was doing at the time with his divers, which was a very boring thing like taking geological samples at the bottom of the Persian Gulf. I filmed under the water and above the water and I directed myself doing it. I took the sound myself, then I went back to Paris, and I had to cut it. This was a film which was entirely shot by one person, completely a one-man operation. That was a great education, because in a matter of a few years I learned everything about the technique, which is something that of course has helped me tremendously because I can discuss microphones with the sound man or I can discuss lighting. I've really done all of that. Especially editing. A lot of the editing that I did for Cousteau was very helpful. Then we ended up with a feature documentary which was called *The Silent World*. I was twenty-three and Cousteau was really a gentleman: since I had worked so hard on it, he gave me credit as co-directing it with him. It was a *"film de Jacques Cousteau et Louis Malle,"* which was wonderful for him to do. This documentary was extraordinarily successful. It won the Golden Palm at the Cannes Film Festival, a real surprise. It went on to win the Oscar for Best Documentary. I wanted to keep working with Cousteau, but I broke my two eardrums diving, and it's the kind of thing that you don't want to happen twice because it's dangerous. I decided I should stop diving, so I came back to solid earth and went to Paris. One year later, I directed my first feature film, which was called in this country *Elevator to the Gallows*. Then, a few months later, I did *The Lovers*, which was also very successful, and that was the beginning of the New Wave in France. That was it. Then I kept making films once in a while, not very many over the last twenty-five years.

Q: Would you say something about your most recent film?

LM: *My Dinner with Andre* is a very special experience. The one thing I'm really pleased with is that 90 percent of the spectators believe that it's been shot in one afternoon with two cameras and the two actors improvising their lines. Actually, it took them two years to write the screenplay. We rehearsed for months.

There's not one period that wasn't discussed. For instance, it took Andre Gregory six months to learn his lines, because this is easily the longest part in the history of movies. There's never been and there will never be as many lines said by the same actor. I hope not. It was a very elaborate process. For instance, for weird reasons, we ended up shooting it in Richmond, Virginia, and in the ballroom of this great Victorian Hotel called the Jefferson Hotel, which had just closed down, so we took it over. It was a perfect soundstage, and we put up our little pillars and mirrors and panels and made that set the restaurant. Then we started rehearsing, then shooting; we were there for three weeks. The first week we just rehearsed, and I tried to figure out how to film it. I realized very quickly that the one thing that I was not allowed to do was to fool around with the camera, which, of course, was a natural temptation, because when you're stuck with two people seated at the table without even moving for an hour and forty-five minutes, you would like to have a crane and dance around them. I realized very quickly that that was exactly the wrong approach, because the moment the spectator felt the camera, the spell would be broken. A lot of people have told me, "I felt like the third person at the table," which is exactly what I had hoped. Also, you never feel the camera, so that you completely forget that it's even a film. I think a lot of people don't even look at it as a film. They look at it as something weird between theater and I don't know what. For every moment, for every segment of this picture, I had the choice between fifteen possibilities. I shot a lot. For instance, we shot the first week. Then the next Sunday I started at six in the morning and I ran all my rushes, just myself at the editing machine. I realized that I didn't like what we had shot. It didn't feel right, but I realized that some of the angles and some moments really worked, so I came on the set the next day, the next Monday, and I said, "Well, we are going to start all over again." We reshot the entire piece in the next five days, the last five days. The editing was very difficult and pretty long, because again that conversation was meant to seem like an uninterrupted flow. You should not feel the camera, but actually, when you think of it, there are a lot of cuts. Of course, there's a little manipulation of the audience in the way I've used, for instance, Wally Shawn's reaction shots, because one of my points was to make audiences aware that they were not absolutely required to take seriously what was being said. I wanted, actually, to make it clear that they were perfectly allowed to make fun of Andre Gregory, for instance, because he says a lot of funny stuff. It ended up being a lot funnier, and it's one of my great rewards that when I drop in to the theater in New York two blocks from where I live, the theater that's been showing it now for I think twenty-three weeks or something like that, I can hear how much people laugh and participate and really react.

Usually I originate my own stuff. I receive ten scripts a week, but it never happens that you find a script and you decide, "This is it, I want to do it." Well, it happened to me with *My Dinner with Andre*. They came to me with a great script. Also, I felt I was very much on the same wavelength with them. The two of them were friends of mine anyway, so I felt very close to what was going on. I thought I should do it, but, of course, we had a tough time raising the money, which was almost nothing compared to *Reds*. It took like $400,000 to make it, but raising that $400,000 was probably more difficult then raising the $55 million for *Reds*. People would read it and say, "Are you going to make a film about that? This is not a film." And the only thing I could say was, "If I film it, it is a film. What is your definition of a film?" Films in the past have had similar long dialogue scenes, but, of course, there has never been a film like this. People would ask me, for instance, "Are you going to use flashbacks?" And I said, "Of course not. I'm not going to use flashbacks. It's for every spectator to make his own flashbacks." It's a very visual conversation; there are a lot of great images evoked in that script, and if it works people should fly away to the Sahara Desert with Andre Gregory. The thing I'm proud of is that I think I made it work, which was not so probable. I must say I was fighting the odds. But I was always confident. My one obsession was to get the two actors to be as good as possible. Wally Shawn is actually a very experienced actor, but Andre Gregory had never acted before. I mean, a little stage acting, but he's never been on the screen; so when I worked with them I would use a videotape machine, and I would keep filming them and showing them, just like a football coach.

Q: How biographical is the relationship between the actors and the characters they portray?

LM: The film is meant to be like a slice of life, right? It's meant to be about these two guys getting together and talking a lot. It's actually a little more fictional. But there is more to it than that. You have the two originals, Wallace Shawn and Andre Gregory; they turn elements of their lives into a screenplay in which they become characters. Then actors play these characters, but the actors happen to be Wally Shawn and Andre Gregory! It was very incestuous and difficult, and I really encouraged them to look at it as actors doing a job and not as this very difficult thing of playing themselves. What happened at the beginning is that they used to be very close friends, Wally and Andre, and it is true that Andre staged Wally's first play. Then Andre dropped out and went to all these places; actually, he spent most of his time in Long Island. Wally went his way and he started having plays staged; all of them since have been staged at Joe Papp's Public Theater. They got together again a little more than two years ago—now it's almost three years— and they wanted to do something again together. They started discussing, and Andre is such an irrepressible raconteur that I had heard most of these stories just having dinner with him. You know, he would never stop. So they ended up with something like 7,000 pages of transcripts. That's what Wally did by himself, which I think was remarkable. He disappeared for one year and came back with a script which was 180 pages. Then we started working on it, and I said, "Yes, I'll work. I'll do it with you; I would love to do it with you." We started rehearsing every day, and we trimmed it down to about 130 pages. In the process of which, I encouraged them to go more and more into fictionalization, because I felt it would be easier. Of course, obviously there are some very intimate moments when, for instance, Andre Gregory talks about his mother; all of this is true. Everything that's told is true, but it's dramatized in the sense that lots of other things were dropped, and Wally has made his character into this little playwright trying to make a living, when actually he is a very adventurous person. He's spent years in India. He's traveled a lot. In the film he pretends that he never leaves the cigar store in his neighborhood, but it's not quite true. He pretends to be the Cartesian one, the rational one, but about halfway through the film you realize that he's even crazier than Andre. Essentially, the film's something that they decided to do. I know for some time they considered having it take place not in a restaurant, but in a train, going, let's say, from Paris to Zagreb or something like that. But that was not a very good idea. That was too fancy.

Q: Has the script of *My Dinner with Andre* been published?

LM: People keep asking me about it. It's been published by Grove Press, but it doesn't seem to be anywhere in bookstores, and I really don't know why, because the picture is doing very well. I even get letters asking me, "Can we have a transcript of the screenplay?" and I have a ready-made answer Xeroxed, telling people to ask their bookstore and order it. It was published last October.

Q: After coming right off a play, after a sequence of films, do you want to say anything about the experience of directing?

LM: I'm always reluctant to direct a play because I'm a little spoiled as a film director. It's generally accepted now that films are the director's medium. God knows I've worked very closely with, for instance, John Guare on *Atlantic City*, and a lot of what people like about *Atlantic City* he must get the credit for. His brilliance and imagination have done, for me, wonders for that script. But I still very much think of a film of mine as a film of mine; I always take complete responsibility, and I'm the one who makes the final decisions, so it's my show. Now things are quite different when you direct a play, unless you're an egomaniac director—and, of course, I've seen quite a few of those—but I'm not one. I just believe that when you are directing a play, your job is to serve the play and the playwright as well as possible. I did convince John to change a few things in *Lydie Breeze*, especially dealing with the visual aspects and setting and the rhythm, and to make some cuts. The casting was very interesting, and I think one of the best qualities of this production was that we had a remarkable ensemble of actors. Still, I would always feel that this was John Guare's play. Also, there's something very frustrating for a film director, because we started previewing and at the beginning it didn't work too well, but I kept working with them every afternoon and little by little it got better and at some point, scene by scene, they seemed to come exactly right. My instinct was always to say, "Print, print, and put it in the can. This one we've got. Let's get to the next one." And, of course, the next night it would be a little different. I must say this is also the very powerful pleasure and the danger and the excitement of the theater—that anything can happen anytime. It's always a working process and by definition it is live, alive. It was, for me, quite odd. I had not worked on stage for more than fifteen years, and I must say I found it such an interesting experience that I might possibly do it again. I'm considering doing it again one of these days.

Q: What are you working on currently?

LM: A while ago we came up with what we thought was a funny idea, starting from the ABSCAM affair and the FBI arresting a crook, a swindler, and convincing him to work for them and to help them frame politicians with the help of a fake Arab sheik. We started from that, but we moved very quickly to something else. What it ended up being was sort of a political farce. It has a lot to do with the FBI. It's a very funny script. I was very interested in working with Danny Aykroyd and John Belushi, so actually the script was written for them. Now we're a little bit in the middle of nowhere.[1] We are going to recast it, but in recasting it we're probably going to also have to rewrite it, because Belushi was supposed to play this fairly ugly crook, a very wild character. I very much admired Belushi for his invention and his craziness and the fact that he would really push situations to the extreme. I liked him a lot, and I must say it has put us in a weird situation now; so we're probably going to proceed with it, but now we've almost got to start from scratch.

Note

1. John Belushi, who had been cast in the lead role in the film, died on March 5, just two weeks before the interview was conducted.

Interview with Louis Malle:
Au revoir les enfants

Françoise Audé and Jean-Pierre Jeancolas / 1987

From *Positif,* no. 320 (1987): 32–39. Reprinted by permission. Translated from the French by CB.

Question: In the last interview with you that was published in *Positif* (issue 157), the 1974 interview with Gilles Jacob, you talked about the exact subject that would become *Au revoir les enfants.*

Louis Malle: Really?

Q: Yes. You said that you had thought about making it as a prologue to *Lacombe, Lucien,* and that you had given up the idea because you didn't feel ready to do it.

LM: That's very funny. . . . In fact, I've told this story a certain number of times, since it seems that it is the most dramatic memory of my childhood. It appeared in a book called *Histoire de la Résistance,* which was published by the Communist Party and written by a guy named Alain Guérin, in five volumes. I met him when I was preparing *Lacombe, Lucien,* I told him the story, and it takes up two pages in his book. I also told it for another book that appeared in 1979, which is called *Louis Malle par Louis Malle,* a book that went unnoticed because the little publishing house that brought it out went bankrupt a week later. Now that I have made the film, people are essentially saying to me, "You've already talked about that . . . " It's true: for years, it would come to the surface. But in the course of the years—I don't know how to explain it, it's very mysterious—it seems that the memory has changed. It has become enriched. I don't believe that memory is static: as one moves forward in life, one sees things differently. Now that the film is finished, I realize that the story I'm telling doesn't really resemble what actually happened all that much. When I finished the first draft of the screenplay, I verified certain elements of the film which I was persuaded were authentic memories, and I realized that they didn't correspond at all with the reality of what happened in 1944. For example, my brother, who was with me in this school, saw things very differently. In the end, I held on to what I believed to be my memory, knowing very well that it is a bit reinvented. Let's say, in order to simplify things, that in the film it is a bit like how I would have *liked* it to have happened. It's more interesting than what actually happened. My relationship with Bonnet, in the film, is more complicated and more interesting than it was in reality, because what we lacked was the time to develop such a relationship; and I suppose that one of the components of my memory is a guilt that I have kept and that has certainly influenced my life, my way of thinking, and even my work. The idea that what happened was profoundly unjust, that it never should have happened, and that, after all, we were all responsible. I charged Julien with it a bit. In particular, he has the impression that it is he who gives up Bonnet, when he turns toward him in the classroom; that detail, I probably added. But it is also my memory, because in my memory I am a bit responsible for Bonnet's death. . . . One time—only one time, because I don't have the mentality of a veteran—I told the story at a reunion of former students from that school, and I noticed that this story affected me more than it did the others. The others remembered it as a dramatic event, but they didn't remember Bonnet very well, while I have a very precise memory of him. Let's say that I took it personally, and that is why I made this film. It's always like that when one is inspired by a real event and one revisits it forty years after: it is torturous and complicated. . . . Making a film that is only an historic reconstruction had no interest for me, and therefore I believe that I added all the memories I had about this event during all these years. I could have made it as my first film, but I would have been terrified. It was a memory that was still evolving. I'm really happy that I made it today, and I hope that it stretched me a bit.

Q: You made it in 1986. Is there a relationship between the events of the film and what is happening today?

LM: Not only is there no relationship, but there is even a comic aspect to it. When we began showing the film, it was during the Barbie trial, and people said to me, "What timing! It's really great," as if I had jumped on the occasion.[1] There is Le Pen and the rise of racism in France, and there is also the broadcast of *Shoah* on television. In fact, when I began to show the screenplay to people last September, those people, especially the distributors, told me: "Yes, it's been ten years since you were in France; there are too many films about the Occupation; that doesn't interest anyone here." I wanted to make the film in any case. I had the impression that the time had come for me to make it; I had waited a long time. For the few years during which I had been telling myself, "I'm going to have to go back and make a film in France; I have to return to my roots," it had always been obvious to me that it would be on this subject. I took notes; I looked at the subject from different angles. And last summer I wrote it, and I had the impression that it had come at a very inopportune moment, that it was completely marginal to what would interest people.

And obviously, since then, there has been a change, mostly because of the Barbie trial. Last autumn, we had the impression that they were going to leave Barbie in prison until his death; we really thought that his trial would never happen, that it upset too many people. . . . At the same time, I was already preparing the film, and there was the student movement in December, which encouraged me. Nowadays they say, "There was '68, and then after '68." There has been a depoliticization, which everyone has noted, in France, just as there has been in the United States. And we saw at the end of last year that that wasn't at all true. And that pleased me; that encouraged me. I thought that the people in these new generations would find something in the film that would interest them.

In any case, I made the film. . . . I have always made films with the hope of interesting people. But to start a film saying, "I am making it because it's in the wind"—that is a mistake.

Q: When you made *Lacombe, Lucien*, was it an indirect way of approaching the same subject?

LM: The truth is that the very first screenplay of *Lacombe, Lucien*, even before I worked with Patrick Modiano, began in a school, and the character was the Joseph of *Au revoir les enfants*, the kitchen boy who is kicked out and who, in revenge, goes to the Gestapo. And then, very quickly, they took him away. I said to myself, "That is something I will do one day; it's a different subject." *Lacombe* had a complicated origin. In the beginning, it was going to be a young Mexican . . . I also thought about setting it at the end of the Algerian War. It was a character I could have situated in different historical moments. When it became clear to me that I could situate him in the period of the Occupation, I told myself this episode from my childhood, and right afterwards, in the place where I shot the film and where I live, in the Lot, I came upon this historical person who really worked for the Gestapo and who infiltrated the *maquis*. This person pointed me in the direction of a rural young man who was badly treated in his childhood and who would find a sort of social affirmation in his work for the Gestapo: all that made *Lacombe, Lucien*.

In the case of *Au revoir les enfants*, everything was much simpler. I started from something I had really lived. The most accurate things—in relation to my experience—are the sociological elements of the film. The fact that, for example, the children in this little school belong to the same upper bourgeoisie, that despite all the difficulties of the time   cold, hunger—that everyone shared, they were still very protected. There is the character of the mother, the conversation at lunch, the reflections about Léon Blum. . . . I remember to what extent the people in my family hated Léon Blum; he was a horror. There is the character of Monsieur

Meyer, the Jew in the restaurant, who is inspired by something one of my friends told me about his grandfather, a Jewish member of the upper bourgeoisie who was arrested in a restaurant. For him, it was unimaginable that they could arrest him, hassle him. He felt completely French; I think that Pétain himself had given him a military medal at Verdun. The idea that they could have considered him as a "dirty Jew" seemed absurd to him. He died during the deportation. . . . It was more in the story of the two children that I invented things.

Q: We were struck by the violence that exists in the boarding school.

LM: There was, first of all, the general dimension of the time period, which was a very hard one. And it is true that, compared to the children of today, even if I was depicting a protected childhood, life was much tougher. From the start, beginning with the first draft of the screenplay, I wanted to put in the stilts game, which doesn't exist today—they got rid of it, or outlawed it. It was incredibly violent. But it was an affirmation of virility. . . . Like the scouting game in the forest. And in that case, I even toned it down a bit. The principal of the school, Father Jean in the film, sent us out at night, after the military blackout time, to look for a treasure in the Fontainebleau forest. It was crazy: we were terrified, and there was a real risk, which provoked protests by the parents. It was intended to build character. And I think this violence exists in all boarding schools. Relationships between the students that are based on force. The way they treat Bonnet is almost normal: he's the new kid, he's not like the others. Aside from Julien, the others are not curious enough to look beyond the immediate differences. I believe that it is a fairly common social behavior: outsiders are viewed badly.

That said, I am very happy that you noticed this violence: once the film was finished, I even asked myself if it was apparent enough. I have a memory of this time of violence in its naked state. There was an almost Darwinian notion of the relations of force within a social group: those who took control were allowed to do what they wanted. There were victims and bullies. But what seems important to me in the film—even if there were the dominated and dominating among the children—is the intervention of the violence of the adult world: it is more abstract and superimposed. For the children, it is inconceivable. While the violence of the children is natural—I would say almost biological—when the militiamen arrive, and then until the end of the film, everything becomes unbelievable, in any case for Julien. "What is a Jew?" It's terribly difficult. Also, even Vichy had a hard time defining the Jew before deporting him. It was simple at first: they began by deporting everyone who wasn't French—German refugees and refugees from central Europe—but then . . .

Q: In the film, there are Germans who are almost sympathetic: the Catholic Bavarians, or the officers who intervene in the restaurant, even if it is simply to make themselves look good in front of the mother.

LM: It would be a cliché if all the Germans were bastards. Most of those who occupied France were guys who had been sent there without asking their opinion. . . . In the restaurant, they are decorated aviators. The character who kicks out the militiamen is a career officer, who is obviously an aristocrat, who is also drunk, and who is annoyed by French people who are political. They say that among themselves, in German. It's very ironic. It seems to me that this was just a way of saying that a large part of the Germans who were in France were not very influenced by Nazi ideology. That is why, when the Barbie type arrives. . . . The guy who is from the Gestapo in Melun was essentially a guy in the Barbie mold: an efficient man who took down several Resistance cells. His name was Kopf. Because, you have to realize that these monks, these Carmelites, were active resistants. The head monk of this order was on the national council of the Resistance. And the principal of the school found it entirely natural to round up the Jewish children: it was a deliberate political involvement . . .

It's a bit like *Lacombe, Lucien*, except that it is another view of the period, another view of the French people. There were all kinds, as you know. When we try to define people by large social categories, we commit grave errors. Those who say that the bourgeoisie collaborated and that the workers carried out the Resistance. . . . In my family from the upper bourgeoisie, there was an uncle who was deported to Dachau, and one of my older cousins went through Spain to join de Gaulle. Perhaps because we are from the north of the country and the Germans were our traditional enemies. It wasn't about ideology: they were just as anti-Communist as any other bourgeois, but for them the Germans were occupying France, and therefore they would fight against the Germans. It is always dangerous to simplify things. People will say that I am trying to reset things, as I did in *Lacombe*: that it's the proletarian who denounces people. . . . It's true that Joseph is a younger cousin of Lucien, but I believe that his behavior is explainable. The situations, the relationships, are complex.

My parents were supporters of Pétain. Until 1942, they thought that Pétain was very good. After 1942, they found that he was messing up. And then there was Laval. For my parents, you could be a supporter of Pétain at the same time as being anti-German. They began to perceive that Laval was really a collaborator. There was a shift. That is why there was the following exchange between my brother and my mother: "Is he still a Pétainist?" "No one is a Pétainist anymore." It's just a word, but it translates a reality. As for myself: before being a student in this middle school, I was at a school run by the Jesuits in Paris, and they went door to door selling portraits of Marshall Pétain: "I gave myself to France." This was in 1941–42, when I was nine years old. People were a bit intoxicated: there was the business about a national revolution, of a return to traditions, which was well received in the milieu I came from. For example, I found it funny that when the students are lost in the forest, in order to encourage themselves, they start singing, and they sing, "Marshall, here we are" and "You have given us hope . . . " And even Bonnet sings! They brainwashed us all with that. I always tried to answer this question while bringing up my memories: "What was it like to be eleven years old in that period?" What experience did we have of the outside world? Where did these absurd conversations the children had about Pétain come from? After these events, I was in another middle school, and then there was the liberation. And I have another memory, fairly precise and also shocking, of a procession of women with shaved heads, on trucks, their hands attached behind their backs. At Montceau-les-Mines. It was the liberation of Montceau-les-Mines.

Q: The conversation between Julien and Bonnet about *The Three Musketeers* is a strong moment in the film. Was it based on a memory?

LM: I have a precise memory, though I'm not sure if it happened at this time or later. I have a memory of reading *The Three Musketeers*, at night, by pocket lamp, and being fascinated by it. But I don't think I discussed *The Three Musketeers* with Bonnet, or at least with the real Bonnet.

Q: Books have a great importance in the lives of children. They read in stolen time.

LM: That is one of the things that connects Julien and Bonnet from the start. The first time that we see Bonnet, when Father Jean takes him to the dormitory, he takes out lots of books. The other boy looks at him and comments on it. That intrigues him. The choice of which books—I don't know, it came naturally. It is only afterwards that one asks these questions. These are memories . . . *Thousand and One Nights*, the eroticism of the *Thousand and One Nights*, in this decadent, delirious symbolist translation by Doctor Mardrus, is a strong memory; it was really a dirty book that we passed around.

Q: And the bound book, in which Julien discovers the true identity of Bonnet? Did you really discover it in that way?

LM: Not at all. In fact, I never discovered the identity of Bonnet. We didn't know he was Jewish. And that is a question that has tortured me all these years: if I had known, how would I have behaved? I have imagined how I would have liked it to happen. In accidentally discovering that Bonnet is Jewish, Julien absolutely does not know what to do about his discovery. I remember when I was still in Paris, before the summer vacation of 1943, when we met people who were wearing a yellow star, and my parents told us: "We have to be nice to them," and that was it. All the rest was abstract. So, Julien asks his brother: "What is a Jew?" The answer doesn't satisfy him. In the final analysis, the definitions of a name by which people decide that someone is part of a group do not correspond to anything. For someone who is discovering the world at the age of eleven, it is really very mysterious. The world of adults is very complicated.

Q: There is another stable center in Julien's life: his mother. Is there a distant connection with the mother-son relationship in *Murmur of the Heart*? Is there a common inspiration for the two films?

LM: It's a bit like variations on a theme. Even though the two characters of the mothers are quite different. I suppose that the mother in *Au revoir les enfants* is more like my mother than the one in *Murmur of the Heart*. Also, in the case of *Murmur*, I was inspired by someone else. But in *Au revoir les enfants*, it would also be very simplistic to say that it was my mother. During the shooting, I was shocked by something Francine Racette, the actress who played Julien's mother, said to a journalist. She said, "Louis Malle came to ask me to play his mother, and I couldn't say no." I never asked her to play my mother! She doesn't look like her at all. And besides, she is Canadian. . . . But the character she plays, the upper-bourgeois character with her lack of social consciousness, her humor, and her tenderness, borrows a lot from my mother. Let's say that this very strong attachment that one finds in both films, and this violence, are another transposition. Once again, I suppose that I would have liked things to have been as passionate as they are in the two films. There is one thing that corresponds well to my life as a child: it is that the mother is an important presence. My father was very absent. There were good reasons for that: he was very busy. But it's true that this absence of the father must have left an impression on me. The only time in my life when I had anything to do with a psychoanalyst, I didn't talk to him about my mother. I talked to him about my father, even though my father had always been nonexistent. I realized that this absence of my father had played a large role in my life.

Three quarters of the film—the characters, the situations, and the details—are invented. But at the same time I don't believe that there is anything that doesn't have a weight, or that there is a moment in the film that I wrote or shot with impunity. The essential things in the film, in the relations between Julien and Bonnet, are infinitely more interesting in the film than what I had with the true Bonnet, but at the same time that is the way in which I changed them. When Bonnet arrives, Julien finds himself confronted with an experience that is outside of the norm, tied to particular historical circumstances.

I'm going to generalize, and I hate doing that, but in my films I have been interested in characters who find themselves in a situation where something lands on them which makes them leave their path. Which unhinges them. Which takes them in another direction. Which forces them to ask themselves questions, something that people do quite rarely in everyday life. From that point on, they come out of their milieu and their routines, their norms, and that is the subject of the film. Julien doesn't know what to do about Bonnet, who intrigues him, bothers him. The dramatic arc of the film is Julien's curiosity. When I say that it is this event in my childhood that has pushed me to make films, that seems absurd. In the years which followed, I didn't ask myself so many questions about what happened that day. However, I would like it to be true that it was the entrance of Bonnet into my life that changed me. If not, perhaps I would have been better off manufacturing sugar.

Q: Did the children understand the film during the shooting?

LM: They understood it very well. I chose the two principal actors very carefully, boys who were both remarkably intelligent. It was difficult for them to put themselves in the skin of a child of those years, but when it came to essential things, even with their contemporary sensibility, they were completely able to react as if they were from that era. My criteria for choosing them had nothing to do with their physical appearance, or with their capacity to speak a text, but rather with their capacity to understand: their sensibility, their intelligence. I did tests, trying to see how they would make sense of a scene. How they would feel the emotion of a scene. Which made me understand that the forty years of distance didn't matter. Someone who is eleven years old today has to ask himself the same kinds of questions. . . . What encouraged me was, when the cops killed Malik Oussekine, the revolt among people who were not born in 1968. They didn't understand it. When one of their own was stupidly shot and died, the reaction was: "This is not possible." Their protest was supremely important, very affirmative. It seemed to me that it was very close to what I would have wanted Julien's emotion to have been, even if 1944 was a more violent era, and death was more present.

Q: It was a more secretive, more opaque era.

LM: That's true. There is always this question that comes back: "Did people know?" Someone asked me the other day: "Did you know that Bonnet was going to die in the concentration camp?" I think people knew, and that they put the question out of their minds because it bothered them. They say that the Germans didn't know that the camps existed, that the inhabitants of Dachau didn't know. . . . People forget. When I was at Sciences Po, I found articles from *Paris-Soir* describing the concentration camps, in 1937, so people shouldn't just say any old thing. In *Paris-Soir*, which was the *France-Soir* of the time, there were articles about the camps. That said, on that day, in the courtyard, we never would have thought that all four of them were going to die. Especially the priest. In his case, the Germans didn't want to make him a martyr, but there was a concurrence of circumstances, and he wanted to leave with the others. That doesn't change the essential fact, which is that when the Gestapo man says, "This boy is not French; this boy is a Jew," that is the shock.

Q: The only really mean moment in the film is when the nun gives up the two other boys.

LM: It is perhaps my old depths of anticlericalism. Let's say that it seemed to me that it would be good if Joseph was not the only bastard in the film. This nun is a real coward: it is out of fear that she gives up Négus. But while shooting the film, I tried to make her a fairly ambiguous character. There are people who don't notice it. In making this film, I told myself that for the first time in my life I was describing priests who were admirable. That was actually my experience in the school: they were great people. There is also a portion of the clergy that collaborated. The nun in the film treats Négus badly; she is fearful; I'm not even sure that she knew that Négus was Jewish, but, "You are going to get us all arrested . . ." I think it is appropriate that there is this nun who behaves badly.

Q: This nun is not in a fixed employment. Neither is the cook. It is as if subaltern kinds of work engender meanness.

LM: The cook treats Joseph badly, as well as the students. This is really based on a memory of this fat woman who never stopped yelling at this poor boy. Yes, they are the two workers of the school; I didn't think of that. People ask me so many questions, and I discover things . . .

It's a screenplay that I wrote very quickly, as with *Murmur of the Heart*. I wrote the first draft in ten days. And then I thought about it from different angles, and I changed it a little. It was important for me that it began as a simple chronicle of the period: what it was like to be a child then, in a middle school. And then it had to turn into a drama. That movement from chronicle to drama is what made the most work for me. I moved scenes around, made transitions, but the twenty essential minutes of the film came to me right away. Afterwards, I made changes, so that Julien would be more and more alone. I made one change at the last minute. In the screenplay, it was made clear to everyone that it was Joseph who denounced them. I said to myself that it would be more interesting if it were Julien's secret, in the same way that it was Julien's secret that Bonnet was Jewish. It would be better to have their meeting be in the little courtyard, cut off from the others, and that it would be he who would carry the weight of knowing. As if lucidity almost brought about culpability. As for me, I have always carried a sense of guilt about the death of Bonnet.

At the age of eleven, I was part of a world in which it was possible that someone could be arrested and deported. I knew much later that the three children had been transported to Auschwitz, very quickly, and that they had been gassed immediately on getting off the train. The Germans had kept the lists; we found the documents. At that moment, I obviously didn't know. But over the years, I developed a sort of double guilt. First, there was a general guilt about feeling that I belonged to a society in which things like that could happen, and second, there was a guilt which came from my curiosity, my lucidity. Curiosity implies an engagement. . . . In the shooting, with the boy who played Julien, and this very intense gaze he has, I could use this heavy gaze to discover things. When one is more curious than other people, one is engaged in things through this curiosity. Many of my friends from this era went back into life; it was an episode from their childhood which did not profoundly affect them. Maybe some of them are even racists today. I could not do that; that is the difference. When people ask me, I have a cliché response: "You know, in my case, it is curiosity that keeps me moving forward." And it is true. I make documentaries. I don't like to repeat myself. It is more than a simple behavior: it is an ethics.

Q: *And the Pursuit of Happiness* also resulted from a curiosity which becomes a form of engagement.

LM: *And the Pursuit of Happiness*, in fact, comes from the same attitude. In the United States, the new arrivals, immigrants, have always interested me. Americans said to me: "You have made a film about immigrants because you are an immigrant yourself." I never really was one. Or, I was a luxury immigrant. I don't look like a Pakistani who has to survive clandestinely; that is obvious. I had a particular interest in those who arrived, in what America was doing to them, and in what, ultimately, they were doing to America. What interested Americans is, "Are those people going to change us, to invade us?" But what America does to them is extremely interesting: for those who come from traditional cultures and who are exposed to mass culture in America it is a shock, a gigantic shift. There are people who jump forward three centuries in a few months. In a bizarre twist, before making *Pretty Baby* I had worked on the story of a young Mexican who had crossed the border clandestinely and who was trying to find work in Los Angeles. I had worked with Jean-Pierre Gorin, who was in California—a professor at the University of San Diego; he is still there—and I found him and together we filmed the scenes at the border in *And the Pursuit*.

In 1976, I had a contract to do two films with Paramount, and I was going to do this film on the young Mexican. I had abandoned it because I thought I had not lived in the United States for long enough, and that I risked falling into clichés, readymade ideas. But the idea stayed with me. When I had some free time after *Alamo Bay*, a television chain offered me the opportunity to make a documentary. I took this project out again. It pleased them, because it came in the anniversary year of the Statue of Liberty. . . . I said that I didn't want to make a nostalgic film, nor a film about memories of Ellis Island. I would show people who were arriving at this moment. For all the people whom we show in the film—with a few exceptions like the Somoza family, where we know why they are there—we ask the question: "Why did they come?" There are readymade answers, like "to give a chance to their family," or "to make more money." In the case of the Mexicans, it is obvious why they come: the economic situation in Mexico is disastrous, but through their stubbornness, and their enthusiasm, they are able to adjust to American society. For others, I don't understand it very well: the way in which they very quickly lose their roots, or sometimes don't. Behind the uniformity of the façade of American society, there are lots of different ways of behaving. Actually, all the variations on this theme interest me. I made the film at a moment when I was in a state of rupture with America. I think that way less now, but at the time I thought that I had done my time in the United States. The Americans saw that. At the same time, there was the making of *Alamo Bay*. In *Alamo Bay*, I could have treated it in the form of a documentary, except that it concerned events which had happened four years earlier. We would have had to reconstruct them, which would not have been possible.

Q: In *Alamo Bay*, and in *Au revoir les enfants*, your way of filming has evolved toward a drier style. Is that a conscious decision? Is it a consequence of your practice as a documentary filmmaker? In *Black Moon* and *Pretty Baby*, there was more prettiness.

LM: That depends on the subject, and also on the setting. I don't try to impose a style that I could artificially proclaim as mine. I almost make that a declaration of principles. When I arrive for a shoot, I have ideas about the way of filming the screenplay, and those ideas disappear after one week. When I was young, I made more systematic films. For example, *Les Amants* is made in sequences, in a way that is at times very artificial. When I see it again today, I sometimes want to have a gaze from Jeanne Moreau, something more intense. Starting with *Le Feu follet*, I let myself go: the problems of writing seemed to me to resolve themselves naturally and to be a function of the texture of the subject. For *Le Voleur*, for example, I got yelled at by Jean-Louis Bory, and that struck me, because his critique was an intelligent one. He said something like, "Louis Malle has put a high hat on his camera," and it is true that the film got drowned in the décor. But the film was about someone who was reclaimed by his milieu. The opulence of the décor was the main attraction of the film, and even of the psychology of the character. I did the same thing with *Pretty Baby*: the decadence, the New Orleans houses of prostitution at the beginning of the century. Child prostitution, officially proscribed, was so accepted that the senators came to the house. These houses were incredibly luxurious. With my cinematographer Sven Nykvist, I treated the décor, the luxury of it, as a metaphor for luxuriousness.

On *Alamo Bay*, the physical setting was obviously very different. There was sunshine, and there was an ugliness that was very offensive. . . . On *Au revoir les enfants*, I said to my cinematographer Renato Berta: "I don't want this film to be in black-and-white because that would be easy, but I have a memory in blue, grey, and black." The period was a hard one, and I don't have memories in warm colors. The children are in navy blue, and the priests in dark brown. I told Corinne Jory, who made the costumes, "I don't want to see red in the film." There is a coldness and a hostility in the environment which are important. We had good luck: that winter, the weather was terrible. We had snow, and in Provins the children were shooting scenes in the courtyard in temperatures of twelve below zero, in short pants. They made mist when they talked.

In terms of the way of filming per se, I believe that *Au revoir les enfants* is perhaps the most . . . Fordian of my films. It is in that sense that the cinematic style is based entirely on the gaze. If I look at it from that point of view, it seems to me that the direction of the film has a more assertive aspect. What often happens, and what the critics rarely notice because it is not their business to notice it, but which I see very clearly in films, is when the director is comfortable with the screenplay. When he isn't, he protects himself, he goes in all directions, and he shoots several versions of things. I know this from personal experience. When I see a film, I can see when the director is not sure of his characters, when he has doubts about the screenplay, and sometimes when he has problems with certain actors. That can be beautiful: it can create a space of instability, and sometimes the director pulls it off quite well. And sometimes not. I had problems with the screenplay for *Alamo Bay*. . . . On the other hand, aside from a scene that I cut, in *Au revoir les enfants* the screenplay worked well. First of all, it's a screenplay by me, and I spent time on it, and I worked with the child actors. That allowed me to give it a strong direction. I didn't have to protect myself much.

Q: Have you made films to order?

LM: I have made one or two that belong to the category of films to order. *Vie privée* was to order. But that can be good, making a film to order: some people manage it royally. In my case, it never works. The other one, *Crackers*, did not come out in France. I refused to make it for two years, and then I agreed to do it, telling myself that I was going to manage it brilliantly, and then I fell flat on my face, and then in the editing. . . . Faced with a screenplay that someone brings to me, if it is something that I don't deeply want to make, I become awkward. I don't have the faculty of certain American directors who are so brilliant when dealing with conventional situations, and who know how to make great variations on them.

Q: That is quite a different approach to the cinema.

LM: Yes, but if I work in American cinema, it puts me in a terrible position of inferiority. Sometimes people offer me interesting subjects which I am obliged to refuse because I would be on dangerous ground.

I will give you an example. David Puttnam, today the biggest producer in the world, offered me *The Killing Fields*. Already, when Sydney Schanberg's short story had appeared in the *New York Times*, certain things in it had interested me. So, I had a good reason for making it. Then Puttnam acquired the rights. I said, "Too bad." Two years later, Puttnam sends me a voluminous screenplay, written by a brilliant English screenwriter. In reading it, I saw what Puttnam had in mind. It was to make a spectacle film, what they call in English a "value production." There were war scenes, a large quantity of blood, and pieces of legs all over. . . . What had interested me was a part of Schanberg's story which took place at the French embassy, when all the foreigners in Phnom Penh find themselves there with a certain number of Cambodians the Khmer Rouge is looking for, and who are given up one by one. This is just one episode in Joffe's film, with details that were not retained. For example, at one moment the journalist loses himself in the corridors of the embassy, and he opens a door and finds four French policemen in the process of eating enormous steaks that they had stashed away, while others didn't have much to eat. What interested me was not making an enormous film. David Puttnam, who is a good producer, knew that in order to make the film do well, there had to be spectacle. I was not in agreement with him, and that's where we ended up.

Q: Why did you have an American career?

LM: It's difficult to give a simple answer, and I am going to repeat myself. I can give five reasons. I was always curious about American cinema. There was an admiration from childhood for that and for jazz, and it was very important in my adolescence. In the sixties, after the international success of *Les Amants*, the Americans, knowing that I spoke English well, began to offer me screenplays. I waited; I knew there was a long tradition of unfortunate experiences of European directors going to work in the United States. In the middle of the seventies, I wanted to turn the page. I wanted to give myself—this is a bit self-indulgent—the impression that I was starting from zero. Which was, at the time, both true and not true, because I arrived in the United States with a reputation. The Americans were extremely warm and hospitable in the beginning. If you wish, the real reason why I went to the United States was *Pretty Baby*, a film that I cared a good deal about. It was a way of assuaging my great passion for jazz; it was a period in New Orleans that I knew well: the story of the photographer Bellocq and that of the girl. *Pretty Baby* was my acclimatization, and I have to say that it was very hard. I had problems with the screenplay. It is a film that I care about enormously, and yet one that does not really resemble the one I wanted to make. At most, it is a film I would really like to *remake*. My good luck was to come upon Brooke Shields, who was an extraordinary object, but there are a lot of things in the film that do not correspond to what I had in my head. . . . On that film, I paid my dues. I stuck it out, during the time it took to arrive, to write the film, to acclimatize, and the production delays imposed by the studio, which could not decide whether it wanted to make the film or not. I said to myself: "I don't want to stay in half checkmate"—however, the film was well received in the United States, though I was not satisfied with it. I decided to stay, without thinking that

I was going to stay for long. Perhaps I stayed because I was stubborn. The time passed very quickly. I shot *God's Country* in 1979, and I only edited it years later. Then some Canadian producers came to see me with tax-free money, and they absolutely wanted to make a film, and they gave me carte blanche. I made *Atlantic City*, with a very brilliant American writer, John Guare, who had collaborated on *Taking Off* with Milos Forman. The film was received with complete indifference in France, but in the United States it did very well. In the mix, I made *My Dinner with Andre*, which was also very well received. And during a certain period, I had the impression that I could make whatever I wanted in the United States. These were both low-budget films: the second one, *My Dinner with Andre*, cost $400,000, which is chicken feed there; and *Atlantic City*, which was obviously more expensive, was made outside of the American film industry, as a French and Canadian production. I had the impression that I could make the films I wanted to make there as well as I could in France. My problem with American cinema is something I see clearly now: it is really an industry; they are obsessed with money; the be-all of cinema is to make money, and there is nothing else. At most, one could say that they are more honest than the French: for the French it is the same thing, but they don't dare to say it. In the United States, you have to accommodate yourself to it. When a producer tells you, "Your screenplay is very interesting, but I don't think it will interest people," it is sudden death! That is what happened to me before making *Au revoir les enfants*.

I had a project for a comedy, which all the studios thought was too sophisticated. You have to know that whatever the prestige of the directors and sometimes the actors involved in a project may be, it is the laws of the industry, the study of the market, which prevails. The result is that one wastes enormous amounts of time. American directors, even the most famous ones, have five projects under their belts at the same time, with the thought that there will be one of them that will actually come out. Once again, in my case, I am incapable of doing that; I can only work on one thing at a time.

After *My Dinner with Andre*, I had a project for a fairly aggressive comedy about the corruption in American political life, with John Belushi. And because I had Belushi, who was interested in the project, I immediately got a contract with a studio. It was a complicated film, expensive, very funny—really a film for the studio system. Belushi was going to make it, and then he died. The project was immediately buried. Since I had an enormous desire to make it, my brother Vincent and I tried to put it back together with other actors. Dan Aykroyd, Belushi's sidekick, who was also involved with project, tried to help us. That went on for months. That's why I made *Crackers*. I became aware that I had not worked for two years, and I had become very nervous. When you live in Los Angeles, there is an extremely unhealthy paranoia, which has ruined a lot of careers. In the cinema, you always have to know how far you can go with compromises; in American cinema, it's even harder—you have to go through a certain number of humiliating circumstances. The whole *Crackers* affair was unbelievable. In the beginning, a guy who was the head of Universal had been able to convince me to make the film by offering me very favorable, comfortable conditions—putting the studio at my disposal—because he was convinced the film would be a great success. I was interested in one particular element of the film: you know that *Crackers* was adapted from the screenplay of *Big Deal on Madonna Street*, but I had connected it with the crisis that was at that moment affecting the American economy. I had discovered the Latin American neighborhood of San Francisco, which had been strongly affected by unemployment, and this neighborhood fascinated me: once again, it was something about immigrants who were going in circles. I had shot half the film on San Francisco exteriors. And the rest of it, I had shot at Universal, in this enormous production machine: there were twenty sets being used, eighteen of them for television, with just Brian De Palma and me making films for the cinema. I had gigantic equipment, and crew members who changed every day because they were employed by the year and went from one set to another. And while we were shooting, the production head of Universal was replaced by another guy, who thought the idea of the film was abysmal. The entire *Crackers* affair, with previews that were not going well, and then the re-editing of the film, was nightmarish. This experience explains everything about American cinema: how the director has no autonomy, and lacks the power of decision-making he is given in Europe.

Q: Because in the US, you didn't have final cut?

LM: I had it. I absolutely had it! This remarkable thing happened to me, which is that I had this producer who had Universal behind him, who offered me *Crackers*, and who was a good guy. I had said to him: "I want final cut." He said to me that it wasn't possible, which was actually true. In the United States, no one gives final cut anymore, even to the biggest directors. But he gave it to me anyway: it was either that or I wasn't going to make the film. He gave it to me. But I didn't notice, until the time when I was working on problems with the re-editing, that he *himself* didn't have final cut. He had completely taken me for a ride, even though he was very nice. I consulted a lawyer, and he said the decision could stand. In France, the law protects the creator absolutely: the author's rights are sacred. In the United States, absolutely not. The laws favor money; they are oriented in that direction. They didn't ask me to change anything or put anything back in; it was more of a harassment, and at a certain moment I had had it up to here. Nothing happens with violence: it's a progressive sliding, and you get to the point where you say: "What am I doing here?" I would gladly never have had this experience, and the only thing I learned from it is that you should never do that. I believe that I will never again make a studio film, a film in the industry. *Alamo Bay*, the next one, was a marginal film, made with a small crew, financed by a distributor. All in all, I had the impression in the United States that I was wasting a lot of time; but when I look at the positive side, America is such an interesting country, so complicated, that I am not sure that I would never want to work there again.

When I make a film like *Au revoir les enfants*, I am in completely familiar terrain, because I am talking about my childhood. If it was a question of making films on current subjects, I have to ask myself if I know America better than I know France. I have the impression, because it's a country that has always interested me and that I have studied for all these years, that I know America well. At the same time, I love living there: I love being an exile, being displaced. I have always been a great fan of Conrad: I love this literary tradition of people who are displaced in another country, whether they are talking about their own country or being elsewhere, or whether they're observing a society that is not theirs but which they know well. When I made *Au revoir les enfants*, we worked in the most complete secrecy, a bit at the margins of French cinema. It was a low-budget film, financed by Marin Karmitz with no problems: we worked in Provins—it's ninety minutes from Paris, but even so it is really deep in the provinces—and I had the impression of reinventing my past, but of being in the margins of the present.

Should I make films in France, reinventing the past, and alternate them with films that take place today? It's funny: all the films that I have made in France are films with a distance in time from the present. With an historical distance, even if it is a small one. Except for *Elevator to the Gallows*. Even in *Les Amants*, absurdly, I told myself that there would be a gap of three years from the present. I even indicated it in the screenplay. *Le Feu follet* took place in the present, but when you look at it, there is a gap: there was a play with time, and it worked much better than if it had been an historical reconstitution. On the other hand, in the United States—except for *Pretty Baby*, which is almost a French film made in the United States—I made contemporary films. I don't have roots there, so what interested me—whether in the form of documentaries or in the form of fiction—was capturing the America of today, the things that strike me and that Americans often don't see.

I liked Otar Iosseliani's film *Favorites of the Moon* (1984) enormously. He was able to tease out the strangeness of Parisians as no one else had done it. I was living in the United States at the time, and I went to see it with my wife, Candice [Bergen]. It made her laugh a lot. She is American, and she finds the French very bizarre. She is sensitive to the gap that Otar so wonderfully, so subtly detected. And that amused me, because I believe that what Americans liked about *Atlantic*

City was exactly that: a somewhat distanced gaze that captures something they themselves don't necessarily see about their own behavior.

Note

1. Klaus Barbie was head of the Gestapo in the French city of Lyon from 1942 to 1944. His much-publicized 1987 trial resulted in a sentence of life imprisonment.

Interview with Louis Malle

Ginette Gervais-Delmas, Bernard Nave, and Andrée Tournes / 1987

From *Jeune cinéma*, no. 184 (November 1987): 4–15. Reprinted by permission. Translated from the French by CB.

In our discussion with Louis Malle, we decided not to talk about *Au revoir les enfants*. The reason for this was that in Venice, where Malle spoke for the first time about his new film, it was quite upsetting for him, and we didn't want to return to it in another interview. We were intrigued by Malle's entire career, and above all by the fidelity to the documentary that Malle has displayed ever since *The Silent World* and up to *And the Pursuit of Happiness*, which was acclaimed at the Cannes Film Festival.

Louis Malle: When I began studying at IDHEC, I, like all my friends, had just one idea: to make fiction films. I wanted to be Bresson; I wanted to be Renoir. What is really funny is that at the moment when Jacques Cousteau came to ask the director of IDHEC for an intern who knew how to swim, I jumped at the opportunity. What Cousteau was doing at the time didn't interest me, and I said to myself, "I'm going to spend three months on Cousteau's boat, and I'm going to learn to dive." I was going to do what I could to help, but I didn't intend to stay on. I got the job, being the only candidate: the others had all disdainfully rejected the offer. When the three months of summer had gone by, I had to go back to IDHEC, but Cousteau asked me to stay, because the person who was in charge of filming on his ship, the *Calypso*, had left. I couldn't refuse this extraordinary offer: I decided not to go back to IDHEC, where I had been bored, and I therefore found myself, at the age of twenty, responsible for everything having to do with filmmaking on the *Calypso*. It was a dangerous move on the part of Cousteau, because I didn't have the training; I didn't know how to do anything. I had just had a little practice making 8mm films, and I was a good swimmer! At least that was something.

For years, I basically thought that this time with Cousteau had been just a technical apprenticeship. But it was fascinating in a human way, and I learned my trade. Being with Cousteau for four years and making *The Silent World* as my first film, I had to capture the images, record the sound, do the editing, and direct the actors. . . . No, that's a whole other question! I went back to Paris, and I wanted to make fiction films: that was my deepest ambition. I was Bresson's assistant on his beautiful film *A Man Escaped*. After that, Cousteau needed me and I went back. But I really wanted to make fiction films. At the time I said to Bresson, "The only job on the set that interests me is yours." And he answered, "I understand: I was never an assistant director."

So I went back to Paris. I wanted to make a film, and I was very much helped by the success of *The Silent World*, which, much to our astonishment, had won the Palme d'Or at Cannes. Cousteau had generously added me as a co-director, and that facilitated my entrance into the profession. When I made *Elevator to the Gallows*, I was twenty-four years old! It was only later that I realized how this time with Cousteau had influenced me much more than I thought. Undoubtedly, after stringing together *Elevator to the Gallows*, *Les Amants*, and, after a slight pause, *Zazie dans le métro* and *Vie Privée*, I needed to take a bit of distance. That was in 1964. I went to Algeria with a camera; it was the end of the war. After the cycle of fiction films that I had made in rapid succession, with that bulimia that one has when starting out, I needed—both for my mental equilibrium and for my work as a filmmaker—to do something different. I had wanted, after the years I had spent in Paris, to go back to a more direct form of cinema. Cousteau had tried to get me back, and I had tried to do it, but I wanted to make a kind of direct cinema that was more personal; I wanted to express myself with a camera and to look at the world, to put myself in a situation, to record it. That was, as you know, an important part of my work, and at times also important to my mental health. I remember that I had a discussion with Truffaut. He had just made *Une nuit américaine*. He told me, "I feel like I'm going in circles," and I said, "Well, yes! It's obvious. When you make film after film and do nothing but that, your lived experience is only that of making films, and you end up making a film about film," which he did brilliantly. He said, "Yes!" He had decided at that point to take a break and had written the book about Hitchcock. A lot of filmmakers had that temptation to speak about what they knew the best: the film set. I told myself that before getting to that point I would have to step back a bit, move away from the set, from actors, from this world which is so beautiful but which is fictional. I would have to question the things that awaken your curiosity, the things you want to know more about, and to convey it to others, which is even more fascinating. All of that came from my experience making *The Silent World*. I have a friend in New York who thinks that my style as a filmmaker is very much like being underwater. He has a whole theory about it. In fact, it's true. I recently watched *Elevator to the Gallows* again, and there is something about the nocturnal walks of Jeanne Moreau: we followed her in her wanderings with a very fluid camera, in the same way we would have followed a school of fish. It's true that that experience influenced me.

The influence was primarily on my style as a director. Like everyone else, I had a style that was a bit. . . . You know, when you start, when you make your first film when you're very young, you act clever: you still have to master the cinema as a means of expression, so you act with a bit of swagger. It's normal and even a bit innocent: you want to show what you know how to do. For example, at the time of *Les Amants*, the sequence shot was in vogue. I quickly realized that this was not my style, but I had to do these long, complicated shots of four, five, or six minutes. It was the kind of film that you put together in a week because there is nothing to do then other than glue together very long pieces of film. In putting it together—because editing is the opportunity to look at your work—I noticed when I looked more closely that that was not really my style: it created problems with rhythm that I could not control. There were important things that it would have been necessary for the camera to be able to do without it being seen. I would have had to be able to go in search of a detail or to capture a gaze: my cinema is a cinema of gazes. The sequence shot is a very aestheticizing kind of cinema which makes actors and objects move for the camera, which is particularly visible in the cinema of Miklos Jancso. In each of these long shots there were really only twenty seconds that I would have wanted to catch, but I had embarked on this aestheticizing sinuosity. Well, OK: it was the style and these shots are complicated . . . or no, they're actually easy but long. In short, that wasn't my style.

In my next project after that I made *Zazie*, which was an important film for me. At the time, it was an exercise in style, or at least that's what I believe, one that gave me the opportunity to make a kind of inventory of cinematic techniques, the equivalent of what Queneau did in his novel on the level of literary writing. That allowed me to put myself into a box, and inventory different styles. It was from that point on that I realized that I had been marked in an indelible way by my beginnings. The important thing for me was the gaze: the gaze at what I was looking at but also my *way* of looking, the more subtle and invisible relationship between the camera and what was in front of it. The cinema as direct capture, which is the central fact of documentary, was my true approach, and I could transpose it into fiction. The difference was basically a very simple one. Finding yourself in front of something which is in the process of happening, and having to capture it very quickly, you notice in the editing that you have already interpreted it without thinking about it. That forces you to make continual choices which are unconscious but which express something: choices in the way of placing the camera or what you leave out are important. That is no different from working on a fiction film. There, through a screenplay, actors, rehearsal, and very patient work, a very elaborate process, there is finally a moment of truth. You shoot, and at that moment there is no difference between the gaze that you bring to bear on this world that you have invented or reinvented—it is not necessarily a reconstitution—and that which you bring to bear in a documentary. In that sense, the return to documentary is a purification: it led me to simplify, to strip down my work as a fiction filmmaker.

What is great in documentary is its spontaneity. You ask yourself after shooting something why you went towards it: why you filmed that and not the other thing! In fiction film you have to discuss things with the cameraman; you have to work in a way that is more reflective; you have to have a point of view but also prevent the camera from being noticed. There has to be an osmosis between the way of filming and what you film, without the spectator being conscious of it. In what I have done the best, the camera doesn't display itself. It's like in documentary: the way of shooting counts as much as what you shoot.

Question: We would like to come back to *Zazie*, and ask whether the film is really just an inventory, and, if not, what really interested you about it.

LM: It's always the same thing. When I read the book, which I loved and which I wanted to make a film of, they told me, "You don't want to make a film about that; it's pure literature!" What interested me was the theme. Strangely, I notice today that it reminds me of the theme of *Au revoir les enfants*, which I made long afterwards. It is the situation stolen from Queneau of this little girl who in forty-eight hours, at the age of ten, barely younger than Julien in *Au revoir les enfants*, discovered the absurdity and the incoherence of adults. And there was this great line in the film: "What did you do there? I got older." It's the end of the book and also the end of the film. I found an echo in it of what I had experienced. *Zazie* is certainly a comedy, but it's a disturbing work, a disquieting work, and the film is too. You remember the arrival of the fascists: Trouscaillon becomes Mussolini. That was in the book and it struck me, and without knowing it was a first draft . . . it was a way of witnessing what had been my own childhood trauma. I noticed it much later, since the memory of this event was still present. That was what interested me more than the stylistic exercise and the game: the first draft of what I had not dared to talk about at the time. I rediscovered a press release from back then, and I didn't talk about it at all.

Q: Do you often have personal pretexts like that?

LM: Oh yes! Especially in the beginning of my career. *Le Feu follet* is a good example. I didn't make it with impunity. There was something that had happened to me and that resembled the story by Drieu La Rochelle. His story involved the death of Jean Rigault, who was a friend of Drieu. He never stopped saying, "I'm going to commit suicide," and then he killed himself. Drieu felt guilty, and he wrote the book in order to free himself from that guilt. For me, it was the same process with one of my friends at the end of the 1950s. I was getting close to my thirties, a difficult moment. You say to yourself that you have to either accept becoming an adult or do something. I therefore had this screenplay with this suicide which created a lot of difficulties for me. I remembered the book that my brother had given me when I was very young, and I found it convenient to hide myself behind Drieu. But I made the film as if it was personal: like Maurice Ronet in the film, I had an intimate relationship with the character. There was a continuity between Drieu, Rigault, and Maurice: we had all been through it. Rigault and my friend had been through it definitively. I transposed the story into the 1950s because I was directly involved.

I also did that for *The Thief of Paris*, because I discovered myself in the character of the thief. There was the great book by Georges Darien that I had read as a student and that Jean-Jacques Pauvert had rediscovered and reissued. I told [Jean-Claude] Carrière that I wanted to make *The Thief*, and I know why I did. There is something in the fate of this character that resembles, in a somewhat transposed way, what happened to me. But, in fact, this character who is revolting against his environment—I felt the same way at the time—and who pushes this rebellion to the point of going over to the other side, becoming this thief who robs upper-class homes and who conducts himself as an enemy of society with anarchic connotations—there was that very strong scene with Charles Denner as a politicized anarchist . . . I tried to pull that character toward what I was personally feeling at the time. And beyond that, the thief manages to be recuperated; he becomes rich and famous, and he finds himself in his house with his fortune restored, and married to his cousin who had refused him before. The ending is sad: he continues to steal until he is arrested, because of an unreasonable loyalty, even after having lost his enthusiasm for it. And for me, in the 1960s, my work as a filmmaker had permitted a rebellion, and yet I was in the process of becoming a filmmaker who was destined for the Légion d'honneur and for membership in the Académie Française!

After *The Thief of Paris* I made a big break: I went to India, and I stopped making fiction films. That was a big turn! I remember that at the time I reminded my cinematographer, Henri Decae, that on the same stage, in the same studio, seven or eight years earlier, we had done the same tracking shot in *Les Amants*, and I said, "I'm going to get stuck in a routine," and he didn't understand. It was absurd, but I had the feeling I was being recycled, an idea that was fairly unacceptable to me. So, it often happened at the beginning of my career that I made films based on literary works with subjects that corresponded to moments in my own experience.

After the interlude of the Indian film, which was outside of my previous work and very enriching, I was freer, in the 1970s, to bring myself closer to things that concerned me. For example, *Murmur of the Heart* was the first film where I was able to bring in elements of my biography, and it was my first return to childhood, even though in *Les Amants* I had related about something that happened in my family, in the milieu where I grew up, and through this story from the eighteenth century I was able to tell about something that had made me indignant and that was close to my heart. In that film, I hid myself a little because I wasn't completely ready for—how to put it?—immodesty. There was a certain resistance, which I believe was good, because you have to wait until you're ready and not force things. People always ask me: "Why did you wait thirty years to make *Au revoir les enfants*?" The answer seems obvious to me: I couldn't, and I didn't want to, and these last few years it seemed not only possible but necessary. All my important films are the ones I felt an urgency about making. After having circled around a theme for years, I have to make it quickly.

Q: Did you feel that same urgency in the American period?

LM: In certain films, yes. If I take them in order, the first was *Pretty Baby*. It was a project I had thought about in a mature way and that I had wanted to make for a long time. That was, among other things, the reason for my move to America: the desire to shoot a film in New Orleans, which I couldn't reconstitute in Marseille. It was an ambitious project that was not without a relationship to *Lacombe, Lucien*, but instead of dealing with politics it was—to simplify—about the theme of social morality. For me, it was the continuation of the work of questioning things, of looking at what seemed unacceptable and seeing. . . . I had read a fascinating story about the history of Storyville, the red-light district of New Orleans where jazz was born, and at the end of the book I had found an interview with a grandmother who was living in a suburb of a little town in the South. She told me that she had been a child prostitute, that she was born in a house of prostitution—a luxurious mansion, that she was born in a seraglio, and that for her, with an inverted morality, this world of prostitution had strict rules. The first man she had sex with, at the age of twelve, was her first communion. Weren't morals a question of point of view, of the society one lived in? There had been a mini-society there, with inverted rules. In addition, as in *Lacombe, Lucien*, it interested me to point out the hypocrisy, and a certain cowardice, of the period in which child prostitution was, if not legal, at least accepted, especially in the puritanical country that America was at the time. They were shocked by *Pretty Baby*, just as the French were by *Lacombe, Lucien*, and everything that *Pretty Baby* told about was exactly true.

Then I lost the sense of urgency. It was my first experience of the difficulty of making films in the US. Time stretched out, and a year passed between my decision to make the film and the beginning of shooting. It was too long. When I feel that it is time to make a film I like to move fast. That's what happened with

Au revoir les enfants: I decided to make it at the end of September, the start was difficult what with having to find money and having to choose the child actors, but I knew that we had to start shooting in January, and it only took one trimester, which was good. With *Pretty Baby*, I had lost the sense of urgency, which was why by the time it was finished the film had lost the energy and the hardness it should have had.

What was very fortunate, on the other hand, was the next experience on *Atlantic City*. It was a small, marginal film, and not even American since the investors came from Winnipeg and profited from a tax shelter system! We were always joking about that! We had to tighten the schedule because the film had to be finished by December 31! Other than that, I had free rein: they trusted me. I wanted to work with a writer from New York, John Guare, who had never worked in cinema except in a collaboration with Milos Forman on *Taking Off.* At the same time, I was reading extraordinary stories in the *New York Times* about this city, which had played a big role in the 1930s and 1940s—there is a scene from *Citizen Kane* that takes place in Atlantic City—and then went to sleep in the following years, becoming a real ghetto. We took a car down there with Guare, and I saw that it was a marvelous metaphor for America. . . . We started working on it at the beginning of August, and we began shooting in early October. I tried to put in the contradictory impressions that America had made on me. I had already spent two years there, and started *God's Country*. I thought about a subject for what would have been a great documentary! I would take a 16mm camera and shoot what was happening! OK, I had already started making the fiction film, but the subject was *Atlantic City* in any case. We would really be there, with direct capture, to see what was happening with the buildings that were falling, and those that were rising, this way of abolishing the past, this American hardness. The film struck Americans because they took it as a revelatory look at the America of today, a look that was capable of capturing it because it came from elsewhere. *Atlantic City* was a big success, the best received of any of the films I made in America.

God's Country was begun in 1979. In the position of observer where I had placed myself, direct cinema came naturally. *God's Country* was supposed to be the first in a series called "America Seen by Louis Malle." It was for public television, which is excellent but with no financial resources. I hadn't finished it: the documentary was very expensive because the editing was so long. I did other things, and then I started on the editing again, both before and after making *Alamo Bay*. I sensed the need to go back to Glencoe. I had stayed in contact with those people, with whom I had become friends. I came back to see them with a camera. In the time since I had been there before there had been a terrible financial crisis in the US, and the farmers had lost their land. This return trip gave weight to the film: the five-year gap had given the film a darker and more pessimistic vision.

There was a fascinating experiment in documentary: it was made by an Englishman who filmed a group of children for the BBC. Seven years later, he came back to film them again, and then again seven years after that. And he told me, "In seven years, I'll do it again." He thinks he will be able to organize all this material, but that is very difficult. We talked about it, because everything having to do with documentary interests me.

Then I made *Crackers*: that was my one bad American experience. It was the only time I worked within the system! Which was unhealthy! They gave me the reasoning that they give to all creative people: make this film, which is going to be commercially successful, and then you will be able to do whatever you want! In the US, you are only worth what you are worth at the box office. I knew that I would never be capable of having a popular success in the US. In short, I had worked for a year and a half on a very difficult subject about political corruption, which was based on a real scandal. With my writing partner John Guare, I had written a comedy for John Belushi, who was a big star and whom I loved. He died, and the project was down the drain. I wanted to shoot something, and I accepted the ludicrous idea of making a contemporary remake of *Big Deal on Madonna Street*. I ended up accepting it—after two years—because we had found a Hispanic neighborhood in San Francisco where we had the impression of being somewhere other than the United States, a neighborhood with a great energy, where people were looking to survive day by day, by means that were often illegal! I thought that I could transpose the environment of the film to there. One could write a whole book about the making of *Crackers*! I said, "I'll read the screenplay, and if I don't like it I'll leave." I asked the fundamental question—is it important to me?—and the answer was no, but I did it anyway out of friendship, out of loyalty, and we started the shoot. The guy who was overseeing the project changed studios, and his replacement—that's how it must be for Puttnam at Columbia—said, "What is this thing?" I felt that I was in danger. At my studio in Los Angeles there were twenty soundstages. I was a machine in a factory. The film was horribly expensive, but you don't see that on the screen. It cost twelve million dollars, while *Alamo Bay* only cost four million! It turned into a nightmare, and when the film came out, I was insulted. And, for once in my life—not that I refuse to accept responsibility—I had taken on a film that came to me by a fluke. I should mention that I had also made *My Dinner with Andre*. It was two hours with two guys in a restaurant, so I thought I could get myself out of any situation. *Crackers* cost me dearly: people would tell me, "Just don't make another *Crackers*." I wasted time on it! The real problem in the US is time: my friends all have five or six projects in the works: it's unbelievable!

Fortunately, what saved me—and sunk me at the same time—was *Alamo Bay*, which I made next. That was in 1984, and it was about events that had taken place four years earlier. I had gone to the location at that time, with my camera on my back, thinking that I could film them, and finally, after *Crackers*, wanting to make another fiction film, I started working on it. That film said a lot about America today: it fascinated me in the same way *Lacombe, Lucien* fascinated me: seeing how racism begins, the situation of these Vietnamese who were victims like the *harkis* in Algeria, and who were forced to leave Vietnam either because they were from the South, or because they were Catholics who rejected the regime. They were objectively victims of the war, and they were treated as Vietcong, as if the war was continuing in the little ports of Texas! That film annoyed Americans. That surprised me, because I had the somewhat naïve idea that Americans accepted criticism, but obviously not of everything. One could feel a deep sense of irritation among film critics. They accused me of describing a subculture of Texas without understanding it, when they were New Yorkers with no knowledge of what was happening in other places! I had spent a year there, and the portrait of the little town was very precise. In the provinces, the press went even further, saying, "Why is this Frenchman getting mixed up in things that are going wrong in our country?" That depressed me, and I said to myself, "I've done my time in America."

And yet, it was really in the tradition of the Warner Bros. films, and very consciously so. Talking with my screenwriter, who really knew the cinema of that time, we said to each other, "We're going to try to rediscover the cinema of the Hollywood of another era, which was a cinema of social denunciation." We thought about *High Noon*. We had read the screenplay, and we imitated the structure, which leads to this moment when the characters go into action. There is the woman who goes against her family, and the Vietnamese man who is following a moral code. There were obvious analogies with *High Noon* and other generous films of that time. Probably it was a question of timing that made Americans unable to receive the film. But it's a film I'm proud of.

Now, with the appearance of videocassettes that have given a second life to films—the critics come back to them—something is happening. Andrew Sarris, the pope of the *Village Voice*, who massacred the film at the time it came out, wrote, "We were wrong about Malle's film. It's a beautiful film." I wrote to him that it would have been more fair to have said it sooner.

Q: In the end, did you make what you wanted to make in the US?

LM: Yes, except for *Crackers*, where they really wore me out. I've spoken about it being an exile, but in a positive sense: putting yourself in a foreign land, getting out of your own culture, changing . . . it was a voluntary exile.

A Seminar with Louis Malle

American Film Institute / 1988

From AFI's Harold Lloyd Master Seminar with Louis Malle, December 7, 1988. ©1988, used courtesy of American Film Institute.

Question: What was it like to go to film school in France in the early 1950s?

Louis Malle: It was horrible. The film school, IDHEC, was in terrible shape when I went to it. It had no money. And it was all theory and no practice. I never finished. They forced me to accept the degree years afterwards because they wanted to put my name on their list of students! But I actually left after two years to join Jacques Cousteau. The good thing was that going to film school was an opportunity to see a lot of films. One of our teachers was Georges Sadoul, who wrote one of the first histories of French cinema and was a wonderful man. We hardly attended classes: we were always at the Cinématheque. But I did study all the different aspects of filmmaking: editing, directing, and cinematography. And then I ended up working with Cousteau, who needed an apprentice for three months. After the three months, he wanted me to stay, and he told me, "Now you are in charge." So I had to train first to become a diver, and then to be an under-water cameraman. And most of my work was on the cinematography, as well as a lot of editing. After three years, we came up with this underwater documentary, *The Silent World*, which was extraordinarily successful. And Cousteau was a real gentleman, and gave me a co-credit as director. I was twenty-three, and it gave my career a big push.

Q: Throughout your career, you've often returned to documentaries. Since the early 1960s, you have shot documentaries in a number of locales: India, France, the US, and elsewhere. What was it that first drew you to the fiction film? And what was it that, after becoming a success in fiction films, took you back to documentaries?

LM: I've always loved documentaries, and, if I had not met Cousteau, I intended to make documentaries of my own. I remember at IDHEC that the other students had great contempt for documentaries, so it was very easy for me to get the job with Cousteau, since no one else was interested. Everyone wanted to work with René Clair, or with Henri-Georges Clouzot, but nobody wanted to work with a documentary filmmaker. I was also the only one in the school who could swim! They were not very into physical things; they were intellectuals. And it was such a fascinating experience to work on the documentary with Cousteau that after I had made four or five fiction films in a row, it was important for my sanity to be able to grab a 16mm camera and go somewhere and try to look at something with my own eyes, without any screenplay. The first documentary I worked on and never finished was in 1962: it was the very end of a difficult moment in French history, the very end of the Algerian War, the last French colonial war. I went to Algeria with a tiny crew in those last days of colonization, and I stayed until the new regime, the Algerian nationalists, took over. That was what I was most interested in: being a witness, with my cameraman and my sound recorder. I was not pleased with what I shot, so I never edited it. That became a sort of pattern in the following years. Every three, four, or five years, I would drop out in a way and work on a documentary, or sometimes several at a time, and then I would go back to features. I think I'm one of the few feature filmmakers to do that. It's a wonderful experience, even if you just do it for practice. You learn a lot from this kind of filming from the hip. You film, and then you wonder "why did I film it that way," and you spend weeks and months in the cutting room wondering what you were doing. But you're always trying to learn more. And documentaries can be very personal. For me, the notion of objectivity in documentaries is ridiculous, because whatever you do is going to be a choice. You are continually choosing points of view. So it's better to declare from the start that this is your view of certain people and situations. It's always *my* reaction to what was happening in front of the camera. I never try to pretend that it was the truth, or that it is an objective version of reality.

This is all to say that I love making documentaries. The problem is that it's impossible to make a living making documentaries, and it's very difficult to get them shown. They're essentially a labor of love.

Q: I saw *Phantom India* at the British Film Institute. It was spectacular. Could you talk a little bit more about making that film? I heard there were some problems after it was shot.

LM: Well, yes, I was banned from India for many years. I never quite understood why. I went to India, traveling with a selection of French films I was showing to film societies around India. I had never been to India before. I stayed about three months, and I was absolutely blown away by India. Those were the days when there were hundreds and hundreds of hippies going to find revelation in India. That was not my interest. What I was confronted by in India was a culture that I could not understand. I was amazed! I thought it would be good for me, at that point in my life and my career, to take a long sabbatical, to go back to India with a camera and two good friends. And I spent a long time there, and we became quite literally drifters. We started in Calcutta and we stayed there for a month. The first of my series of films, *Calcutta*, which was released in Europe theatrically, was sort of a portrait of the city. Then we went south. I had no idea what I was going to do with the material, and I couldn't care less. I was just happy to be there, not trying to understand it, but trying to be part of it. Very quickly, we gave up on the notion of even having an itinerary. There were days when we were not even shooting. My cameraman and sound person finally had enough, and they went home.

And eventually I returned to Paris as well. I spent another year and a half "in India"—because I was in the cutting room trying to make sense of everything we had shot. So this was a very important moment in my life, and in my work, too, because, if you've seen the films, I'm never trying to say, "This is what it is." I film something, and then I think I have an interpretation. And then I realize a few days later, or even in the cutting room, that it's not about what I thought it was about. So it's always a reevaluation of everything.

When I came back from India, I was not quite sure that two plus two was four: that is what it did to me. It was a completely different system of values, and I'm grateful to India for having forced me to start all over, as if I was a five-year-old again. So it was really important to me. And I think it shows in the films, which are about someone trying to find out not just about India, but about himself. These are possibly the most personal films I have made. The narration is just a series of moments of disarray, and the visuals and the sound in India are so stunning. All of that is conveyed in the films, but I regret not being able to convey the smells of India!

Q: What inspired you to make a story like *Lacombe, Lucien*? Does it have anything to do with your own personal experiences with people like Lacombe?

LM: Well, yes and no, because I've always been interested in making a film in which the central character is somebody who, basically, I find very difficult to understand, somebody with a completely different background. I had been exposed to this kind of behavior during the French Algerian War, because I had a few encounters with French soldiers who were drafted to go to Algeria, sort of like Vietnam, because there was a war going on. And within six months, some of them, because it was a guerilla war, ended up torturing people to get information. I remember one of them in particular, who was going to be an accountant (and probably is one now). He was from my hometown in France, and this guy was what they called an "information officer," which meant he was torturing people. One night he told me all about it. I couldn't believe what was going on in his head. He was perfectly normal; there was nothing about him that was sadistic or brutal. He ended up saying, "Somebody has to do it." We had a terrible fight, but the result was that I kept wondering: How does it work? How does somebody become that? And I worked on that particular story for a while, and then I thought that the Algerian War was the wrong war, and I ended up with World War II, with this character of Lucien Lacombe. Now, this character comes from my own background, in a way. If you see *Au revoir les enfants*, it's very obvious that the kitchen boy in *Au revoir les enfants*, who goes to the Gestapo and denounces people, is a cousin of Lucien Lacombe, and he was my starting point. I very quickly decided to separate the two stories, because even then, in the 1970s, I knew I would eventually do *Au revoir*. In this country, you had the My Lai trials, and I remember there was one guy who had gotten a Purple Heart, and then a month later he was on trial for war crimes. And he was saying, "You have to make up your mind: am I a hero or a war criminal?" There was a great piece about it in *Esquire*. And I thought, "We're always dealing with the same story: the banality of evil, or how people in special historical circumstances, people who could have lived perfectly normal lives, do these things." These people are not animals, not vicious, not sadists. And so I came up with this character, and because I knew so little about this character, I did an enormous amount of research. I started working with a young French writer, Patrick Modiano, because I needed a lot of help. That film created a huge controversy: I think in a sense it was good, because the French have a problem with that part of their history. French history is complicated during that period, because we had a Vichy government that was very active in collaborating with the Nazis. They were reporting the Jews, and fighting against the Resistance. This topic had been avoided for many years, and then Marcel Ophuls's film *The Sorrow and the Pity* came out, and then my film, which focusses on a collaborator who is very young, not a monster, and a member of the working class. So I knew that I was going to get myself in trouble, because nobody could deny that these things happened, but it was not easy for the French public or even for many French intellectuals to accept it. But I think it was good, because I always try in my films to force people to reevaluate stereotypes and preconceived ideas. So with *Lacombe, Lucien*, I was right on the money, and there was a lot of discussion. And I think that now, in the 1980s, the French are finally coming to terms with that muddy episode. I think that of all my films, *Lacombe, Lucien* is my best work. I saw it again recently, and it's almost exactly what I like to do. It's complicated and simple at the same time, and the truth is very convoluted, if there is any truth; but at the same time I think that everything about the film is very authentic. And it's also disturbing. And everyone in the film is an unknown: there were practically no professional actors in it. If I had to remake it, I think I would make it pretty close to the same way, with just a couple of changes.

Q: Did your experience in India open up your way of making films or change your project for making films? The first film you made after coming back from India was *Murmur of the Heart*.

LM: Well, *Murmur of the Heart* was a long time after, but I don't think I would have made the film if I hadn't been to India. I came back from India after a long and deep experience, and I felt quite free and loose. So what happened with *Murmur of the Heart* was that I wrote a screenplay in one week. And I wrote it practically with what the surrealists called automatic writing. I was very surprised by what I had written, and I decided to shoot it more or less the way it was. I think it had to do with working on a subject that is as heavy as incest, which as you know is one of the last taboos in our society. And, of course, the fact that I was dealing with incest as comedy material was interesting. And I worked for months trying to improve the first draft, but essentially the screenplay just came, after years of not wanting to deal with it. So I was working with a lot of elements of my own adolescence, and it was scary to shoot it, but I felt I had no choice.

Q: In *Au revoir les enfants*, it's a story you've been wanting to tell for fifteen years.

LM: Yes, but *Au revoir* was something I felt—when I started out as a filmmaker—that I would never deal with, because it was too difficult and too personal, and there was not even a story. And it was mine; it was *my* story, so why should I give it away? It took years and years, when I was not even talking about it with anybody. When I was working on *Lacombe, Lucien*, it came back very strongly, and it was only then that I knew I would eventually have to deal with it. The reason I waited so long is that it was *the* event of my childhood, and I felt that I had to do it right. And I was also naïve enough to believe that I was getting better as a filmmaker, and that I had a little more control. One of the things I have learned over the years, and that I do well now, is directing children. I made a film called *Zazie*, my third feature, and I knew nothing about directing children, and I had to learn on the spot. Over the years since then I have worked with children a lot, and each time I have felt I was improving, first of all in choosing them, and then in directing them, getting the best out of them. I'm not saying I have any kind of technique, or any tricks. It's just a matter of knowing what to do and what not to do in each situation.

The key for me in *Au revoir les enfants* was that I needed remarkable children. And that's why I didn't hurry, because I knew that this was something I was doing better and better. In that sense I think was right, because the one thing I'm proud of in *Au revoir les enfants* is those two boys. They were, for me, a sort of miracle—except that it took me nearly six months to find them, to work with them, to get them used to the camera, and to prepare them for the shoot. And so I felt very strongly that it was worth waiting, and also because, as you grow older, many things from your childhood come up, a lot of things that you've blocked. I certainly remembered vividly every moment of what happened to my friend Bonnet in the school in 1944. But there were lots of other things that, little by little, were coming back. It's usually after your forties or fifties that these things come back. It's no accident that in recent years you've seen Bergman do *Fanny and Alexander* and John Boorman do *Hope and Glory* and even Woody Allen do *Radio Days*, and I could name a few more. It seems like, at a certain time in your life you feel almost obliged to deal with your childhood, or something very intimate about what happened to you in those years. So I did, and, of course, I was absolutely scared to death, because I would never have forgiven myself if something had gone wrong. And when you watch the film, I suppose it could seem very simple. The structure of the story seems to flow absolutely naturally, and it could even be a bit boring in that sense. But when I was shooting the film, I remembered something my cameraman Sven Nykvist told me when we were shooting *Pretty Baby*. I worked with Sven twice, and I was very impressed by him. There's something about his lighting that is very simple. He doesn't light shot by shot; he lights the whole scene. And he works fast, and it always seems the simplest possible way, and also the most logical way: it's very poetic. And I asked him, "How do you do it?" And he said, "It took me all these years to get rid of everything that was not completely necessary, all the tricks. It took me twenty years to achieve simplicity." And I thought about that when I was making *Au revoir*, because I never thought of the camera as one of the characters. Some directors do, and some do it brilliantly. But I'm not of that school. I like the spectators to forget, in a matter of minutes if possible, that there is a camera. And by doing so, it seems to me, I bring them infinitely closer to the characters and the emotions of the story. I am really trying to get to what is essential, and in that sense the film is almost austere in telling that story, and it seems like it is deprived of any sort of cinematic fireworks. But as far as my approach to filmmaking is concerned, I really think it's, so far, what I've done best, because it's exactly what I've been trying to achieve all these years: simplicity. That's why I think it was worth waiting.

Q: From your comments, it sounds like the two young boys in the film are not professional actors. Where did you find them?

LM: Oh no, I never work with child actors, because they're monkeys, even after making one film, and especially if they've been anywhere near a television production. They learn the tricks. This may be very unfair of me, and I'm sure there are wonderful exceptions. When you start casting a film like *Au revoir les enfants*, that has children in it, the hardest part is finding the right children. When I started *Au revoir les enfants*, I said, "Let's see what twelve-year-olds have been in films or television recently," and I was really horrified! It's almost sad. I don't think it's right for a child to do it professionally. It was the same for *Murmur of the Heart, Zazie, Lacombe, Lucien,* and even *Pretty Baby*—Brooke Shields was unknown then. But what I was doing was trying to find remarkable children. So I worked with a group of casting people, three girls who were great, and we tried to define the direction in which we would go. We knew it would be a long process, and it took five months.

Basically, it's very boring, because it means you advertise. You put little articles or ads in the magazines and the radio stations and television programs that those particular children you are looking for are watching. You ask them to get in touch, to send photos. It's a selection process that takes forever, and it's actually quite boring. But eventually, you're going to meet someone who's going to be stunning. We decided that we would limit our research to Paris and to certain *lycées* and certain schools, because we wanted children of a certain background. It was arbitrary, but we had to limit the field in some way. Eventually, the girls who were helping me with casting and I went to the outside of schools with video cameras—we were really voyeurs, and we had problems with school principals. It's a weird occupation. And eventually I remember about one month after the start, they called me and they said, "We think we found a terrific kid," and that was Gaspard, the boy who played Julien. He came on his own. He'd read about it, and he came, and right away we felt that there was something quite unusual about him, something quite remarkable. He was extremely poised, very smart, and slightly arrogant. He was very fast, very quick, like quicksilver. He couldn't stay in the same place for two seconds. And everything about him was perfect. And of course, what I always had in my mind was that I wasn't going to choose one boy before choosing the other one. The chemistry had to work: they had to work well with each other.

And then it took us forever to find the other boy. I told the production people, "Listen, I know we have to start, at the latest, by the end of January, because shooting it in winter is so important. If not, we'll have to wait a year." And about mid-December, just before Christmas, I still hadn't found the boy to play Bonnet, and I told them, "If I don't find this boy and I don't feel completely enthusiastic about him, I would rather postpone," which would have been a disaster, of course. But just around Christmastime, Raphaël Fejtö came. That was very interesting, because when Gaspard came into the casting office, I knew right away that he was right for the part, but with Raphaël it took me two weeks to make up my mind, and even then I was afraid I'd made a terrible mistake. There was something about him that was very closed and very introverted, although he was also incredibly arrogant, which seems to be a quality that I like. And he was not so crazy about the idea of being involved; he was very laid-back.

I always have my little 8mm video camera with me, and I keep taping them all the time—when I talk to them, when we go to lunch. It's boring for them, but I keep doing it because I'm always trying to look at a lot of footage of them. What they look like in life is interesting, but there's always something that happens on the screen which is completely different. You know, there's this strange mystery that is called "screen presence." People can be terrific in life, or they can give you a great reading, but when you make a screen test you see there's nothing going on on the screen. There's no explanation for it: it's just this mysterious quality that certain people have and certain people don't have. Whether you're an actor or not is not the point: some great stage actors don't do anything on the screen, whereas you can pick up someone on the street who is great.

And at some point with Raphaël, the boy who plays Bonnet, I saw a moment where he was quite extraordinary: his eyes, and something like a curiosity, a certain way of looking at the camera, a sort of inquiring look that was absolutely right for the character. And then we worked on scenes, and it was endless. After the first couple of days of shooting, things went very smoothly. The great thing about working with children is that they are not going to be able to give you something they don't have. Or if there's something in the dialogue that's not right, you can hear it right away and fix it. Professional actors always say, "I'll find a way to make it work," which can be very dangerous. But with kids, if it sounds wrong, if it sounds out of tune, you have to change it. You can work on it, and it might get a little better, but if they're right for the part and there's something that sounds wrong, you change the line. You don't change the boy.

During the shooting of *Lacombe, Lucien*, it went even further. The boy I had chosen, through this same excruciating process—his background was so close to the background of the character. He came from the lowest of the peasant families in that part of France, and he had no education. He had dropped out of school very early, and his work was cutting wood. He was very wild, and he had never seen a movie in his life—just to explain how remote he was from all of it. This boy, who was also very smart and very sensitive, could understand this character infinitely better than I could. So eventually what happened was that he not only played the part, but he was also my technical consultant for the part, helping me to understand the character. I was always asking him, "How would *he* do it?" And he was the one I would listen to, rather than to myself or to historians. And I have to say that, as good a director as you are, a mistake in casting will cause you trouble. I think 50 percent of directing actors is choosing them.

So we would go to rushes, and these kids kept surprising us, because in a way they were always better than I expected. I would say to Renato, my cameraman, "They're great; how come they're so good? It certainly has nothing to do with *us*. They're just great." We try to help a little, but essentially it came from them. And if I'm proud of one thing, it's of having found them and chosen them.

Q: Did you take a different approach, or structure your films differently, during your American period?

LM: Not really. First of all, I always try not to think about audience reactions. The minute you start to worry about how the audience is going to react, you're in trouble. What happens with successes and failures in our business is very surprising, and it's absurd to make any connection between the quality of a film and its commercial success. I could give you examples of all four possibilities: a good film that is successful and a good film that's not, and a bad film that is successful and a bad film that's not. We could argue about the definition of a bad film for hours, but. . . . I've been lucky not to have had to make too many compromises. I've been able to make my own mistakes, and I've never been forced to take a star for the lead role, or to change the ending. That's never happened to me, so I can't say, "I wish I'd done it differently, but I was forced to do that." There are films of mine that I don't like too much, but it's all been my mistake.

I think you have to work from the point of view of your own satisfaction, and of what you're trying to achieve, and your instincts, because if not you will end up with something that is not what you wanted to do, and also not something spectators will want to see. Because if you do something you wanted to do and it doesn't work with audiences, too bad. You just have to move on. I can think of examples from my films of things I should have done differently, or perhaps, in the case of one American film, where I should not have done it at all. But other than that, I have never considered that because I am working in this country I should do things differently. On the contrary, what I have tried to do is be a good observer of the American scene, because I know this country pretty well. I have been living and working here since the 1970s, so this is a country that I know almost as well as my own. But I wasn't born and raised here, so I have a different view of it. I'm still surprised by certain things that you take for granted when it's your country and your culture. There is no point in me in becoming an American director, but what people liked about *Atlantic City* is that it was from a slightly different angle.

The only adjustment I have had to make is that working in this country requires a lot of patience. Because there is so much money involved, things are extraordinarily slow. To get things going, to get the money, to get the approval of the cast, to get the contracts . . . it takes so long, and I like to do things quickly. I like the momentum. And it kills me that it can take a whole year, and by the time you get to make the movie there's no energy left for making it. I see that happening a lot around me.

I've been lucky in the sense that my films have gotten financed. When I made *Atlantic City*, I had a project that had been turned down by every studio, and then two Canadians came to me and they had money. It was a Canadian tax shelter, and it was July and the money had to be spent by the end of December. They didn't have any project in mind. So I told them, "I've always wanted to work with a writer in New York named John Guare." They said, "John who?" And I said that he was a playwright in New York. So I went and talked to John, and gambling had just been legalized in Atlantic City, and there were articles in the *New York Times* about it. So John and I got a car and drove down to Atlantic City and spent a couple of days there, and then I talked to the Canadian producers, and they said, "It's already the end of July, and you would have to get started by the end of December." And we were actually able to start shooting in October! I was able to use a lot of my documentary experience, because the film is a lot about the city itself. And the fact that there was such great momentum in getting the film made was wonderful.

Then there was another project I worked on with John Guare, which I was tremendously excited about. It was an outrageous political comedy about political corruption in this country. And fairly quickly, we were able to put together a deal, because the central character was going to be played by John Belushi, who was a big star at the time. So we started working on the screenplay, and it was big budget, and there were the lawyers, and the Hollywood pace which drives me nuts. And eventually we gave the studio a first draft, and then I had to go to Paris. While I was in Paris, I got a call from John Guare saying that Belushi had died at the Chateau Marmont, and at that moment we knew that the project was also going to die. I kept struggling to keep the project alive for a year, hopelessly trying to come up with ideas for replacing Belushi. They were not bad ideas. I suggested Bob Hoskins, who is quite big now, but at the time nobody knew who Bob Hoskins was. And I thought of John Malkovich, but nobody knew who he was. So I went straight into making another film, *Crackers*, which was probably one of my mistakes. I felt that I had devoted all my time for the past two years to this one project, which was called *Moon over Miami*. And I felt like, "I'm not getting any younger. I can't take too many more meetings with these people." And I kept thinking that I should be able to do something as quickly as possible. That's my main problem with working here, and that's why I'm not anxious to work within the studio system anymore. Outside of that, I don't have any horror stories.

I don't think filmmaking is very different in different countries. Films can be very different, but the way of *making* films is the same everywhere. It varies with individuals, and with their techniques.

Q: Could you discuss *My Dinner with Andre* and your approach to the material? Was there a danger of it being just a filmed play?

LM: I knew Andre Gregory as a friend, and I knew Wally Shawn as a very interesting playwright. He had actually played a small part in *Atlantic City*. The two of them kept telling me, "This is a terrific project, and we want you to direct it." I knew that it was about these two guys, Wally and Andre, discussing in a restaurant for two hours, and I said, "Oh, my God, do I really need to do that?" I was hoping that it would never happen, because Wally is a very slow writer.

But eventually they sent me the script, and I read it, and I thought it was quite extraordinary. I called Andre after I finished reading it, and I said, "Listen, I'm willing to do it. At least I think I'm willing to do it. But it's absurd. It's not a movie! I don't know what it is." But what I liked most about it was that I felt close to both characters. I was terribly interested in them. Then I told them, "We're not going to be able to do this unless we work very hard." Because Wally was only vaguely an actor, and Andre was a stage director. I even told them at the beginning, as a sort of provoking thought, "Maybe these are perfect parts for Robert Redford and Dustin Hoffman, and then we can get financing." They were not amused! They really wanted to do it themselves. So I told them, "We're going to have to rehearse." I don't usually rehearse that much, but in this case I knew we had to. The first couple of weeks, I had them play the opposite parts, because I wanted to make sure that they were thinking of themselves as actors playing a part, and not as themselves. If not, they weren't going to be able to get anywhere. Then I realized that Andre had what was easily the longest part ever written—the greatest number of lines in film history. We ended up in rehearsal for three months!

We came to the point where it was supposed to be the first week of shooting, but it was still really rehearsal. And then I found a way to do it. The film basically has two camera angles: shot on one character and then reverse shot on the other. But each camera position could be made slightly different from the one before. There could be a particular angle on one shot of Andre , and then the next shot of Andre could be slightly higher. So it became very subtle. It was a bit like *Au revoir les enfants* in the sense that the only way it was going to work was if Andre and Wally were really extraordinary. And since they're not really actors, I had to "catch" them. After one week of shooting, I knew that when I wanted Andre to look angry, I had to shoot him in three-quarter profile, and if I wanted him to look sincere, or look like he was joking, I had to shoot him from a different angle. So it was incredibly byzantine. But for me, that was the only way to do it, because if not it would have been really boring and meaningless.

Editing the film was also an enormous amount of work, because it was meant to look absolutely seamless, like there were just these two guys talking, whereas in fact there were an incredible number of cuts. It was shown at the Telluride festival, where it was extremely well received. I take it as one of the greatest compliments I ever got when a friend of mine, the wife of a producer, told me, "I saw *My Dinner with Andre*. It's great, it's wonderful; it's very funny; it's very interesting. But what did you do, exactly? I saw your name. I understand you directed it, but what did you *do*"? I realized that that was exactly what I was trying to achieve. Most people are convinced that it was shot with two cameras in one afternoon, with two guys improvising their lines and being more or less themselves.

My Dinner with Andre was an extraordinary experience for me, because it was the ultimate achievement in directing. The control, the ability to work on the face. And the fact that it was absolutely not meant to be cinematic. And I learned a lot making it, especially things about dealing with actors. And then I went back to normal filmmaking. I was really pleased that it became such a cult success, contrary to what I expected.

Q: Could you talk about working with Brooke Shields? How do you work with an adolescent girl in a very sexually oriented subject?

LM: Well, let me put it this way. Casting the girl for *Pretty Baby*, like with the boy in *Lacombe, Lucien* and the two boys in *Au revoir les enfants*, was the key, and it was extraordinarily difficult because the story was about a child who, because of her background, lived in a society where sex was really part of her daily life. So she had to be a lot more sexually mature than a girl of twelve would normally be. We knew that was going to be the main problem with the casting. I found Brooke Shields quite early in the search. She was a model, and she was doing a lot of modeling in New York. Maureen Lambray, a photographer friend of mine, mentioned her and showed me photographs of her, and I met with her. Brooke was twelve at the time, and I think she had been modeling since she was three months old: her mother put her to work very early! What immediately struck me, aside from the fact that she was extraordinarily beautiful—she's still extraordinarily beautiful, but when she was twelve, she was just incredible, one of the most beautiful human beings I'd seen in my life—was that, because she'd been modeling, she'd been, in a way, selling her body. I'm not trying to say that modeling is prostitution, but there is a fine line. In a way she was used to taking those poses, so I think she was psychologically better prepared for the part than any other girl I saw.

I saw a lot of girls, and we did a lot of interviews. But Brooke really seemed the only way to go, despite her mother having a bad reputation at the time. I knew it wasn't going to be easy, and she had certain limitations. The other side of it was that she had dried up a bit emotionally. So, before I cast her, I worked with her: we did lots of tests, and I could see there was a limit point. It was very difficult for her to let go emotionally, which I needed for certain scenes. And I realized that I wasn't going to get that from her. I hesitated in casting her for that reason, but I realized that I didn't have any choice, because another actress might not have been able to deal with the kind of role she had to play. So I went with Brooke, but I had to cut a couple of scenes in the cutting room because she wasn't quite up to it.

It's interesting that we have been talking mostly about actors, because for me working with actors is the most interesting thing there is about directing. When I was young, I was very interested in the camera. I remember in my second film, *Les Amants*, there was the longest tracking shot that had ever been done in France: it went on for half a mile! And I was terrible with actors, because I came from directing fishes! I had had no experience directing human beings. I was tough with actors because I was scared of them. I can't give you a method for working with actors, but if you are directing a scene with two actors, you realize that they have to be directed in two completely different ways. And you realize that one of them is going to be the best on the first or second take and go downhill from there, and the other one is going to warm up until take ten. So what do you do? This is a problem that you have to deal with constantly.

To come back to the question about Brooke Shields: she was very interesting, and she gave a lot to the part. She was not exactly the part, so I had to adjust, but that's what you are doing constantly in this profession.

Q: Since you are not as involved with the camera anymore, how do you deal with cinematographers and other members of the camera crew?

LM: This might be a place to talk about the difference between working in Europe and working here. It's not an absolute rule, but cameramen here are expected to take care of camera setups much more here than they are in Europe. Most American directors will discuss the scene and the way they want it shot with the cameraman, and the cameraman will set up the shots. I don't work that way because, first of all, I *was* a cameraman, and second, the placement of the camera is an important part of my way of putting together the scene. I work in close collaboration with the cameraman, and we work a lot on the lighting. I know enough about lighting to be able to immediately see what the cameraman is doing. Sometimes they don't like that! It's not difficult to check what your cameraman is doing. I've worked with a lot of cameramen. I don't know why, but I change cameramen pretty often, whereas I have mostly worked with the same sound man. The sound man is doing something very mysterious, which is difficult to check. You don't even hear the sound until the rushes, and even then they tell you, "This isn't how it's going to sound in the final version." So I like to work with technicians I can really trust, and that's especially true for the sound man. I'm very confident about technique, because I started as a technician. I let everyone do their thing, and I like it when they participate. I love it when the dolly grip will tell me, "Maybe we can go from position five straight to position seven instead of position six."

In *Au revoir les enfants*, we had a crew of about fifteen people—a very lean, efficient crew—and they were really interested in the story. They were very involved. And it's great when people come to me and give suggestions. But then, at some point, you are the director, so you have to make the decision. You're all alone, and you have to make this horrible decision. They can help you a bit, but not really. It's like you're building a house together, but at the same time you're really alone. There's a real solitude about directing, which is sometimes very tough.

My Discussion with Louis: An Interview with Louis Malle

George Hickenlooper / 1991

From *Cineaste* 18, no. 2 (1991): 12–18. Reprinted by permission.

Unlike most of his colleagues in the generation of the French New Wave filmmakers, Louis Malle has become a transatlantic director, making critically acclaimed films both in France and in the US over a nearly forty-year period. While Malle's films have over the years won their share of Golden Palms and Golden Lions and other major European awards, they have also frequently been honored in Hollywood by the Academy of Motion Pictures Arts and Sciences. Three years ago, his *Au revoir les enfants*—Malle's autobiographical account of his childhood friendship in World War II France with a Jewish boy being hidden from the Gestapo at a Catholic boys' school—was nominated for an Academy Award for Best Foreign Film. In 1982, *Atlantic City* was nominated for five Academy Awards. And Malle actually received an Oscar for Best Documentary, an honor he shared with his co-director, Jacques-Yves Cousteau, who had discovered Malle studying in Paris at the Institut des Hautes Etudes Cinématographiques (IDHEC). Malle was studying cinematography there after majoring in political science at the Sorbonne, which had been preceded by an austere Catholic education at the Jesuit school in Fontainebleau. Born into one of France's wealthiest industrial families, Malle says, laughing, "I knew that fate would somehow bring me to the cinema."

After his auspicious debut with *The Silent World*, Malle's later landlocked assignments included a brief apprenticeship with Robert Bresson (on *A Man Escaped*), before his directorial debut, at the age of twenty-five, with *Ascenseur pour l'échafaud* (*Elevator to the Gallows*) in 1957. *Les Amants* (*The Lovers*, 1958) stirred controversy because of its uninhibited exploration of human sexuality; the visual tour-de-force *Zazie dans le métro* (1960) marked a radical change of pace, while *Le Feu follet* (*The Fire Within*, 1963) was praised for its compelling portrayal of the last days of a suicidal alcoholic. In those early years of the French

New Wave, Malle didn't achieve the same celebrity status as Truffaut, Godard, or Resnais, but his films were praised for their poignant and often explicit look at human relationships and established his reputation as a versatile director.

After subsequent efforts such as *Viva Maria!* (1965), starring Jeanne Moreau and Brigitte Bardot, and *Le Voleur* (*The Thief of Paris*, 1966), with Jean-Paul Belmondo, Malle returned to documentary filmmaking in 1967 with two very powerful portraits of poverty in India—*Calcutta* (1969) and *Phantom India* (1972). In the early seventies, he produced several of his most accomplished French films, including *Le Souffle au coeur* (*Murmur of the Heart*, 1971) and *Lacombe, Lucien* (1974), a provocative character study of a young French collaborator with the Gestapo.

In 1977, Malle moved to the US, where he worked in opera and theater and directed his first American film, *Pretty Baby*, starring Susan Sarandon and Brooke Shields as mother and daughter in a New Orleans brothel, followed by the critically acclaimed *Atlantic City* and two insightful documentary portraits of America's heartland: *God's Country* (1985) and *And the Pursuit of Happiness* (1986). When Malle's work conformed to no particular genre, he made one up, such as his surprise hit *My Dinner with Andre* (1981), a feature-length dinner-table conversation between theater director Andre Gregory and playwright Wallace Shawn.

Although Malle has found success on both sides of the Atlantic, when we meet for this interview he explains how strange he feels to be back in Los Angeles. This time, however, it is not business, but a personal visit to see his wife, actress Candice Bergen. "Paris, New York, Los Angeles," he sighs, "long distance marriages are very difficult." Just then, Malle breaks into his satchel and pulls out an old black-and-white photo of a younger version of himself (bearded) with Jean-Luc Godard and François Truffaut. "This was at Cannes in 1968," he says, "shortly after the Cinématheque incident and the general strikes." The photo shows Malle and Truffaut sitting in folding chairs, nonchalantly looking up at the ceiling, while Godard, gesticulating wildly, shouts into their ears. "It was a very crazy time," he says, chuckling. It is then that Malle explains that his latest film is an indirect portrait of that turbulent period in French history.

George Hickenlooper: How autobiographical is *May Fools*?

Louis Malle: It's certainly not as autobiographical as *Au revoir les enfants*, but it's still inspired by family and childhood memories. *May Fools* is not really about the May '68 events in Paris, because it takes place in a house in the country in a very remote part of France. The matriarch of the family has just died and, when the various family members arrive for the funeral, they find themselves stuck in the family home where they all have a lot of childhood memories. So what's then going on in Paris is like a distant echo for them. In fact, they only hear of the events in Paris on the radio.

For two weeks, while the country was on strike, there was no electricity, no mail, and no public transportation of any kind. In those remote parts of France, the telephone was still manually operated; you had to go through a switchboard in a neighboring town, so there was not telephone service either. In that sense, *May Fools* is about the end of an era. It's not that 1968 was by itself a turning point. During the sixties, cities like Paris were already into a completely new approach, almost like a new culture, but in the outer provinces of France you could still find people living the way their grandparents had lived in the nineteenth century. That very traditional way of life was all turned around in the seventies.

In many ways, the film is also really about my life during that period. Shortly before the May '68 strikes, I had been making a documentary in India. I had been there for a long time, and coming back to Paris was very disorienting. Suddenly, everything just exploded in Paris, at the university, and at the Cinématheque with the Langlois affair. The utopian experience of May '68 was not so much about ideology or politics, but rather about a different way of looking at things. It didn't go very far, of course, and it wasn't long before people took their holidays and everything was back to the way it was before. But there was a sort of dream that lasted for about six weeks.

GH: The mother's funeral appears to function as a metaphor for the end of an era. Do you consciously try to incorporate such metaphors for their narrative resonance, or do you prefer to leave that to the critics?

LM: Oh, I definitely prefer to leave that to the critics—sometimes they find them, but sometimes they find something else. These kinds of ideas don't usually occur to you in advance—and I think they're dangerous if they do—but sometimes they're brought to your attention by someone who reads the script. Most of the time my themes are visualized. For *May Fools*, I dreamed for months about a house I knew many years ago and I saw a series of images of people stuck there and cut off from the rest of the world.

GH: Childhood memories also provided the basis of *Au revoir les enfants*.

LM: You know, it's interesting that a lot of filmmakers—the best known example, of course, is Truffaut—based their first films on childhood or adolescent memories. But in recent years a number of major filmmakers have made films about their childhoods rather late in their careers—Ingmar Bergman's *Fanny and Alexander*, Woody Allen's *Radio Days*, John Boorman's *Hope and Glory*, and a few others. I was discussing this with Boorman, and he said he'd been thinking about doing that film for years but it was only recently that he remembered exactly the way he felt as a child.

I've always wanted to deal with the story behind *Au revoir les enfants*. In my case, it's a story that's particularly traumatic, and I really wanted at some point to pass it on. For some strange reason I almost felt like I should buy more time, that I should really wait and save it. Then at a certain point my memories came back with a vengeance. While I was shooting *Alamo Bay* in those little towns on the Texas coast, where you're really far away in a different world, my memories came flooding back and they became obsessive. That's when I really started to think of a structure for *Au revoir les enfants*. In the little spare time I had, on Sundays, I would try to put together some ideas for the screenplay.

I carried those memories for many years without being sure I could get a screenplay out of them. I didn't know how to approach them. But at a certain point it seemed natural; it's almost a Proustian way of dealing with memory by allowing things to open up. Suddenly, little remembrances float to the surface of your conscience, and you realize it is material you can use, whereas before you felt uncomfortable dealing with it. I repressed a lot of my childhood memories, including the story of Bonnet in 1994; for many years, until I was past thirty. I didn't want to deal with it. I didn't even want to talk to anyone about it.

GH: Do you think French viewers are more willing now than they have been in the past to accept films about French collaboration during World War II?

LM: Yes. I don't think *Au revoir les enfants* offends the French the way *Lacombe, Lucien* did. *Lacombe, Lucien* was a fairly negative view about France during the period, whereas *Au revoir les enfants* is just my own memory of the time. There was a sort of split between people like those priests behaving heroically and those who succumbed to the Nazis and turned in their friends. A lot of ugly things happened under the Vichy government, which was overzealous about obeying German orders to track down Jews. But several thousand Jewish children were hidden and saved. There are children of my generation, for example, working in the film industry in France today, who were hidden in schools and elsewhere and who were saved. Very often their parents were taken away and killed.

GH: Was making the film cathartic for you?

LM: I felt immense relief because suddenly I was working in my own past, on my own ground, in my own language. It was a lot easier. I felt like I was in control 100 percent, whereas in Hollywood I was at best 80 percent in control.

As you get older, memory becomes almost omnipresent. That's why I'm so happy living in Paris these days, because that's where all my memories are. I can turn a corner while walking and something comes back to me which took place in 1964. I remember the corner and somebody who lived in an apartment near there. I'll walk some more and on the next block I'll see a café where I remember something else from my past. It's sort of the geography of memory, because I spent most of my adolescent and adult life in Paris, and it's like walking into my past. That's why lately I've enjoyed making films that deal with my memories.

GH: As a director, it must also be easier for you to work from your own script rather than the words and ideas of someone else.

LM: It's a lot easier because I don't have any problems in changing the dialogue. Or if someone else comes up with a better line. That's the main reason I prefer to write my own screenplays. I learned from working in Hollywood that I don't want to write in English because I'm not good enough. When it's your own script, with your own dialogue, in your own language, I always think—being a director more than a writer—of how I'm going to shoot it. Compared to my American films, making *Au revoir les enfants* was like shooting a documentary in the sense that it's my own material.

In the case of someone else's screenplay, even if I'm involved from the very beginning and work very closely on it right up to the production date, trying to adjust to the way I want to shoot it, you usually don't find out until you're on the set that a scene doesn't work for you. Then you're in trouble, because you either have to fix it by having the writer on the set or you have to do it by yourself with the actors. Neither is very good, because it's done sort of hastily, and sometimes you don't have the distance. When I work from my own screenplay, it's easy for me to adjust and to make changes because I know it so well.

In *Au revoir les enfants*, as opposed to some films I shot in English, I almost never had to say, "Wait, there's something wrong with this scene!" I think it happened only once in a scene that was essentially cut. I find the location months before we start shooting, and the shooting script is always adapted to the location, so I can make all the changes that are needed to make it flow more naturally. The simple problem of being in the middle of a scene and thinking "this doesn't work"—which any director who is candid will admit happens in every movie— wasn't a problem for me in *Au revoir les enfants*.

GH: Did you have a lot of rehearsals with the children, who were all non-professional actors?

LM: Once we had the cast set, about a month before shooting, we started to meet regularly to read the script, discuss the scenes, and allow them to get used to each other. Then we rehearsed five days in the key location, which was the classroom with all the children, and then we did some more rehearsals in the courtyard and got them used to the camera. We acted as if we were shooting, except that I was watching them. The cameraman was watching them. They were watching us. We were sort of getting used to each other, and they were getting used to the strange process of filmmaking.

It was very slow, very repetitious, and, frankly, for children, very boring. It's even boring for adults, so the big problem when you work with children is to keep them interested or amused in order to keep up their stamina. Usually what happens is that they're great in the morning, after lunch they give you one or two good hours, and then they collapse, which is perfectly normal because film-making takes so much concentration that it's unusually demanding for children.

GH: Did you schedule the more demanding scenes in the early stages of production?

LM: That's not always possible. In *Au revoir les enfants*, the most important scene is when the Gestapo officer comes into the classroom and Julien seems to betray his friend by a look. That was shot during the first week, because we had to deal with that particular classroom during the first week of shooting. That was fine with me because we'd rehearsed, but I find that you're better off doing your most difficult scenes right in the middle, because that's when they're really at their peak. Also, by the end sometimes they have become actors. They tend to know too much; they get used to the camera and they start becoming too precocious. It's best when everybody, especially children, has a pretty loose relationship with you but at the same time really stays concentrated. At the end, it's much more difficult because they're too familiar with the crew and it starts becoming like a game. The last week of shooting was a nightmare for me because there were all these ongoing inside jokes, and it was very difficult keeping it together.

GH: You've explained that stylistically you tried to achieve an objective approach because you were afraid of the film becoming too sentimental.

LM: I was terrified of that, because the story was so easy to play sentimental. I had to almost fight myself. I don't think my films are sentimental, but in this case, because it was so close to me, I really had to hold back.

GH: Is that why you waited thirty years to make the film?

LM: That had to do with the choice of the film's voice. You know, I could have picked children with a lot more sweetness and charm, and I had to be careful during the shooting and editing. Film is a very manipulative medium, as we know well, especially in this town. It is so easy, if you know a little bit about this medium, to manipulate audiences with music, with a close-up, or with editing by two more seconds on a close-up. It's a Pavlovian medium in the sense that you can almost mathematically get any reaction you want. I try to avoid that kind of cheap manipulation and try to impress the audience on a higher level, not to force them but to trust them to make their own choices.

I think the strength of *Au revoir les enfants* came from its being so restrained. That's why everyone seems to find the ending so devastating: because it's all been very restrained, but it's also been building up, and it all comes out as we reach the moment when Bonnet is taken away and Julien knows he's never going to see him again. There's a moment there which is pure emotion, and it has stayed with me for more than forty years. I wanted things to slowly mount to that moment, and to stay away from anything before then that would allow people to let go with their emotions.

GH: Do you think the success of a performance derives from the casting?

LM: Yes, it often happens that way. *Au revoir les enfants* was the best casting I've had as a group, because we did it very carefully and most of them were not professional actors. Even half of the adults in the film were not professional actors.

I've worked with wonderful actors many times, and I've often written parts for certain actors, like Michel Piccoli, who I like to work with; but as a director, my greatest experience of watching someone work in front of a camera was with the seventeen-year-old boy in *Lacombe, Lucien.* Before the film, he had worked in the woods as a woodcutter and had never seen a movie in his life. He didn't know anything about the medium and was really sort of a creature from the wild. But he came up with the most interesting performance I have ever seen. He was very close to the character which I had written, but he also brought a lot to the character which I was incapable of conceiving, and I kept being amazed by that.

GH: Do you think it was his lack of experience that added an extra dimension?

LM: I wouldn't say lack of experience, because that was overcome in three days. He knew his marks so well. We had some very complicated shots where he had to take six to seven different marks. He would sort of rehearse it and his feet would come naturally into position. He had an extraordinary sense of rhythm, and film acting is a lot about rhythm. He acquired the technique of film acting in just three days. What no actor could have given me was his personal experience, his intimate knowledge of the character, because he had the same background as the character. He was wild, he had family problems, he had been socially humiliated, and he had a really tough childhood, so he really knew this character. He was not only playing the part; he was also a technical consultant for the part, and helping to conceive the character. That doesn't happen very often.

GH: Is working with actors easier than working with nonprofessionals?

LM: It's very different, and how to handle actors is something you have to learn. My biggest problem at the beginning of my filmmaking career was with handling actors. After working with Cousteau for four years, I directed my first feature film. Technically I could deal with any problem, and I knew enough to discuss them with the sound man, the editor, and the cameraman. When I was working for Cousteau, I was practically a one-man crew. At the age of twenty-three or twenty-four, I had a real technical knowledge of my craft, but I knew very little about actors. I remember my terror, during the first two or three features that I did, in dealing with actors, because at that point I was really only experienced in directing fishes! [*laughs*]

It's not always easy working with actors, because you often have to deal with their egomania or their insecurity. You sometimes have situations where you have to direct three actors in a scene, and each of them has to be directed differently because their personalities are different, sometimes almost opposite. Some actors you have to make nervous, because they're too confident. You have to terrorize other actors because that's what they need most. Most actors need to be fathered and sort of patted on the back and helped. You have to hold them to the camera.

GH: Is that more true in America?

LM: I think it's true everywhere. My problem with American actors is the Method. Not so much the ones who actually worked with Lee Strasberg, but all the actors who have this sort of inferiority complex and try to use the Method without really knowing too much about it. They're building the "character arc" and they're using this—what do they call it?—"sense memory," which sometimes borders on the ridiculous and can actually be counterproductive.

In the case of *My Dinner with Andre*, I was constantly having to loop the loop because the film was more or less about Andre and Wally themselves. The whole thing started from a series of encounters between them after having not seen each other for several years. They had done theater before, and then they went their own ways. Andre began traveling, and Wally stayed in New York and started having his plays produced. When Andre returned, they decided to work together again. Originally they wanted to do something on stage from their conversations, so they began taping them. I think they had twenty-five hours of tape. Wally worked on them for two years and came up with a screenplay about these two characters who were Andre and Wally, somehow transposed. Andre and Wally were set to play these characters, but not quite as themselves. I read the script and I said, "Yes, I'll do it." I knew both of them quite well at the time. Wally even had a small part in *Atlantic City*. When we had our first meeting, I said, "You know, it doesn't have to be you playing these parts." I said we could conceive of Robert Redford and Dustin Hoffman.

GH: What did they say to that?

LM: They were shocked. You see, from the beginning, I wanted to make clear to them that they would have to approach acting the parts, and not just say, "It's me, I'm just playing myself." I wanted them to become professional actors being asked to play a part. It became very confusing and it took a long time to sort of get the necessary distance. I realized very quickly that I needed to keep breaking this confusion between the character and the actor, or I was not going to make any progress. I would be stuck in this messy confusion about who they are, and I really needed for them to have this distance so that they could look clearly at their characters and their weaknesses.

I wanted Andre to be almost completely ridiculous in the first twenty minutes. I think that was my input into the screenplay. I knew that if this film was going to work, we must get laughs or we will be buried. The first time I read it, I laughed a number of times, but, of course, they took it very seriously, especially Andre. Wally was much more into the humor of Andre's sometimes being so solemn. I got Andre to understand that his character had to be pompous and then open up. I needed that distance, because otherwise the film would have been neither documentary nor fiction, but a mess.

GH: What is your approach to editing?

LM: I have always been tremendously interested in editing. It is a tool that gives you immense possibilities. Speaking as a documentary filmmaker, editing is always about "after." You don't write a screenplay for a documentary; you just go out there and shoot it. It's all improvised, and then the cutting room becomes purgatory, because you spend months trying to put it together. It's not so much trying to make sense of it, because there is no sense. The way you've shot it has a meaning. You just have to find it, order it, and clarify it. It takes forever because you now have to do all the homework you didn't do before. I spent a lot of time in a cutting room when I made my India documentaries.

I believe the editing should not show. You spend a long time, and you find out it's a question of two frames, more or less, of matching cuts, and that can take forever, but it's not meant to show. On *Au revoir les enfants*, I kept telling my editors, "If you ever win an award for editing, I won't work with you anymore. That means your editing shows."

I had a terrible time editing *My Dinner with Andre*, because Andre and Wally, as good as they are, are not professional actors. Andre had the longest speaking part in the history of the cinema. I don't think anyone's ever had so many lines to say in a movie. There were ups and downs in there; we had many takes, and I used a lot of reaction shots, especially in the first half hour. My big worry about the first half hour was people leaving the theater, because it includes the endless monologue of Andre's, which is very important. I wanted to keep a distance from what Andre was saying, and the perfect way to do it was to use Wally's reaction shots, which were great. They would get a laugh, and give us the distance from this very pompous aspect of Andre's character before he mellows and becomes a little different.

I think we succeeded in a way that is almost unnoticed by the audience, because when people watch *My Dinner with Andre*, they think they see a continuum, but they don't really. It's a heavily edited film. You have no idea how many cuts there are. It's basically two angles, except that sometimes it's here, sometimes it's there. It varies only minimally. *My Dinner with Andre* may appear on one level to be a very simple approach—just putting a camera on one person and another camera on the other and then rolling the cameras when they start talking—when actually it was all very studied, very rehearsed. The whole point was to give the sense that it was completely improvised, almost like *cinéma verité*, and a lot of that came from the editing.

GH: Creatively, are you more restricted working in the US than in France?

LM: I don't think it has anything to do with the system or the economy. It has to do with the fact that I'm more comfortable working in my own language.

GH: Do the studios ever prevail on you to make changes?

LM: Not really. I have made all my American films in complete freedom. I don't blame the system for being oppressive or destructive. I just blame myself for not being comfortable with the system and for not being able to adjust. When I was shooting *Crackers*, there were 110 people on the crew, and I didn't know what to do with them. I just don't understand Hollywood stages. I like to work with the minimum number of people. I'm not saying you can eliminate key jobs on the set, but there's nothing more pleasurable for me than to go out with my documentary crew, just myself and two other people.

GH: Do you ever see yourself coming back to Hollywood to work?

LM: If I did, it would only be to make a documentary about Hollywood. It's funny, you know, because I've made a film about Calcutta, which is a city of physical and economic despair. And I've often thought about making a film about Los Angeles, another city of despair—obviously not economic or material despair, but rather a spiritual and ethical despair that stems from lifestyles saturated by popular culture. Los Angeles has its own mini-culture that has grown to serve as the rhetoric for the rest of the industrial world.

American popular culture really comes from here. A little bit comes from New York, on a subtler, more sophisticated level, but the real popular culture—movies, television, commercials, music—comes from Los Angeles. Not only popular culture, but a whole way of life—this obsession with health, for example—all that stuff comes from here. I think people in this town are mutants. They're a different species.

So I might like to come back to make this documentary, but working in fiction here is totally uninteresting to me because you fall into all the traps. I did it once on *Crackers*, and I'll never go that route again! I made all the mistakes, one by one, just like in a catalog. I suppose everyone has to do it once. Everyone was very nice—a nice writer, a nice producer, a nice studio, wonderful actors. That's what kept me from quitting, actually. I had a great group of actors: Donald Sutherland, Sean Penn, Jack Warden. They were a nice cast. What I'm saying is that it doesn't make very much sense for me to become another Hollywood director.

Interview with Louis Malle

Michel Ciment / 1994

From *Positif*, no. 419 (January 1996): 29–32. Reprinted by permission. Translated from the French by CB.

Michel Ciment: You, more than any French director, have had strong relationships with the American film industry. How do you see the possibilities for working within it?

Louis Malle: I have made films that are completely marginal in relation to their system. Each of my attempts over a twenty-year period to move inside of the Hollywood industrial system has been unfortunate, because I have bad habits. Without taking myself for an auteur, I estimate that a film is 100 percent my responsibility, and I want to decide everything about it. Whether it is a failure or a success is on my shoulders. I have a very hard time inserting myself into a system where, in the crushing majority of cases, the producer is more important than the director, as is also the screenwriter, and more often than not the actors. For me, as for many Europeans, the director is the main contractor, the architect charged with building the house. In the United States, it doesn't happen exactly like that. I think I am right in saying that this year more than half of American films have had their endings changed on the basis of previews. This custom, which consists of finding adolescents in some suburb and making them the representatives of the public and the arbiters of the fate of your film, is abominable to me. To the extent that the American system is entirely geared toward the search for profit and nothing else—they are honest in recognizing it, as opposed to the vast majority of French producers—their point of view is logical. Even so, they have the custom of replacing a director, a cinematographer, or an actor if they don't please the studio, which has the definitive final word.

MC: As a French speaker, living in France, you have nevertheless made four fiction films and as many documentaries in the United States. You therefore have a privileged observation post.

LM: I went there because America interested me a lot, and I continue to go there because it is a much more complicated country than one thinks, and very fascinating. Whether I would say that it taught me anything in terms of the means of production.... I have never really worked in Hollywood in the way that, for example, Paul Verhoeven—who has integrated himself into it perfectly—has. When I arrived in the United States, I remember that Milos Forman said to me: "I'm going to give you some good advice. Don't co-sign your screenplays: it's looked on very badly here!" In France, when a director and a writer work together, they are both credited. And it is true that Forman writes his screenplays meticulously over months, and that he has never signed any of them in the United States, while the number of films he has made there is equal to the number of his Czech films. This renunciation of a writing credit is significant for me, even if it doesn't bother me all that much because I consider myself to be a director above all. If I try to be positive, what I admire in American cinema is that it comprises a booming industry that has imposed its films on the entire world. They have maintained a hegemony, and they have even reinforced it further in these last few years. That said, I keep my distance from it in the sense that I have always affirmed that my goal is not to make films that please everyone, a concept that dominates the cinema made by the studios. The systematic search for the "blockbuster" seems to me to be very unhealthy, because it goes against everything we know about the history of art. It is difficult to make original and different things if one has as an exclusive ambition to satisfy the maximum number of people within the embrace of mass culture.

The power of American cinema is so great that the independents and those at the margins are, unfortunately, irresistibly attracted by the system, and they end up being recuperated by it, one after the other. It even seems that it is their deepest ambition, no doubt because of the attraction of both legitimacy and money. Personally, I would have no excuse if I made films simply for money, since I have the privilege of not having problems with that side of things. As I have always made a good living making films, that has given me the freedom of choice.

MC: Your four fiction films made in the United States—*Pretty Baby*, *Atlantic City*, *Crackers*, and *Alamo Bay*—must have been very different experiences for you.

LM: *Crackers* is the extreme case. I could write a book on the subject, to the extent that, on the insistence of a very sympathetic producer, I put my finger into the gears of the system in doing a remake of the admirable film *Big Deal on Madonna Street* by Mario Monicelli. After three years of resisting the idea, and in the aftermath of a project that was never completed because of the death of my main actor John Belushi, I agreed to make a film where, every morning, I had to ask myself what I was doing on the set. It is an experience that I will never repeat. After *Atlantic City* and *My Dinner with Andre*, which had critical and commercial success, I no doubt felt too sure of myself and I thought that perhaps I could film the phone book! And I fell flat on my face! And I was very unhappy. On the other hand, when I arrived in Los Angeles and had made a deal with Paramount for the project of *Pretty Baby* in the middle of the seventies, they left me completely alone. They were very respectful, very nice, but it is true that it was a very small budget. I had decided to make films in the United States, not because I wanted to work there, but because the action of the film took place in New Orleans. *Atlantic City* had Canadian financing. As for *Alamo Bay*, it was a film that was close to being a documentary, with a very small budget. TriStar financed it without it really being a studio film.

MC: Were you involved as a producer in these films?

LM: Yes, all of them except for *Crackers*. For *Atlantic City*, I was not a producer, but I had a percentage. For the two other films, I had a role as producer.

MC: That shows that cooperation is possible!

LM: Except that there is no co-production treaty between the United States and France. The Americans don't have a central cinema organization; they don't have federal regulations; and there are no restrictions and no economic aid. It is a 100 percent capitalist industry that functions in a totally Darwinian way, according to the law of the most powerful. What I have come to realize over the years—let's say, the last twenty years—is that the influence of cinema made in languages other than English has diminished considerably. Foreign films have a more and more difficult time penetrating the market. It has to be admitted that the attitude of the Americans is magnificent: on the one hand, they refuse to do dubbing, and on the other hand they have a harder and harder time watching films with subtitles! For example, we recently gave a prize to Jean-Louis Levi, the producer of *Un coeur en hiver* [*A Heart in Winter*], the French film that did the best business in the United States last year. And it only made one and a half million dollars. At one time, *La Cage aux folles* or *Diva* made seven or eight million! The little slice of the cake represented by the foreign art film is getting smaller every year.

MC: For you, then, the success in the United States of films like *Chariots of Fire*, *The Crying Game*, or *Four Weddings and a Funeral* has resulted only in seeing their directors get vacuumed up by Hollywood?

LM: American cinema has always been fertilized by Europe. It is true that a number of British directors, like Adrian Lyne, the Scott brothers, Neil Jordan, Roland Joffe, and others, have had a lot of success on the other side of the Atlantic. If one is bilingual—and even better, Anglophone—and if one puts oneself entirely at the service of the Hollywood system, one can perfectly well succeed there. Because as long as the film comes out in their language, it interests them.

In my case, things were simple. Either I made American films, or English films like *Damage*, because their subject was English, or I made French films. When *Au revoir les enfants* came out in the United States, one of the major American producers said to me: "Ah, my dear friend, you should have made it in English." It was really insulting and in poor taste to tell me that: I never would have made a film like that, about a painful French childhood, in English. The film has done well, but its success would have been considerable if they had spoken in American! After the initially favorable results of the film, they dubbed it, but that version bombed.

MC: Given the threat of seeing European directors having to make their films in English in order to have a chance of selling them on the American market, is it possible to encourage the Americans to dub the films and make them more successful that way?

LM: What is going to gnaw into and perhaps destroy European cinema is that they are going to make more and more films in English that have no reason to be in that language. I always refuse to do it, and besides, it usually doesn't work. The problem with dubbing is that the American critics refuse to see the films in that format. Paradoxically, it is in the name of purism that European cinema finds itself restricted from a greater penetration in the American market. But at the same time, when they dubbed films, it was often a commercial failure. In fact, dubbing—which is not an ideal solution—is a question of money, of time, and of talent. I know that for *Les Visiteurs*, Gaumont asked Mel Brooks to direct the dubbed version. I would be curious to see the results. I think, in any case, that the attempt is an interesting one. However, the dubbed version of *Au revoir les enfants* has practically not come out in theaters, and on the video market 90 percent of people have bought the subtitled version.

MC: How do you explain the decline in European cinema?

LM: I think there are two phenomena at work. During the sixties and the first part of the seventies, it was a period of change which was troubled both politically and culturally, and in which the Americans of that generation were more curious. At the same time, it corresponded with a very brilliant period for European cinema, one that had begun in the fifties. A lot of things were happening, and directors like Bergman and Fellini benefited from a real cult following. The sixties were also a time when American cinema was losing money, when the studios had splintered, and when there was hardly any regeneration. Since the seventies—the time when I was working with Paramount—the industry has righted itself, started to make a lot of money, and opened movie theaters everywhere.

MC: Can we envision a source of financial aid to American distributors of European films?

LM: Given the fact that the French cinema is probably the most heavily supported by the State of any in the world, it seems to me that it would be very important and useful—rather than having a French film festival in Sarasota—to help with the financing of subtitles and distribution, to have the distributors come to Paris. The situation was completely different in the past. I remember that my films like *Le Feu follet, Murmur of the Heart*, and *Lacombe, Lucien*, when they were presented at the New York Film Festival, already had a distributor in the United States, or, if they didn't, it was an excellent opportunity to find one. Today, French films arrive in great numbers at festivals and then go back to France, often without a distributor. That, I believe, is characteristic of what is happening. If a film does come out, it is because Fabiano Canosa, a true lover of film, has programmed it at the Public Theatre, which pays for the subtitles. There are a few places like that for cinephiles—Don Talbot's theaters among others—but it stops there. We have a little niche that gets smaller every year. It is interesting to discuss this with the people at Sony Classics, Fine Line, Goldwyn, and Miramax, who distribute foreign films. It turns out that, based on their calculations, it is difficult for them to make it economically viable. For them, it seems infinitely easier to release a British film, or an independent American film, than a film from the European continent.

MC: What, then, are the prospects for the future?

LM: I have a theory which makes me seem old-fashioned. I believe that freedom in the cinema is the acceptance of working in modest conditions. The more money one has, the less free one becomes. The proof of this is in the American independent cinema. The current system in France, which consists of wanting to compete with American cinema on its own terrain, seems naïve to me. Aside from a few exceptions like *Cyrano de Bergerac*, it is a dangerous game, because Americans know remarkably well how to make spectacle for the lowest common denominator. If you want to imitate them, it will mean, in any case, working in the English language. The other alternative is to make films that are firmly anchored in their particularism. I believe in that old cliché that the more something is culturally specific, the more it is universal. It would be criminal to renounce our differences. European cinema does not exist as such. The power of Europe is the sum of all our cultures.

Selected Resources

Billard, Pierre. *Louis Malle: le rebelle solitaire*. Paris: Plon, 2003.

Carrière, Jean-Claude. *Les Années d'utopie*. Paris: Plon, 2003.

Chapier, Henri. *Louis Malle*. Paris: Seghers, 1964.

Crisp, Colin. *The Classic French Cinema, 1930–1960*. Bloomington: Indiana University Press, 1993.

French, Philip. *Malle on Malle*. London: Faber and Faber, 1993.

Frey, Hugo. *Louis Malle*. Manchester: Manchester University Press, 2004.

Frodon, Jean-Michel. *L'Age moderne du cinéma français: de la nouvelle vague à nos jours*.
    Paris: Flammarion, 1995.

Gitlin, Todd. "Phantom India." *Film Quarterly* 27, no. 4 (1974).

Hawkins, Peter. "Louis Malle: A European Outsider in the American Mainstream." In *European Identity
    in Cinema*, ed. Wendy Everett. Bristol: Intellect Books, 1996.

Higgins, Lynn. "If Looks Could Kill: Louis Malle's Portraits of Collaboration." In *Fascism, Aesthetics, and
    Culture*, ed. Richard Golsan. Hanover: University Press of New England, 1992.

Jeancolas, Jean-Pierre. *Histoire du cinéma français*. Paris: Nathan, 1995.

Kedward, Roderick. "*Lacombe Lucien* and the Anti-Carnival of Collaboration." In *French Film: Texts and
    Contexts*, eds. Susan Hayward and Ginette Vincendeau. London: Routledge, 2000.

Malle, Louis. "Le Cinéma français et le star-system." *Le Film français*, no. 8 (1974).

Mallecot, Jacques, ed. *Louis Malle par Louis Malle*. Paris: Editions de l'Athanor, 1978.

Met, Philippe, ed. *The Cinema of Louis Malle: Transatlantic Auteur*. New York: Columbia University Press, 2018.

Nicholls, David. "Louis Malle's *Ascenseur pour l'échafaud* and the Presence of the Colonial Wars in French
    Cinema." *French Cultural Studies*, no. 7 (1996).

Prédal, René. *Louis Malle*. Paris: Edilig, 1989.

Sellier, Genèvieve and Ginette Vincendeau. "La Nouvelle Vague et le cinéma populaire: Brigitte Bardot
    dans *Vie privée* et *Le Mépris*." *Iris*, no. 26 (1998).

Singerman, Alan J. "Histoire et ambiguité: un nouveau regard sur *Lacombe Lucien*." *French Review* 80,
    no. 5 (2007).

Southern, Nathan C., and Jacques Weissgerber. *The Films of Louis Malle*. Jefferson, NC: McFarland, 2006.

Williams, Alan. *Republic of Images: A History of French Filmmaking*. Cambridge:
    Harvard University Press, 1992.

Index

About the Editor

Christopher Beach is a film scholar and author of several books on film and literature, including *Class, Language, and American Film Comedy* and *The Films of Hal Ashby*. He was named an Academy Film Scholar by the Academy of Motion Picture Arts and Sciences for *A Hidden History of Film Style: Cinematographers, Directors, and the Collaborative Process*. He is editor of *Claude Chabrol: Interviews*, also published by University Press of Mississippi.

Printed in the United States
by Baker & Taylor Publisher Services